AMERICAN EDUCATION

Its Men

Ideas

and

Institutions

Advisory Editor

Lawrence A. Cremin
Frederick A. P. Barnard Professor of Education
Teachers College, Columbia University

The Founding of
American Colleges and Universities
Before the Civil War

Donald G. Tewksbury

ARNO PRESS & THE NEW YORK TIMES
New York * 1969

Reprint edition 1969 by Arno Press, Inc.

*

Library of Congress Catalog Card No. 79-89246

*

Reprinted from a copy in Teachers College Library

*

Manufactured in the United States of America

Editorial Note

AMERICAN EDUCATION: *Its Men, Institutions and Ideas*
presents selected works of thought and scholarship that have
long been out of print or otherwise unavailable. Inevitably, such
works will include particular ideas and doctrines that have been
outmoded or superseded by more recent research. Nevertheless,
all retain their place in the literature, having influenced educational thought and practice in their own time and having provided
the basis for subsequent scholarship.

Lawrence A. Cremin
Teachers College

The Founding of
American Colleges and Universities
Before the Civil War

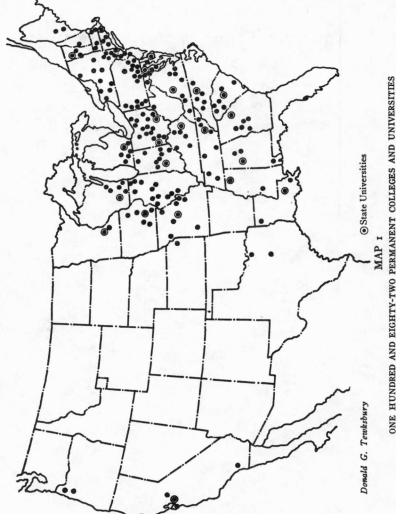

Donald G. Tewksbury   ⊙ State Universities

MAP I

ONE HUNDRED AND EIGHTY-TWO PERMANENT COLLEGES AND UNIVERSITIES
FOUNDED BEFORE THE CIVIL WAR

The Founding of
American Colleges and Universities
Before the Civil War

WITH PARTICULAR REFERENCE TO
THE RELIGIOUS INFLUENCES BEARING UPON
THE COLLEGE MOVEMENT

By

DONALD G. TEWKSBURY, Ph.D.

Teachers College, Columbia University
Contributions to Education, No. 543

*Published with the approval of
Professor E. H. Reisner, Sponsor*

BUREAU OF PUBLICATIONS
Teachers College, Columbia University
NEW YORK CITY
1932

Printed in the United States of America by
J. J. LITTLE AND IVES COMPANY, NEW YORK

Foreword

The need for a general survey and interpretation of the move-ment for the founding of American colleges and universities is recognized by all who are familiar with the literature of the history of higher education in this country. The present study was under-taken as a preliminary step in meeting this need. The field of the history of higher education in this country is largely unexplored. Only recently have the general historians of American life given attention to this significant phase of our social and cultural history. At this time, when higher education is in the midst of an era of reorganization, a study of some of the forces that have played a part in making our institutions of higher education what they are today seems especially appropriate. The present study is neces-sarily limited to certain aspects of the general movement for higher education in this country. Other aspects of this movement require further study. It is hoped that others will be induced to carry on research along these lines in order that the history of higher educa-tion may be more adequately represented and its values more fully appropriated by the leaders in higher education in this country.

The author is indebted to a number of persons for their interest and coöperation in the present study. Initial encouragement was given by the late Professor R. J. Leonard, Director of the School of Education, Teachers College, Columbia University. Stimulation in the general field of the history of education and valuable criti-cisms of the study itself, were received from Professor Edward H. Reisner, who kindly consented to act as sponsor for the study. Professor Isaac L. Kandel and Professor F. B. O'Rear, acting as advisers for the study, were generous in giving their time to an examination of the manuscript. Professor Dixon Ryan Fox of Columbia University, Professor Donald P. Cottrell, and Pro-fessor Erling M. Hunt read the entire study and made valuable suggestions. To these, and to the large number of persons represent-ing the various colleges and universities who have coöperated in

v

the study, the author wishes to express his appreciation. Responsibility for such errors as may exist in this study rests with the
author. The table of contents has been made as full as possible in
order to serve in lieu of an index. The unusually large number of
quotations from primary and secondary sources included in this
study were used for the purpose of making more vivid and realistic
the movement for the founding of colleges and universities in this
country. These quotations are given general acknowledgment in
this place. To the Carnegie Institution in Washington and to the
American Geographical Society in New York the author is indebted
for permission to use certain maps which are to appear in the forth-
coming *Atlas of the Historical Geography* of the United States.

D. G. T.

Contents

Tables and Maps

TABLES

The Founding of
American Colleges and Universities
Before the Civil War

Chapter I

THE MOVING FRONTIER AND THE AMERICAN COLLEGE

We cannot look on the freedom of this country, in connection with its youth, without a presentiment that here shall laws and institutions exist on some scale in proportion to the majesty of nature. . . . It is a country of beginnings, of projects, of designs, and expectations.[1]

—Ralph Waldo Emerson

Our country is to be a land of colleges.[2]

—Absalom Peters

American social development has been continually beginning over again on the frontier. This perennial rebirth, this fludity of American life, this expansion westward with its new opportunities, its continuous touch with the simplicity of primitive society, furnish the forces dominating American character.[3]

—Frederick J. Turner

THE AMERICAN COLLEGE AS A FRONTIER INSTITUTION

THE American college was typically a frontier institution. It was designed primarily to meet the needs of pioneer communities, and was established in most cases on the frontier line of settlement. The frontier conditions under which Harvard, the earliest of American colleges, was founded were reproduced on each successive line of settlement across the continent. In the course of the westward expansion of the American people, as the forces of frontier life gained a cumulative power, a distinctive American institution was evolved, an educational institution shaped and adapted to the peculiar needs of an advancing people. In this process of continuous remaking on the frontiers of American life,

[1] Emerson, Ralph Waldo, "The Young American" (1833), *Nature, Addresses and Lectures*, pp. 370-371, 1876.

[2] Peters, Absalom, *Discourse before the Society for the Promotion of Collegiate and Theological Education at the West*, p. 13 (pamphlet), 1851.

(This Society is hereafter referred to in the footnotes of this study in abbreviated form, viz., S.P.C.T.E.W.)

[3] Turner, Frederick J., "The Significance of the Frontier in American History" (1893), *The Frontier in American History*, pp. 2-3, 1920.

I

the American college came to depart radically from its European antecedents, and to acquire characteristics and functions which made it truly an indigenous institution. In its type of control, in the nature of its curriculum, in its standards of admission and selection, and finally in its ideals and aspirations, the American college came in large part to represent the essential frontier character of our civilization.[4] Attempts made at various times to modify or transform this institution so that it would be more in accord with French and with German patterns in higher education were successfully resisted before the time of the Civil War. Numerous statements from contemporaneous sources testify to the fact that our colleges and universities were being shaped and molded by the forces of American life into truly native institutions of higher education.[5]

In the settlement of the great spaces of the west, and in the building up of a frontier civilization and culture, the colleges that were established during the period before the Civil War served as the agents of a cultural and religious advance on a wide front. Born, on the one hand, of the ideals and aspirations of a frontier society, and nourished, on the other, by the effort and zeal of the older settlements in the east, the American college came into being, a unique institution, destined to play a significant and dramatic rôle in the development of American life. It is not within the purpose of this study to set forth in any comprehensive way this truly epic story of the evolution of the American college on the successive lines of frontier settlement across the country, but rather to sketch some of the larger features of the general movement for the founding of colleges in the period before the Civil War, and to present a body of factual material bearing on the colleges that were founded on a permanent basis during this formative period of our national life.[6] In this chapter, the founding of American colleges will be considered as one phase of that vital expansive movement in American life which may be summed up under the term, "the moving frontier."

[4] It is recognized that forces other than the frontier played a significant part in the shaping of American institutions of higher education. For a recent essay on the limitations of Turner's frontier thesis, see Wright, B. F., "American Democracy on the Frontier," *Yale Review*, Winter Quarter, pp. 349-365, 1931.

[5] See, for example, Anderson, M. B., *Voluntaryism in Higher Education*, p. 15 (pamphlet), 1877.

[6] A number of important aspects of the college movement have not been included in this study on account of the limitations of space, e.g., the founding of women's colleges, the rise of manual labor institutions, the development of boards of control, and the financial aspects of the founding of colleges.

THE MULTIPLYING OF COLLEGES ON THE FRONTIER

The unusually large number of small colleges founded in America constitutes one of the most distinctive features of our development in higher education. No other country in the world reveals such a multiplicity of institutions of higher learning. Henry P. Tappan, later president of the university of Michigan, made the statement in 1850 that "we have multiplied colleges so as to place them at every man's door." [7] It is evident that America had already become the land of neighborhood colleges.

In the absence of a compelling sentiment in favor of a state-controlled and monopolistic system of higher education in most of the states of the Union, charters were granted to large numbers of private college ventures. The forces of frontier democracy demanded the decentralization of educational facilities in higher education, as in elementary and secondary education. President Philip Lindsley, of the University of Nashville, in describing the state of higher education in America in the year 1837, made the statement that

Whoever has studied the history, genius, character, government, modes of instruction, endowments, revenues, and all the concentrated ways and means and facilities of communicating knowledge, which distinguish the most celebrated European universities, will be able to comprehend our meaning when we speak of them as an order or species of institution altogether unknown in the United States. We have nothing like them or approaching them. . . . Whether we ought to essay the creation of precisely such institutions among us, or whether, if established, they would be duly patronized and sustained by our busy, restless, speculating, money-making people, are questions open for discussion. . . . For the ordinary purposes of educating boys, generally between the ages of fifteen and twenty-one, we have no hesitation in giving preference to such colleges as we already possess; provided always, that they be made in fact what they assume and profess to be in name. Such institutions, scattered over the land, at convenient distances from each other, are better adapted to the habits, wants, and circumstances of our widely dispersed and comparatively poor population. [8]

A contemporary writer, Absalom Peters, maintained in 1851, that

It was never intelligently proposed to concentrate these advantages in a single University, "cum privilegio," nor to confine them to a few Colleges,

---

[7] Tappan, Henry P., *University Education*, p. 64, 1850.
[8] Halsey, Le Roy J., Editor, *The Works of Philip Lindsley*, vol. 1, pp. 404-405, 1864.

at great distances from each other. The wide extent of the country, the prospective increase of population, the form of the government, the independence of the States, and above all the Protestant principle of universal education, have forbidden such a design; and the Colleges have adapted themselves to their appropriate spheres, in accordance with this state of things. They have thus trained the public mind to feel that a College, in each district of convenient extent, is a great blessing to the people. It is therefore placed beyond all doubt that our country, in the whole extent of it, is to be a land of Colleges.[9]

Theron Baldwin, the "Father of Western Colleges," noted in 1854 that

It is one of the glories of American colleges, that they are not concentrated into one vast University, but scattered far and wide among the people; each one filling its sphere, availing itself of local associations and local sympathies, and standing up there as the visible and ever present representative of liberal and Christian learning.[10]

In the absence of a "standing order" in religion in the new nation that came into being after the Revolution, numerous religious denominations and sects arose and flourished, especially on the frontier.[11] Thus a multitude of rival colleges representing various competing religious interests were established during the so-called "denominational era" of our history. America proved indeed to be a virgin land for the multiplication of religious sects and for the development of colleges designed as agents for the advancement of the interests of these religious groups.[12] As early as 1829, it was observed that

A principal cause of the excessive multiplication and dwarfish dimensions of Western colleges is, no doubt, the diversity of religious denominations among us. Almost every sect will have its college, generally one at least in each State.[13]

President F. A. P. Barnard, of the University of Mississippi, and later of Columbia University, made the statement in 1856 that

Nearly all our colleges are, furthermore, the creations of the different religious denominations which divide our people. They are regarded as important instrumentalities, through which the peculiarities of doctrine which

[9] Peters, *op. cit.*, p. 13.
[10] *Eleventh Report of the S.P.C.T.E.W., 1854,* p. 43.
[11] For a discussion of the rise of denominations in the middle period of our history, see pp. 69-70.
[12] See Mode, P. G., *The Frontier Spirit in American Christianity,* Chap. 4, 1923.
[13] Halsey, *op. cit.,* p. 254.

distinguish their founders are to be maintained, propagated, or defended. It is this which has led to the great multiplication of collegiate institutions in our country, and which is daily adding to their number.[14]

In the absence of class and social distinctions on the frontier, the privileges of higher education came to be regarded as the right of all. Thus the select institution of European heritage was transformed into a large number of "colleges for the people." It was claimed by Theron Baldwin in 1856 that

It is one of the glories of our American colleges, that their doors are alike open to all classes in society, and that the only nobility known within their walls has its basis in intellectual power, high attainment and moral worth, . . . Within the walls of an American college all factitious distinctions vanish. There the rich and the poor not only meet together, but they commence their intellectual struggle under a full knowledge of the fact that no hereditary dignity or inherited wealth, on the one hand, can entitle to special privileges and honors; nor, on the other, like inexorable fate, can they repress the aspirations of genius.[15]

President Tyler of Amherst stated in 1856 that

American colleges bear a general resemblance to the English colleges, from which they sprung; not, however, without important modifications, which bring them into nearer conformity to the genius of our institutions, into closer connection with the wants and wishes of the people. . . . the people have built them with their own hands, and cherished them in their own hearts. They are the people's colleges. . . . Scarcely anything in America is more distinctively American than the relation between the colleges and the common people. The people have made the colleges what they are, and the colleges have, in no small measure, made the people what they are. All classes have contributed to the establishment and the support of colleges, and all classes have reaped the benefit.[16]

Finally, in the absence of an established culture and scholarly traditions, except in a few of the older states, standards were lowered so that almost any enterprise setting up a claim as a collegiate institute, seminary, college, or university was given the right to confer degrees and dispense the benefits of a liberal education.[17]

[14] Barnard, F. A. P., "On Improvements Practicable in American Colleges," *American Journal of Education and College Review*, vol. 1, p. 176, January, 1856.

[15] *Thirteenth Report of the S.P.C.T.E.W., 1856*, p. 20.

[16] Tyler, W. S., *Colleges: Their Place Among American Institutions*, pp. 9, 11, 26 (pamphlet), 1857. Some rearrangement has been made in the order of sentences.

[17] In many cases, institutions of higher education were built up before a sufficient number of secondary institutions warranted such a development. In consequence many so-called colleges and universities were obliged to undertake a considerable amount of instruction on the secondary level. The general relation of the academy movement in this country to the college movement remains to be adequately studied.

Thus scores of unworthy, as well as of worthy, institutions were established on the principle that in a democracy the facilities of a cultural education should be placed within the reach of all the people. It was in this way that a democratization of culture was eventually achieved in this country. In reviewing the situation in 1823, the directors of the American Education Society expressed themselves as follows:

The multiplication of Literary Institutions is dreaded by some, as being in their view, unfavorable to the substantial progress of our national literature. But for ourselves we can say that it seems to us no inauspicious omen. We hail it as a token of a spirit in this community that will not rest, till it has brought within the reach of every enterprising youth the means of a liberal education.[18]

Rev. Lyman Beecher, in a statement made in 1836, argued that

Colleges and schools are truly the intellectual manufactories and workshops of the nation, and in their design and results are preëminently republican institutions. They break up and diffuse among the people that monopoly of knowledge and mental power which despotic governments accumulate for purposes of arbitrary rule, and bring to the children of the humblest families of the nation a full and fair opportunity of holding competition for learning, and honor, and wealth, with the children of the oldest and most affluent families . . . giving thus to the nation the select talents and powers of her entire population.[19]

This same point of view was maintained in 1856 by the Secretary of the Society for the Promotion of Collegiate and Theological Education at the West, in the following more cautious, yet none the less positive, statement:

There are, however, important advantages in the diffusion which distinguishes our American colleges, especially as regards their action upon society at large. This has already reached at one hundred and thirty-five different points, in more than thirty States and Territories. They are thus out among the people, and in sympathy with them—each one entwining itself with local interests, and eminently republican—by their presence giving visibility and consequent power to the great educational argument, and through their Alumni and annual gatherings, awakening a desire for their advantages in the minds of the multitudes of young men, and by their accessibility and cheapness multiplying the number who resort to them for instruction.[20]

[18] American Quarterly Register, *Ninth Annual Report of the American Education Society*, 1823.
[19] Beecher, Rev. Lyman, *A Plea for Colleges*, p. 15 (pamphlet), 1836.
[20] *Thirteenth Report of the S.P.C.T.E.W., 1856*, pp. 19-20.

Another writer stated in 1857 that

> It is also among our benefits that, though our system of education is less
> definitely wrought out in some of its parts than in the older countries, yet
> nowhere is the spontaneous impulse to general culture so widely diffused. . . .
> The elemental forces are at work; it needs only their wise direction to pro-
> duce unequalled consummation.[21]

In the light of these considerations, so vividly brought out in the
quotations from contemporary sources given above, it is possible
to appreciate the reasons that led to the founding of a multitude
of small colleges in this land.

There were not lacking, however, those who even in that day
viewed with grave concern the excessive multiplication of colleges
in America. They were, however, largely powerless to resist the
course of events. At the time of the panic of 1837, a temporary
check was given to the movement for the founding of colleges. This
period of depression worked havoc both on the older and the
younger colleges, and permanently discouraged a number of "wild-
cat" ventures, particularly in the west.[22] It was shortly after this
critical period, moreover, that the Society for the Promotion of
Collegiate and Theological Education at the West was organized.[23]
By its judicious handling of funds and its restraining influence on
the founding of colleges, much duplication and waste in the field
of higher education was prevented. The following quotation indicates the general position taken by the Society in 1847 on the
problem of the excessive multiplication of colleges:

> The tendency to the undue multiplication of Colleges at the West is
> notorious, and by none more deplored than by the members of this Board.
> The whole influence of the Society has been to terminate the day of college
> building, having its origin in the pecuniary interest of individuals or local-
> ities, and to place every movement, having such an object in view, upon a
> broader scale.[24]

The movement for the founding of colleges could not, however, be
checked. In the decade of the forties as many permanent colleges
were chartered as in the preceding decade. A vigorous protest
against the trend of the day was voiced by Henry P. Tappan, in
1850:

[21] Smith, Rev. Henry B., *An Argument for Christian Colleges*, p. 23 (pamphlet), 1857.
[22] See *Sixth Report of the S.P.C.T.E.W.*, 1849, pp. 9, 10.
[23] For a discussion of the general purposes of this society, see pp. 10-11.
[24] *Seventh Report of the S.P.C.T.E.W.*, 1847, pp. 38-39.

The idea of fitting our colleges to the temper of the multitude does not promise great results. . . . We have cheapened education so as to place it within the reach of everyone; we have retained the short term of four years, so that no great portion of life need be spent in study; and we have made the terms of admission quite easy enough. . . . The multiplication of colleges after the same model only serves to increase our difficulties. We set about putting up the same kind of buildings; we create the same number of professors, to teach the same things on the same principle; we get together a few books and some philosophical apparatus; and then we have the same annual commencements, with orations and poems, and the conferring of degrees; and we get under the same pressure of debt, and make the same appeals to the public to get us out of it; and then with our cheap education, to induce many to get educated, we experience the same anxiety to gather in as many students as possible; and since, where we cannot get money it is something to get appearance, we show the same readiness to educate for nothing those who will submit to be educated, but who cannot pay. In all this we are improving nothing; but we are taking away all dignity from our system of education, and proving its inadequacy. . . . To bring about change, we must do something besides multiplying colleges after the same model.[25]

The forces of a frontier civilization continued nevertheless to shape events and policies, for better or for worse, in the matter of college-building. It is significant that in the decade of the fifties, more than twice as many permanent colleges were founded as in the preceding decade. The protests of leading educators were of little avail. The native forces of American society were at work in the field of higher education as in other fields. The wide expanses of new territory and the unlimited resources of a new civilization provided an ever expanding opportunity for individual enterprise and local initiative in education as in other spheres of endeavor. By the time of the Civil War it was clear that America had indeed become the land of colleges. In reviewing the situation in 1876, President Anderson of the University of Rochester indicates the elemental character of the tendencies that brought into being this unique situation in higher education in America:

But we are told that there are too many colleges; and that this result is due to the voluntary system. In a free country, how can this be helped? There are just now too many banks, too many railroads, too many ships, too much iron; but the law of supply and demand is the only possible corrective for the evil. If a college attracts to itself patronage and endowment, it has a right to live; if it does not, it will die. The law of natural

[25] Tappan, *op. cit.*, pp. 65-68. A slight rearrangement has been made in the order of sentences.

selection applies to colleges as well as to the animal and vegetable world. . . .
Time alone can determine whether a college has the right to live.[26]

THE DEPENDENCE OF WESTERN COLLEGES ON THE EAST

In following the movement for the founding of colleges on the
successive frontiers of settlement across the continent, the local
and independent character of many of the western ventures in
college-building is truly impressive, but too great an emphasis on
this feature of the college movement leads to a real misinterpreta-
tion of the facts. There is a larger pattern involved which reveals
a close dependence of the frontier college on the resources of the
older communities in the east. In the founding of many western
colleges the helping hand of the older sections of the country was
evident. The significant and dramatic rôle of the "Yale Band" in
the founding of Illinois College was typical of many instances of
close coöperation in the launching of college ventures.[27] When the
personal and financial resources of the east were not available, many
western colleges languished and died. Their high mortality was due
in many instances to failure to receive adequate support in men
and money in their time of need. Many colleges about to die, on
the other hand, gained a new lease on life through receiving this
assistance.[28] It is apparent, therefore, that in higher education, as
indeed in other spheres of American life, the interests of the two
sections of the country were indissolubly united.

The economic dependence of the western states on the east has
indeed been a feature of the American development from the very
beginning, but nowhere was this economic dependence more striking than in the realm of higher education. In the financing of college
projects on the western frontier this dependence is seen in the
appointment of "agents," whose main function was the solicitation
of funds.[29] College presidents in that day, even as in our own day,
were oppressed with the necessity of appealing to the creditor east
to come to the aid of the debtor west in the common cause of higher

---

[26] Anderson, *op. cit.*, pp. 14, 15.

[27] Magoun, President G. F., *Asa Turner and His Times*, pp. 60-62, 1889. Note also the
rôle of the "Iowa Band" from Andover in the founding of Grinnell College.

[28] *Sixth Report of the S.P.C.T.E.W., 1849*, pp. 9-10.

[29] Reference to the work of college agents in the east may be found in many source
materials of this period. The following reference is typical: *Addresses and Discourse at the
Inauguration of Rev. George F. Magoun as President of Iowa College*, p. 55 (pamphlet),
1865.

education.[30] When the frontier settlements were passing through the throes of economic depression in the years following the panic of 1837, the appeals for help became more insistent and impelling. Many western colleges were placed for a time in a condition of financial insolvency and a considerable number failed to weather the crisis. In this era of financial ruin, so well portrayed in the following quotation, the utter dependence of these colleges on the philanthropy of the east stands revealed.[31]

> Times have changed. The West is no longer an El Dorado. It is a land of public and private bankruptcy, of broken promises and forfeited credit, and suspended banks, and wrecked fortunes. It is in painful and mortifying association with disappointed speculations, bad debts, unwise investments, and the sickening sense of being swindled and over-reached. The carcasses of defunct enterprises of mistaken benevolence, or mistaken speculation, have made the whole land an abomination. The color of the gold has gone. Hues of gloom, disappointment and disgust have succeeded . . . Education has suffered with other interests . . . Colleges, that have meanwhile been quietly, and soberly, and faithfully pursuing their appropriate work, relying on that enlarged and enlightened liberality that founded them, and on the consciousness of continuing to deserve it, find themselves sacrificed among the rest. . . . Subscriptions made in the days of imaginary wealth, have become valueless with the disappearance of that wealth; and Colleges organized upon the supposed validity of those subscriptions, are compelled to appeal anew for aid, or to disband.

With the rapid multiplication of colleges in the west, the sympathies of the east were strained to the utmost, and the demands of the west for financial aid soon became intolerable.[32] Following the panic of 1837, the situation became so distressing that the eastern interests set about to protect themselves from the more aggravating features of "college-begging," and at the same time, to preserve the cause of western colleges, by the organization of Educational Societies. It was at this time that the Society for the Promotion of Collegiate and Theological Education at the West was founded.[33] While this society was but one of many similar organizations, it was unquestionably the largest and most influential. During its long period of service in the cause of western education it

---

[30] An excellent summary of the general management of western colleges is to be found in Sears, J. B., *Philanthropy in the History of American Higher Education.* Bureau of Education, Bulletin, 1922, No. 26.

[31] Post, T. M., "A Plea for Western Colleges," *First Report of the S.P.C.T.E.W., 1844,* pp. 19, 20.

[32] Rammelkamp, President C. H., *Centennial History of Illinois College,* pp. 90, 160, 192, 1928.

[33] The S.P.C.T.E.W. was organized in New York City on June 30, 1843.

exemplified the highest type of statesmanship in its program for the coöperation of the east and west in the field of higher education. Its twenty-six annual reports, written by Theron Baldwin, constitute one of the most valuable sources of information on the development of higher education in the country between the years of 1844 and 1869.[34] The motives that led to its organization are well stated in the following quotation:

And this is the very thing designed to be effected by this Society. It is to unite the appropriate and the best energies of the older and the new States in harmonious coöperation, to concentrate them upon the most important points of the West, and thus to plant and cherish Colleges and Theological Schools when and where they may be most needed, and to aid them in succession, until they shall have in themselves the elements of strength, of expansion, of improvement, and of continuance.

For such a purpose as this our society was called into being, as by the voice of God. It was felt to be needed. A hundred beginnings had been already made, moved, in some instances, by religious principles and a high sense of duty; in others, by the hope of worldly emolument, and the multifarious impulses of a discordant and enterprising people. But they were without concert. Their conflicting applications came to us from every portion of the West. Benevolent men were interested in their appeals. They wished to aid the general cause. But what they gave was, in many instances, scattered and lost in ill-directed and impracticable efforts, and good men were becoming weary of the work, in the exhaustless multiplicity of its demands.

In such a state of things, it became necessary to arrest the progress of causes, which threatened not only to weaken, but even to destroy the benevolent sympathy of the East in the great cause of Western education. Western men desired it, and we saw the necessity of an organization to harmonize the diverging and scattered action which was wasting itself in this impracticable way.

Our object was to protect the churches of the East against the ill-judged and discordant appeals of the West (with which we are thronged), and, at the same time, by a Society, representing the Eastern Churches, to welcome all worthy applications from the West, and combine them into one, and thus commend them to our churches, on the effective and economical plan of a single and concentrated agency, which should have its place among the other agencies of our great Benevolent Societies.[35]

The appeals for financial aid on behalf of western colleges were often met with many objections on the part of eastern philanthropists. These objections multiplied with the increasing number of

---

[34] *Permanent Documents of the S.P.C.T.E.W.* These documents include all the annual reports, and the addresses and discourses delivered before the Society.

[35] Peters, Absalom, "Address," *Fourth Report of the S.P.C.T.E.W., 1847*, p. 34.

appeals that were made during the latter decades of the general period under consideration. Among the reasons urged against further aid were the following: (1) The colleges in the east demanded the prior consideration of philanthropists. (2) The west already had too many colleges. (3) Western colleges were generally schemes for swindling and speculation, "gulling the public with extravagant tales and promising lucrative investment of charities." (4) Colleges in the west were often visionary and improvident, having squandered the funds entrusted to them, thus destroying public confidence in their endeavors. (5) Western colleges were in many cases mere pretenders and quacks in education. (6) Many colleges in the west were hotbeds of social and economic radicalism and the rendezvous of all the "ultrisms." (7) The west would create colleges to herself when they should be required, these colleges coming into being like manufactures only when needed. (8) The east had already given much to the west, but it had effected nothing, as the west was a "bottomless gulf" into which it mattered not how much one threw, it could never be filled.[36]

In the face of such objections the educational leaders were obliged to propose more effective arguments on behalf of their struggling institutions. While the final and most effective appeal, in most cases, was to the deeper religious sentiments of the eastern philanthropists, other motives for giving were at times suggested, and often emphasized, especially in the petitions made to business men with large investments in various parts of the west. Through a well-disguised appeal to self-interest, for example, benefactions of considerable value were secured for western colleges in that era, as indeed in other eras of educational development. In the following quotation one is impressed not only by the potency of the arguments advanced, but also by the fact that in this appeal, as in many similar appeals, the interests of the west were assumed to be inextricably bound up with those of the east.[37]

The learning, religion, and the living ministry bestowed on the great West by these Colleges, unite in special benefit to mercantile morality and hence to the safety and value of business engagements there formed. Eastern merchants have an especial and increasing concern in the commercial integrity of this immense market for Eastern industry. However lightly men think of religion and of the culture attending it, they are "terribly in

---

[36] Post, *op. cit.*, pp. 28-30.
[37] Whiting, Lyman, *Address before the S.P.C.T.E.W.*, *1855*, pp. 15-17 (pamphlet).

earnest" as to the counterfeits and cheats which irreligion and ungodliness impose on them. They forget that, like the pillars of Hercules, Education and Religion define and defend the path of trade. . . . These colleges thus plead, to every enlightened merchant, his own self-preservation, and the perpetuity of the commercial virtues which adorn his own profession. . . . Every corner of the great Eastern workshop ought generously to hearken to the great Western salesroom crying out, "Save yourselves by saving us,— make sure your own interests by timely aid to ours."

Another aspect of the mutual relations of the east and west in the development of higher education to be considered in this connection, is the reproductive character of the college movement in this country. This aspect is brought out clearly in the statement made in 1855 that "colleges at the west are only seedlings from colleges at the east." [38] The frontier colleges were indeed, in many cases, seedlings planted with conscious intent and religious motive in pioneer communities by the eastern churches and colleges.[39] When the larger religious patterns of the movement for the founding of colleges are taken into consideration, it seems only natural that the leaders of that day should regard the institutions on the frontier as the daughters of the mother colleges of the east. Western colleges, modeled on the pattern of the east rather than instituted as independent colleges of the people and by the people on the frontier, may be regarded in a sense as the symbols of the dependence of the west on the religious and cultural life of the east. The term "Yankee College" became in fact a term of reproach in many pioneer communities of that day.[40] The religious and educational control exercised by the eastern interests over the institutions of the west tended in many instances to be paternalistic in nature, and few colleges were bold enough to reject this tutelage. Yet, it is probably true that this situation was to a certain extent inevitable and even desirable within reasonable limits. There is, moreover, undoubtedly a difficult problem of historical interpretation involved in the question as to whether the American college was more nearly the foster child of the east than the true product of the frontier— a frontier with needs distinctively its own and demands that might or might not be effectively met by the more or less exotic institu-

[38] *Ibid.*, p. 5.
[39] The larger patterns of denominational influence in higher education are described more fully in Chapter II.
[40] Boone, R. G., *A History of Education on Indiana*, p. 79, 1892, refers to the prevailing prejudice against "colleges, pianos, and Yankees."

tions thrust upon it by the east. It seems clear, however, that the interests of the two sections of the country were bound up, for better or for worse, with the development of most colleges in the west.[41]

Of the older colleges in the east, Yale and Princeton stand out preëminently as, each in its sphere, the "mother of colleges." [42] The missionary and evangelistic interests of the Congregational Church were centered at Yale during the early nineteenth century, and it was from that "fountain of orthodoxy" that a stream of influence went forth over a wide field of higher education in the west in the period before the Civil War. Successive institutions, such as Western Reserve and Beloit, for example, were known each in its turn, as the "Yale of the West." [43] It is stated that at least sixteen colleges were founded before the Civil War largely under the guiding hand of Yale College and its graduates.[44] Princeton was likewise, within the sphere of Presbyterian influence in higher education, the "mother of colleges." One of the historians of the Presbyterian Church has stated that "Princeton claims that twenty-five colleges in the Union indirectly owe their existence to the exertion of its graduates." [45] Although this estimate may be somewhat excessive,[46] the evidence points to the fact that the Presbyterian interests centered at Princeton were actively involved in the founding of a large number of western colleges, and even of a number of state universities, some of which continued for a considerable period to be associated with the Presbyterian Church.

Two main streams of cultural and religious influence are discernible in the activities of the eastern churches in higher education during the period before the Civil War, one emerging from Congregational New England with Yale as its source, the other from Presbyterian New Jersey and Pennsylvania with Princeton as its source, and both flowing west.[47] If space permitted, other streams

---

[41] A study of the contemporary sources reveals the fact that in many aspects of their life the western colleges were patterned on the eastern colleges.

[42] The earliest reference to Yale as the "mother of colleges" was found in the *Twelfth Report of the S.P.C.T.E.W., 1855,* p. 43.

[43] Haydn, H. C., *An Historical Sketch of Western Reserve University,* p. 15, 1895. Also personal letter of former President Eaton of Beloit College, under date of December 4, 1930.

[44] See *Yale Alumni Weekly* for October 18, 1929.

[45] Patton, J. H., *A Popular History of the Presbyterian Church of America,* p. 119, 1900.

[46] Personal letter of V. Lansing Collins, Secretary of Princeton University, under date of November 28, 1930.

[47] Schmidt, G. P., *The Old Time College President,* p. 25, 1930.

of influence having their origin in eastern colleges might be indicated, such, for example, as those deriving from the original sources of the Methodists and Baptists in the east.[48] Furthermore, it might be pointed out that certain institutions situated in regions that in time lost their pioneer character, such as Hampden-Sidney and Oberlin, became in turn centers of influence for the building up of other colleges further out on the frontier.[49] Sufficient evidence has been presented, however, to indicate the reproductive character of colleges in the development of higher education in America and to call attention to the existence of a wider influence in the early history of higher education in this country. The movement for the founding of colleges in America, to be rightly understood, therefore, must be viewed in the light of this larger pattern, involving the dependence of the west on the personal, economic, cultural, and religious resources of the east.

THE EXPANDING FIELD OF HIGHER EDUCATION

In the period before the Civil War, the legal foundations of one hundred and eighty-two permanent colleges were laid in this country.[50] Many others were founded in the pre-Civil War period, but none of these was able to survive the exigencies of time and circumstances. One of the striking aspects of the college movement in this country has indeed been the high mortality of these establishments. In order to arrive at a strictly accurate statement of the total number founded before the Civil War it would be necessary to undertake an extensive program of research in the legal documents of the thirty-four states that were admitted before 1861, recording the exact number chartered as degree-conferring institutions in each year of our history up to that date. Such an extensive piece of research was obviously beyond the scope of the present study. In order to determine, however, the approximate number that failed to survive, an examination was made of the legal records of all colleges chartered in sixteen states and a general survey was also made of all those founded in a large number of other states. The detailed evidence growing out of this investigation will be presented

[48] Randolph-Macon in the south and Wesleyan in the north for the Methodists; and Brown and George Washington for the Baptists.

[49] Historical statement in Catalogue of Hampden-Sidney College for 1927-28; also Mathews, L. K., *The Expansion of New England*, p. 187, 1909.

[50] This number represents about one-third of the 600 odd colleges of liberal arts and science existing in America today. State universities are included in these totals, but are considered separately in a later section of this study.

in connection with a later discussion of the problem of the mortality of colleges.[51]

A list of all permanent colleges founded before the Civil War has been prepared for the specific purposes of this study, and is given at the end of the present chapter. All statements of facts relating to the colleges founded before 1861 are based on this list, which was prepared from an intensive research in original legal sources. Column 1 of the following table summarizes the data given in the list and indicates the number of permanent colleges founded in each decade of our history up to the time of the Civil War. The approximate figures given by Dexter and Cubberley for the total number of colleges founded during each decade before that time [52] are added in columns 2 and 3.

TABLE I

SUMMARY TABLE OF COLLEGES FOUNDED DURING EACH DECADE
BEFORE THE CIVIL WAR

PERIODS BEFORE THE CIVIL WAR	PERMANENT COLLEGES	ALL COLLEGES (BY DEXTER)	ALL COLLEGES (BY CUBBERLEY)
Colonial Era	9	9	10
1780–1789	10	—	7
1790–1799	6	13 *	7
1800–1809	5	8	9
1810–1819	7	5	5
1820–1829	12	20	22
1830–1839	35	36	38
1840–1849	32	36	42
1850–1861	66	82	92
TOTAL	182	209	232

* This figure refers to the number of colleges founded between 1780 and 1799.

The general trend of the movement for the founding of colleges before the Civil War may be inferred from the figures given above. It is apparent that a marked acceleration took place in the decade

[51] See pp. 23-28.
[52] Dexter, E. S., *A History of Education in the United States*, p. 270, 1904; and Cubberley, E. P., *The History of Education*, p. 705, 1920. The figures of Dexter and Cubberley are largely based on statistics found in the *1870 Report* of the U. S. Commissioner of Education, pp. 506-517, which are, however, admittedly incomplete. Dexter and Cubberley have based their lists on definitions of the "founding" and "standards" of colleges that are different from those used in this study.

of the thirties. The rapid multiplication of colleges taking place in this decade continued unabated in that of the forties, after the recovery from the panic of 1837. The peak of the movement was reached in the decade of the fifties,[53] when more than twice as many permanent colleges were founded as in the preceding ten years. Taking the period from 1830 to 1861 as a whole, it will be noted that 133 permanent colleges were founded. It is significant that these decades of accelerated development in higher education in this country coincided with the period of the great migrations westward. Evidence of the significance of the movement of the population during this period is found in the fact that while in 1830 the regions west of the Alleghenies contained less than one-half as many inhabitants as the area east of the mountains did, in 1860 the population west of the Alleghenies had become actually greater than that in the Atlantic states.[54] It was during this era that America moved west.

The accompanying series of maps shows the density of population for each decade of the census from 1790 to 1860, and portrays in a vivid way the general spread of population westward.[55] The location of the permanent colleges founded in each decade, as given in the Appendix, may be studied in relation to these maps. The essential pioneering character of the American college thus stands revealed. The large number of colleges established on the frontier lines of settlement at every stage of the college movement, and the small number established in the older and more densely populated sections of the country, as indicated on the accompanying maps, emphasizes the fact that the development of higher education in this country was an integral part of a vital expansive movement in the life of America.[56] The founding of colleges in this country is seen to be clearly related to the westward spread of the population. Maps showing the spread of denominational population as given in Chapter II, present an even more significant picture of the college movement. The missionary character of the American college, moreover, stands revealed in no uncertain terms. In the religious, as well

[53] The movement for the founding of colleges, however, continued at only a slightly reduced rate until 1890.

[54] Scribner's Statistical Atlas of the United States, Plates 19 and 20, 1885.

[55] This series of eight maps is used with the kind permission of the Carnegie Institution in Washington and the American Geographical Society in New York.

[56] The term "frontier" is used in this study to denote regions either in the west or in the east that were sparsely settled, i.e., with a population of less than forty-five inhabitants per square mile.

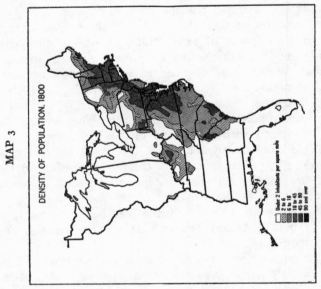

MAP 3

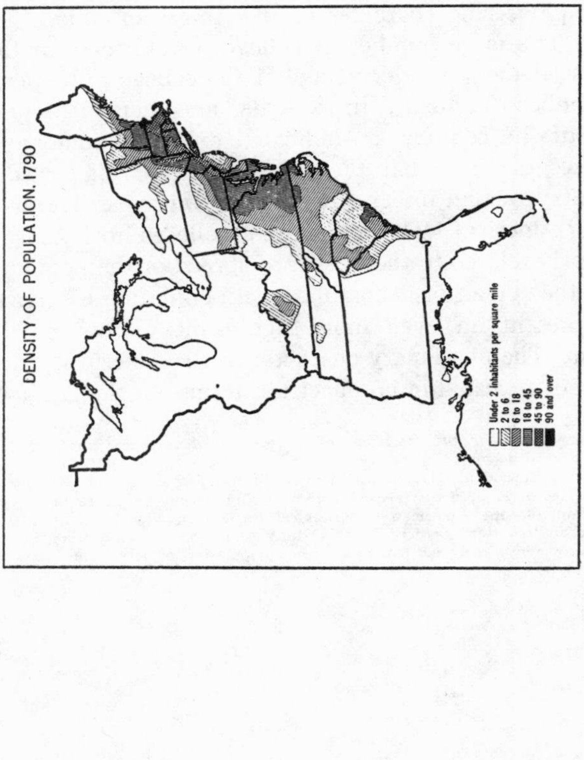

DENSITY OF POPULATION. 1800

Under 2 inhabitants per square mile
2 to 6
6 to 18
18 to 45
45 to 90
90 and over

MAP 2

DENSITY OF POPULATION. 1790

Under 2 inhabitants per square mile
2 to 6
6 to 18
18 to 45
45 to 90
90 and over

Maps used by the courtesy of the Carnegie Institution, Washington, D. C.

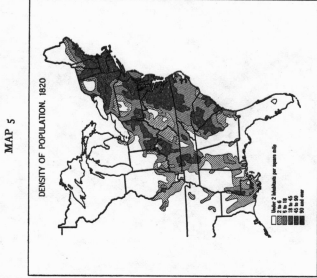

MAP 5

DENSITY OF POPULATION. 1820

Under 2 inhabitants per square mile
2 to 6
6 to 18
18 to 45
45 to 90
90 and over

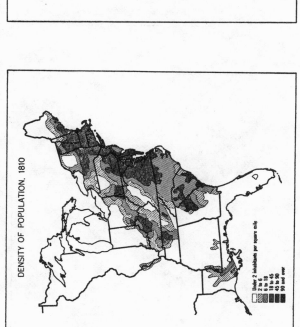

MAP 4

DENSITY OF POPULATION. 1810

Under 2 inhabitants per square mile
2 to 6
6 to 18
18 to 45
45 to 90
90 and over

Maps used by the courtesy of the Carnegie Institution, Washington, D. C.

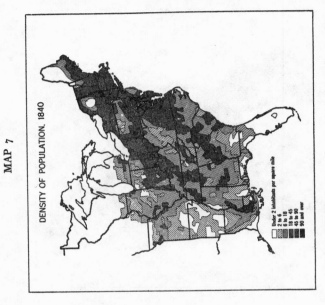

MAP 7

DENSITY OF POPULATION. 1840

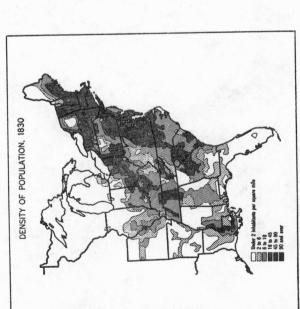

MAP 6

DENSITY OF POPULATION. 1830

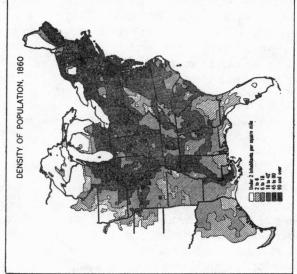

MAP 9

DENSITY OF POPULATION, 1860

Under 2 Inhabitants per square mile
2 to 6
6 to 18
18 to 45
45 to 90
90 and over

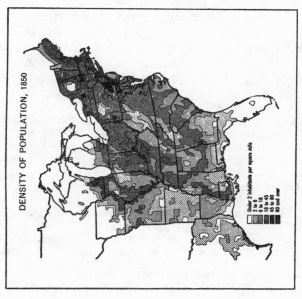

MAP 8

DENSITY OF POPULATION, 1850

Under 2 Inhabitants per square mile
2 to 6
6 to 18
18 to 45
45 to 90
90 and over

Maps used by the courtesy of the Carnegie Institution, Washington, D. C.

as the cultural sense, therefore, the American college was indeed the agent of an advancing civilization and the product of the moving frontier. The following quotation, often repeated in the glamorous days of western settlement, reflects the dominant mood of the pioneers who set out to conquer and subdue a vast continent, as well as of the more foresighted leaders who undertook the task of building up colleges along the broad expanse of territory.

> Westward the course of empire takes its way,
> The first four acts already past,
> A fifth shall close the drama with the day;
> Time's noblest offspring is the last.[57]

Following in the wake of the westward trend of population, and in the path of the spiritual conquest of a continent, the course of higher education in like manner took its way westward. The expanding purposes of a "Christian" society demanded the building up of a series of colleges on the advancing line of a frontier civilization. The story of a Harvard, founded in a struggling frontier village numbering only twenty-five houses, and surrounded by a stockade against the Indians, was repeated on a hundred fronts in the course of this development.[58] The western colleges, thus serving as the agents of a moving population, carried the benefits of culture and religion to the remotest ends of a vast empire. The following contemporary statements reveal the larger designs and purposes of the general movement of the founding of colleges in America, and testify in no uncertain terms to the stirring character and frontier aspect of this educational development:

The quality of Western Society, combined with the bold, prompt, energetic, and adventurous temperament impressed generally upon it by common influences in the life of the emigrant, exposes it to vehement and brief excitements, to epidemic delusions and agitation. Upon this sea of incoherent and vehement mind, every wind of opinion has been let loose, and is struggling for the mastery; and the mass heaves restlessly to and fro under the thousand different forces impressed. The West is, therefore, peculiarly perturbed with demagogism and popular agitation, not only in politics, but in religion, and all social interests. Amid these shifting social elements, we want principles of stability, we want a system of permanent forces, we want deep, strong and constant influences, that shall take from the change-

---

[57] Berkeley, Bishop George, quoted in Tyler, *op. cit.*, p. 15.
[58] Eaton, E. D., *The Inevitable Relation of Congregationalists to Education*, p. 6 (pamphlet), 1923.

fulness and excitability of the western mind, by giving it the tranquillity of depth, and shall protect it from delusive and fitful impulses, by enduing it with a calm, profound, and pure reason . . . the above exigencies of Western society cannot be met without colleges.[59]

When the effervescence of that world of commingled elements shall have subsided, and the race for choice locations in unoccupied territory terminated—when the prize of wealth, to be secured by a single fortunate turn, shall have ceased to dazzle the young men of the West, and the work of felling the forest, and settling the prairie, been in a measure completed—when the people shall have acquired the means of educating their sons, and society presents its thousand openings for educated mind—then we may expect that Western youth will crowd the Halls of Learning which we now erect.[60]

In the history of the West, the age of steam synchronizes with that of missions; and the thunder of its progress westward is no louder than the call upon all who love the kingdom of Christ, or their country, to send into the wide fields, which this great agency of civilization opens, all the creative and moulding forces of Christian society. The year 1826 was signalized by a somewhat remarkable coincidence, viz., the charter of the first American railroad, the organization of the American Home Missionary Society, and the founding of Western Reserve College. The first, inaugurating a system whose grandest developments are to be witnessed on our vast Western domain; the second, opening a channel of benevolence, whose influence upon the evangelization of that land has thus far surpassed, in scope and power, that of any other single instrumentality; and the third, constituting the first, in a series of institutions, destined to carry the light of Christian learning from the Alleghenies to the Pacific.[61]

THE MORTALITY OF COLLEGES ON THE FRONTIER

In the light of the picture that has been drawn of the rapid increase in the number of colleges along the lines of frontier settlement, it would be natural to expect that their mortality rate would be high. One of the most striking and distinctive features of this educational development has indeed been the large number of colleges that have failed to survive the exigencies of a pioneer civilization. Acute observers of the development of higher education in America have noted from time to time this particular feature. President Lindsley of the University of Nashville, for example, in speaking in 1829 of the excessive multiplication of colleges in this country, observed that

[59] Post, *op. cit.*, pp. 26-27.
[60] *Twelfth Report of the S.P.C.T.E.W., 1855*, p. 46.
[61] *Thirteenth Report of the S.P.C.T.E.W., 1856*, pp. 42-43.

Colleges rise up like mushrooms in our luxurious soil. They are duly lauded and puffed for a day, and then they sink to be heard no more.[62]

Theron Baldwin, a well-qualified observer of the American scene, stated in 1864 that

The annalist who should be faithful in respect to these obituary records could hardly fail to swell the list to somewhat formidable proportions— and if a headstone were put up for each, bearing the inscription "In Memoriam," the traveller, after lengthened journies by lake and forest, and prairie, might find himself still within the enclosures of this apparently limitless burial ground.[63]

Among the many factors that have been responsible for the death of colleges in this country, the following may be selected for special consideration, viz., financial disaster, denominational competition, unfavorable location, natural catastrophes, and internal dissensions. Most of the colleges founded on the frontier were faced from the very beginning with serious financial embarrassments. In many cases these institutions were largely dependent, as has been pointed out in a previous connection, on the wealth of the east. This source of support was, to say the least, temporary and uncertain in character; failure to win the support of religious and philanthropic interests in the east generally meant disaster for the frontier college. On the other hand, success along this line made it possible for certain institutions to weather the more serious financial crises, such as the panics of 1837 and 1857, and ultimately to win out in the severe struggle for existence on the frontier.[64] Local sources of support were indeed drawn upon as far as possible, but such support was at best meager, and only a few colleges were able to place themselves during this period upon a sound basis of local support.[65] The history of the sacrifices made by frontier communities during the early years of existence of many colleges is a noble one, but in most cases a sad one. Colleges multiplied with such rapidity in response to the local needs of widely scattered communities that tragedy was an almost inevitable consequence.[66] The course of de-

[62] Halsey, Le Roy J., Editor, *The Works of Philip Lindsley*, vol. 1, p. 213, 1864.
[63] *Twenty-first Report of the S.P.C.T.E.W.*, *1864*, p. 21.
[64] The whole subject of the relation of the college movement to economic factors in the history of this country remains a subject to be adequately studied.
[65] The adoption of "manual labor" features by many colleges during this period was in part due to the desire of institutions to provide for a more stable source of local support.
[66] It must be kept in mind that many questionable ventures in higher education were undertaken during this era of college-building. Among these must be included the "real

velopment of higher education in this country is literally strewn with the wrecks of colleges that met their fate on the rocks of financial insolvency.

The effects of denominational competition on the college movement were particularly disastrous on account of the fact that the struggle for dominance in the field of higher education was accentuated in this country by the inordinate desire of various churches for possession of the "promised land." Colleges were subjected to the special exigencies of a religious campaign for the conquest of a vast continent. This struggle for territory was reenacted on each successive frontier, and thus the effects on the college movement were cumulative in character. Colleges were built up only to be abandoned as the scene of warfare moved elsewhere, and as the strategy of some new advance necessitated the shifting of the forces of the various armies of occupation. The history of higher education in each of the states in the Union during the pre-Civil War period reveals to a greater or lesser degree the costly nature of the struggle between the various denominations.[67] The fortunes of the institutions that were established in such large numbers in each state as strategic centers of denominational advance were closely correlated with the general progress of the campaign for the occupation of the frontier territory. While it is not possible to describe more fully in this connection the struggle for dominance in the field of higher education among the denominations in any one state, it may be said that the general picture that has been drawn is true to the facts revealed by a careful reading of contemporary sources.[68] It was not until the smoke of the battle had cleared away that it was possible to count the cost and to determine which enterprises were destined to remain as more or less permanent institutions of higher education.

Colleges in this country have generally been regarded as the special pride of local communities, but this fact did not necessarily ensure their survival. In the founding of most of them, the question of location was a matter for competition among the various com-

estate" colleges, which were founded as purely speculative ventures. See Halsey, *op. cit.*, vol. I, p. 570.

[67] Kentucky and Tennessee represent states where the struggle was particularly severe, and the mortality of colleges in consequence unusually high. The author is arranging to have the history of higher education in the various states studied during the next few years by graduate students in connection with a course in the History of Higher Education in America.

[68] In the writings of Philip Lindsley, Asa Turner, and J. M. Sturtevant, for example, abundant evidence may be found of the severe nature of the struggle.

munities desirous of seeing the college located in their midst. They were bid for and sold in the open market, the highest bidder generally winning out in the transaction.[69] When it came about that an institution was finally situated as a result of this procedure, the community often found itself unable to contribute further to its support. In this situation the college often found it easier to close up its affairs permanently than to attempt to move to a new location. The colleges of this country were subject to many variable factors in the local situation. In the course of the movement of population westward certain communities, boasting of the presence of a collegiate institution, found themselves losing out in the struggle to build up the town or city of their hopes. When it became apparent that the future belonged to some other settlement for one of a large number of reasons, the college shared with the community in the dwindling of its hopes. In the shifting of denominational population it often suffered the loss of constituencies and was obliged for this reason to move or to close its doors. Thus it will be seen that the high mortality of colleges in this country may be accounted for in part by the exigencies of a civilization subject to rapid changes in the fortunes of local communities.

It is truly amazing to discover the large number that met their fate through the working of natural catastrophes. Destruction by fire was in that day a most common occurrence and a most disastrous one. When the inadequate resources of most colleges are taken into consideration, it will be seen that reconstruction was in many cases out of the question. While a considerable number were eventually rebuilt on the ruins of a former institution,[70] colleges in general were forced, as a consequence of destruction by fire, to resign themselves to their fate. Although great care was taken in most cases to choose locations that were favorable from the standpoint of health, the prevalence of such diseases as malaria, smallpox, cholera, and fevers of various sorts in that day led to the temporary suspension or the permanent abandonment of certain enterprises.[71] Life on the frontier was at best an adventurous affair, and college communities shared in the risks involved. Even in the more settled regions there was constant danger from epidemics of various kinds.

[69] Even in a state such as Connecticut, we find that financial inducements were important considerations in the eventual location of Yale, Trinity, and Wesleyan.

[70] Cokesbury College in Maryland, for example, was rebuilt in 1795 after being destroyed by fire. A second fire, a year later, led to the abandonment of the college.

[71] See Thwing, C. F., *History of Higher Education in America*, p. 216, 1906, for some light on this aspect of the situation.

Proposals for removal to a more healthful location were often entertained and in some cases carried out. When, however, the ravages of some disease periodically afflicted the personnel, it often proved the final blow to an institution already beset by innumerable other difficulties.

Among the causes for the abandonment of college enterprises must be reckoned the internal dissensions that developed to an acute stage in so many institutions. It must be kept in mind that those on the frontier were experiments in institutional management conducted under the most trying circumstances. For one thing, the student body was made up of youth accustomed to the individualistic ways of a frontier existence. Thus the problem of discipline was an ever-present source of difficulty. In striving to meet this problem the faculty were often set off against the trustees, who in that day took a more active part in the internal affairs of a college than is the custom today. Constant friction between these two groups contributed in a number of instances to eventual disruption.[72] Furthermore, the internal life of many of them was seriously affected by the controversies that were waged in society during that day. Factions developed within the institution which reflected the party strife on religious and political questions. Beset within and without by influences often beyond their own control, it is small wonder that many colleges in this country eventually gave way to the favored few in the struggle for existence. The high mortality rate in the states was an inevitable corollary of the situation that has been outlined in the preceding pages. Although the limitations of this study have precluded a fuller treatment of this particular subject of the mortality of colleges, sufficient material has perhaps been presented to account for the large number that have failed to survive in this country. It remains to consider briefly the statistical aspects of the subject.

As indicated in another connection, an intensive study was made of the mortality of colleges in sixteen states for the period before the Civil War, using the Session Laws of each state as a primary source. In these states the average mortality rate was found to be 81%. In this study, a college was assumed to have died, if it is not in existence today (1927-28) as an institution of higher education bearing its original name or a new one. The lists of those that have perished are now filed under the author's name in a

[72] Dickinson College in Pennsylvania is an instance in point.

manuscript in the Teachers College Library. The results of this
particular study are given in the table below. A survey of the situation that existed in the eighteen other states of the Union before the
Civil War led to the conclusion that in twelve states the average
mortality rate was approximately as high as that existing in the
sixteen studied more intensively, while in six states, viz., Maine,
Vermont, New Hampshire, Massachusetts, Connecticut, and Rhode
Island, the average mortality rate was low. In the light of this

TABLE II

MORTALITY OF COLLEGES FOUNDED BEFORE THE CIVIL WAR IN SIXTEEN
STATES OF THE UNION

S.N.	NAME OF STATE	TOTAL COLLEGES	LIVING COLLEGES	DEAD COLLEGES	MORTALITY RATE
1	PENNSYLVANIA	31	16	15	48%
2	NEW YORK	36	15	21	58%
3	OHIO	43	17	26	60%
4	VIRGINIA	32	10	22	69%
5	NORTH CAROLINA	26	7	19	73%
6	MARYLAND	23	5	18	78%
7	ALABAMA	23	4	19	83%
8	TENNESSEE	46	7	39	84%
9	GEORGIA	51	7	44	86%
10	LOUISIANA	26	3	23	88%
11	MISSOURI	85	8	77	90%
12	MISSISSIPPI	29	2	27	93%
13	TEXAS	40	2	38	95%
14	KANSAS	20	1	19	95%
15	FLORIDA	2	0	2	100%
16	ARKANSAS	3	0	3	100%
	TOTAL FOR 16 STATES	516 =	104 +	412	81%*

* Average mortality rate for 16 states.

study of sixteen states and this survey of eighteen other states, it
is apparent that the mortality rate for the country as a whole was
higher than has generally been assumed to be the case.

THE PERMANENT COLLEGES AND UNIVERSITIES FOUNDED BEFORE THE CIVIL WAR

Among the large number of colleges founded along the lines of
frontier settlement across the continent during the period before
the Civil War, one hundred and eighty-two were able to maintain
a legal existence up to the present day. In Table IV, pages 32 to 54,

a list of these "permanent" institutions, arranged in order of their founding, is given. This list has been constructed on the basis of an extended research in legal and official sources,[73] and represents an initial attempt to bring some order out of the prevailing confusion with regard to the founding of colleges in this country. The procedure followed in discovering the exact number that were founded before 1861, and were able to maintain a legal existence up to the present day, was a laborious one. The legal histories of all those existing in 1927-28,[74] which made a claim to have been founded before the Civil War, were examined, in order to establish their right to inclusion in the present list under the definitions set up for the purposes of the study.[75] Leads from various types of sources were likewise followed up in order to make it reasonably certain that no college that should be included in the present list would be omitted.[76]

The need of accurate and definitive data bearing on the founding of colleges in America is apparent to all who are familiar with the literature on the history of higher education.[77] Errors of fact and interpretation abound in such materials as college histories, historical statements in catalogues, general histories of education, and works on higher education in general that make incidental or extended reference to the founding of colleges. Claims and counter-claims are made in various sources, and errors of fact once committed to print have tended to reproduce themselves in succeeding publications. Conflicting interpretations are found in various accounts, and a general lack of definition in the use of terms has added to the confusion in the field. Much of the present chaos with respect to such specific matters as the date of the founding of a college, the changes in name and location, the date of the granting

[73] The Session Laws of thirty-four states were used as the primary sources for this study.

[74] See *Statistics of Universities, Colleges, and Professional Schools, 1927-28*, U. S. Office of Education Bulletin, 1929, No. 38.

[75] A questionnaire entitled, "A Request for Historical Information," was sent to the President of each institution in the country claiming to have been founded before the Civil War. The returns were used in order to give added validity to the study.

[76] The author would appreciate information on any college omitted by mistake from this list.

[77] Two general lists of colleges provided some help in determining the colleges to be studied for inclusion in the present definitive list, viz., U. S. Commissioner of Education, *Report for 1870*, pp. 506-17; and West, A. F., *The American College*, in Butler, N. M., *Education in the United States*, pp. 37-40, 1900. Both these lists proved to be grossly inaccurate and lacking in definition. On the difficulty of compiling a satisfactory list, see Barnard, F. A. P., *On the Regulation and Control of Degree-Controlling Power*, pp. 5, 6, 1880.

of the legal right to confer degrees, and the denominational or other associations, appears to be due in large part at least to the want of some standard reference in which such aspects of the college movement are set forth in an accurate and definitive manner. The present list was undertaken by the author as a preliminary step toward meeting this need.

In the endeavor to make the list definitive as well as accurate, it was necessary to set up at the outset a number of definitions which would serve as guiding principles in the selection of materials.[78] A "college" has been defined for the purposes of the list as an institution of higher education which is legally empowered to confer degrees in the liberal arts. Institutions known as universities, colleges, seminaries, or institutes, if granted the right to confer degrees, have been included in the list. Higher institutions of a technical or professional character are not included in the list, unless they were also granted the right to confer degrees in the liberal arts. The date of "founding" of a college has been defined as the date on which the legal right to confer degrees was granted to the institution either by implication or by explicit reference.[79] In cases where this right was granted by implication, footnote notation to this effect has been made. Changes in name and location are indicated for each one included. The present name and location are given first in every instance in the list, working back to the original name and location of the college. The dates of legal change in name, and the dates of actual removal of location are given in each instance. The exact date, by day, month and year, of the founding of each college is indicated, and page reference is given to the Session Laws where the legal sanction for the establishment of the institution is recorded. The primary denominational or other association of the college during its early years is given in every instance. Confirmation of this association is to be found in other sections of the study where the histories of the various colleges are considered in more detail. The date on which the first degrees in the liberal arts were conferred is indicated in all cases where such dates could be ascertained. Colleges included in the list have been given an index

---

[78] The term "definitive" is used in this connection not in the sense of "final" or "perfect" but in the original sense of the term, denoting a list that is based on data that are selected on certain defined principles of selection.

[79] In the literature on the founding of colleges and universities in this country, the term "founding" has been variously used to refer to the date of the organization or the opening of an institution, rather than to the date of the legal organization of a degree-conferring institution.

number as well as a serial number.[80] The index number, for the purposes of identification, is prefixed by the letter (A), signifying that it was a pre-Civil War (*ante-bellum*) college which has survived up to the present time. In a supplementary list of those, founded before the Civil War, which failed to survive, the prefix (M) is used to signify that it is a dead (*mortuum*) college. The serial number indicates the chronological position which it occupies in the definitive list of those founded before 1861. While priorities in the founding of colleges are established by the use of these serial numbers, it is to be noted that such priorities exist only by virtue of the definitions set up for the purposes of this study. With these words of explanation, the "List of Permanent Colleges and Universities Founded before the Civil War" is presented, together with Table III, "Summary Table of Permanent Colleges and Universities Founded before the Civil War Arranged by States."[81]

TABLE III

SUMMARY TABLE OF PERMANENT COLLEGES AND UNIVERSITIES FOUNDED BEFORE THE CIVIL WAR ARRANGED BY STATES

S.N.	STATE	COLLEGES	S.N.	STATE	COLLEGES
1	OHIO	17	20	CONNECTICUT	3
2	PENNSYLVANIA	16	21	LOUISIANA	3
3	NEW YORK	15	22	NEW JERSEY	3
4	ILLINOIS	12	23	VERMONT	3
5	INDIANA	9	24	MAINE	2
6	VIRGINIA	9	25	MINNESOTA	2
7	MISSOURI	8	26	MISSISSIPPI	2
8	TENNESSEE	8	27	OREGON	2
9	SOUTH CAROLINA	7	28	TEXAS	2
10	GEORGIA	6	29	DELAWARE	1
11	IOWA	6	30	KANSAS	1
12	KENTUCKY	6	31	NEW HAMPSHIRE	1
13	MICHIGAN	6	32	RHODE ISLAND	1
14	NORTH CAROLINA	6	33	ARKANSAS	0
15	WISCONSIN	6	34	FLORIDA	0
16	MARYLAND	5		(DISTRICT OF COLUMBIA	2)
17	ALABAMA	4			
18	CALIFORNIA	4		TOTAL	182
19	MASSACHUSETTS	4			

[80] Colleges in existence today, like Franklin and Marshall College in Pennsylvania, which are the result of a merger of two or more former institutions are listed as a unified institution in the present list, and given one index number and one serial number. In every instance of a merger, footnote reference to this effect is made.

[81] Table III is based on the "List of Permanent Colleges and Universities Founded before the Civil War Arranged by States" given in the Appendix, which in turn is a rearrangement of Table IV.

TABLE IV

LIST OF PERMANENT COLLEGES AND UNIVERSITIES FOUNDED BEFORE THE
CIVIL WAR ARRANGED IN ORDER OF THEIR FOUNDING

Colleges Founded (1636-1776)

S.N.	I.N.	CHANGES IN NAME AND LOCATION	CHARTER-DEGREE DATE
1	A1	HARVARD UNIVERSITY (1780)	
		Cambridge, Mass.	
		Harvard College (1639)	
		Cambridge, Mass.	
		"School or College"................*October 28, 1636*[82]	
		Newtown, Mass.	
		(Mass. Gen'l Court Rec., vol. 1, p. 183)	
		Cambridge, Mass. (1638)	
		(Congregational, then Unitarian) (Degrees 1642)	
2	A2	COLLEGE OF WILLIAM AND MARY.........*February 8, 1693*[83]	
		Williamsburg, Va. (Hening's Statutes, vol. 1, p. 122)	
		(Episcopal) (Degrees 1700)	
3	A3	YALE UNIVERSITY (1887)	
		New Haven, Conn.	
		Yale College (1745)	
		New Haven, Conn.	
		"Collegiate School"................*October 16, 1701*[84]	
		Killingworth, Conn.	
		(Conn. Gen'l Court Rec., vol. 4, p. 363)	
		Saybrook, Conn. 1707	
		New Haven, Conn. 1716	
		(Congregational) (Degrees 1702)	
4	A4	PRINCETON UNIVERSITY (1896)	
		Princeton, N. J.	
		College of New Jersey................*October 22, 1746*[85]	
		Elizabethtown, N. J.	
		(Penn. Gazette for August 13, 1747)	

[82] Although the Act of 1636 did not explicitly grant the institution the right to confer degrees, this right was implied in the establishment of the institution, and degrees were actually conferred, beginning in August, 1642. A full charter was not granted to Harvard until 1650. Quincy, J., *History of Harvard University,* vol. 2, Appendix, 1840.

[83] No explicit reference to the right to confer degrees is made in the charter of the college, but that an implied right existed is clear from the fact that degrees were actually conferred at a later time without challenge. For charter in full, *see* Parsons, E. C., *Educational Legislation and Administration of the Colonial Governments,* pp. 361-378, 1899.

[84] A full charter was not granted to Yale until 1745, but the Act of 1701 provided for the conferring of degrees.

[85] There is no official record of the charter of 1746 in existence, but an advertisement in the Pennsylvania Gazette gives the substance of the charter. On September 14, 1748, a confirmatory charter was granted. Maclean, J., *History of the College of New Jersey,* vol. 1, pp. 90-97, 1877.

Newark, N. J. 1747

Princeton, N. J. 1756

(Presbyterian) (Degrees 1748)

5   A5   COLUMBIA UNIVERSITY (1912)

New York, N. Y.

Columbia College (1787)

New York, N. Y.

University of the State of New York (1784)[86]

New York, N. Y.

King's College . . . .*October 31, 1754*

New York, N. Y.

(Moore, N. F., Hist. Sketch of Col. Univ., p. 12)

(Episcopal) (Degrees 1758)

6   A6   UNIVERSITY OF PENNSYLVANIA (1791)[87]

Philadelphia, Pa.

College, Academy, and Charitable School . . . . . .*June 16, 1755*

Philadelphia, Pa.

(Wood, G. B., Early Hist. of the U. of Pa., p. 17)

(Episcopal, then Presbyterian) (Degrees 1757)

7   A7   BROWN UNIVERSITY (1804)

Providence, R. I.

College of Rhode Island . . . .*October 24, 1765*

Providence, R. I.

(Rec. of R. I. Colony, vol. 6, pp. 385-391)

(Baptist) (Degrees 1769)

8   A8   RUTGERS UNIVERSITY (1924)

New Brunswick, N. J.

(State University of New Jersey [1917])

New Brunswick, N. J.

Rutgers College (1825)

New Brunswick, N. J.

Queen's College . . . .*November 10, 1766* [88]

New Brunswick, N. J.

(New York Mercury, April 20, 1767)

(Dutch Reformed) (Degrees 1774)

9   A9   DARTMOUTH COLLEGE . . . .*December 13, 1769* [89]

Hanover, N. H.

(Smith, B. P., Hist. of Dart. Col., pp. 457-464)

(Congregational) (Degrees 1771)

[86] See pp. 145-146 for a discussion of the changes that took place in 1784 and 1787.

[87] See pp. 146-147 for a discussion of the Acts of 1779, 1789, and 1791.

[88] There is no record of the charter of 1766 in existence. The substance of the charter is given, however, in the *New York Mercury*. General powers were granted to the college, including by implication the right to confer degrees. Another charter was granted on March 10, 1770. In this charter explicit reference is made to the right to confer degrees. Demarest, W. H. S., *A History of Rutgers College*, pp. 57-58, 1924.

[89] See pp. 64-66 for a discussion of the Dartmouth College Case decision of 1819 in reference to the act of the New Hampshire legislature of 1816.

Colleges Founded (1780-1789)

S.N.	I.N.	CHANGES IN NAME AND LOCATION	CHARTER-DEGREE DATE

10 A10 WASHINGTON COLLEGE......................*April —, 1782*
        Chestertown, Md.   (Md. Laws, 1782, chap. 8)
        (Episcopal) (Degrees 1783)

11 A32 WASHINGTON AND LEE UNIVERSITY (1871)
        Lexington, Va.
        Washington College (1813)
        Lexington, Va.
        Washington Academy (1798)
        Lexington, Va.
        Liberty Hall Academy...................*October —, 1782*
        Lexington, Va.   (Hening's Statutes, vol. 11, p. 164)
        (Presbyterian) (Degrees 1785)

12 A11 HAMPDEN-SIDNEY COLLEGE....................*May —, 1783*
        Hampden-Sidney, Va. (Hening's Statutes, vol. 11, p. 272)
        (Presbyterian) (Degrees 1786)

13 A24 TRANSYLVANIA COLLEGE (1915)[90]
        Lexington, Ky.
        Transylvania University (1798)
        Lexington, Ky.
        Transylvania Seminary.....................*May 5, 1783*
        Danville, Ky.   (Hening's Statutes, vol. 11, p. 282)
        Lexington, Ky. 1789
        (Presbyterian, then Others) (Degrees 1790)

14 A12 DICKINSON COLLEGE......................*September 9, 1783*
        Carlisle, Pa.   (Pa. Laws 1783, vol. 2, p. 76)
        (Presbyterian, then Methodist) (Degrees 1787)

15 A13 ST. JOHN'S COLLEGE......................*November —, 1784*
        Annapolis, Md.   (Md. Laws 1784, chap. 37)
        (Episcopal) (Degrees 1793)

16 A14 UNIVERSITY OF GEORGIA....................*January 27, 1785*
        Athens, Ga.   (Ga. Laws, vol. 1, p. 560)
        (State) (Degrees 1804)

17 A15 COLLEGE OF CHARLESTON....................*March 19, 1785*
        Charleston, S. C.   (S. C. Laws, vol. 4, p. 677)
        (Episcopal, then Municipal) (Degrees 1794)

18 A16 FRANKLIN AND MARSHALL COLLEGE (1850)[91]
        Lancaster and Mercersburg, Pa.
        Lancaster, Pa. 1853
        Franklin College.......................*March 10, 1787*
        Lancaster, Pa.   (Pa. Laws, vol. 12, p. 395)
        (German Reformed) (Degrees 1853)

---

[90] Transylvania University was merged with Kentucky University in 1865, but became a separate institution in 1908 under its former name. In 1915 it was renamed Transylvania College.

[91] Marshall College, chartered in 1836, was merged with Franklin College in 1850.

S.N.	I.N.	CHANGES IN NAME AND LOCATION	CHARTER-DEGREE DATE

19 A17 UNIVERSITY OF NORTH CAROLINA.........*December 11, 1789*
    Chapel Hill, N. C.   (Nash Digest, N. C., vol. 2, p. 427)
    (State) (Degrees 1798)

Colleges Founded (1790-1799)

20 A18 UNIVERSITY OF VERMONT..................*November 3, 1791*
    Burlington, Vt.   (Vt. Laws 1791-92, p. 302)
    (State) (Degrees 1804)

21 A19 WILLIAMS COLLEGE..........................*June 22, 1793*
    Williamstown, Mass.   (Mass. Laws 1892-93, p. 405)
    (Congregational) (Degrees 1795)

22 A20 BOWDOIN COLLEGE.........................*June 24, 1794*
    Brunswick, Me.   (Me. Laws 1894, p. 673)
    (Congregational) (Degrees 1806)

23 A21 TUSCULUM COLLEGE (1913)
    Greeneville, Tenn.
    Greeneville and Tusculum College (1868)[92]
        Tusculum, Tenn.
    Greeneville College ....*September 3, 1794*
        Greeneville, Tenn.   (Catalogue and History)
    (Presbyterian) (Degrees 1808)

24 A22 UNIVERSITY OF TENNESSEE (1879)
    Knoxville, Tenn.
    East Tennessee University (1840)
    Knoxville, Tenn.
    East Tennessee College (1807)
    Knoxville, Tenn.
    Blount College......................*September 10, 1794*
        Knoxville, Tenn.   (Tenn. Laws 1794, chap. 18)
    (Presbyterian, then State) (Degrees 1806)

25 A23 UNION UNIVERSITY (1873)
    Schenectady, N. Y.
    Union College......................*February 25, 1795*
        Schenectady, N. Y.
                (By the Regents of the State of N. Y.)
    (Presbyterian and Others) (Degrees 1800)

Colleges Founded (1800-1809)

26 A25 MIDDLEBURY COLLEGE....................*November 1, 1800*
    Middlebury, Vt.   (Vt. Laws to 1824, p. 585)
    (Congregational) (Degrees 1802)

27 A28 OHIO UNIVERSITY (1804)
    Athens, Ohio
    American Western University..............*January 9, 1802*
        Athens, Ohio   (1 Sess. 2 G.A.T., p. 161)
    (State) (Degrees 1815)

[92] Tusculum College, chartered in 1844, was merged with Greeneville College in 1868.

S.N.   I.N.   CHANGES IN NAME AND LOCATION   CHARTER-DEGREE DATE

28   A27   WASHINGTON AND JEFFERSON COLLEGE (1865)[93]
                      Canonsburg and Washington, Pa.
                      Washington, Pa. 1869
                      Jefferson College........................*January 15, 1802*
                              Canonsburg, Pa.   (Pa. Laws 1802-5, vol. 17, p. 33)
                      (Presbyterian) (Degrees 1802)

29   A26   UNIVERSITY OF SOUTH CAROLINA (1906)
                      Columbia, S. C.
                      South Carolina College (1890)
                              Columbia, S. C.
                      University of South Carolina (1887)
                              Columbia, S. C.
                      South Carolina College (1882)
                              Columbia, S. C.
                      South Carolina Col. of Agric. and Mech. (1880)
                              Columbia, S. C.
                      College of South Carolina (1878)
                              Columbia, S. C.
                      University of South Carolina (1866)
                              Columbia, S. C.
                      South Carolina College.................*December 14, 1805*
                              Columbia, S. C.   (S. C. Laws 1805, p. 83)
                      (State) (Degrees 1806)

30   A30   MIAMI UNIVERSITY......................*February 17, 1809*
                      Oxford, Ohio   (Ohio Laws, vol. 7, p. 184)
                      (State) (Degrees 1826)

                        Colleges Founded (1810-1819)

31   A31   HAMILTON COLLEGE...........................*May 26, 1812*
                      Clinton, N. Y.   (By the Regents of the State of N. Y.)
                      (Presbyterian) (Degrees 1814)

32   A48   UNIVERSITY OF MARYLAND...............*December 29, 1812*
                      Baltimore, Md.   (Md. Laws 1812, p. 177)
                      (State) (Degrees 1862)

33   A33   GEORGETOWN COLLEGE [94] (1844)
                      Washington, D. C.
                      College of Georgetown....................*March 1, 1815*
                              Washington, D. C.   (Catalogue and Questionnaire)
                      (Catholic) (Degrees 1817)

34   A37   UNIVERSITY OF VIRGINIA (1819)
                      Charlottesville, Va.
                      Central College.......................*February 14, 1816*
                              Charlotteville, Va.   (Bruce, P. A., History)
                      (State) (Degrees 1849)

[93] Washington College, chartered in 1806, was merged with Jefferson College in 1865.
[94] The name "Georgetown University" is used in practice, but the legal name remains "Georgetown College."

S.N.	I.N.	CHANGES IN NAME AND LOCATION	CHARTER-DEGREE DATE

35   A34   ALLEGHENY COLLEGE........................*March 24, 1817*
           Meadville, Pa.   (Pa. Laws 1816-17, p. 240)
           (Presbyterian, then Methodist) (Degrees 1821)

36   A35   CENTRE COLLEGE (1918)
           Danville, Ky.
           Central University (1901)[95]
           Danville and Richmond, Ky.
           Centre College ....*January 21, 1819*
           Danville, Ky.   (Ky. Laws 1819, p. 618)
           (Presbyterian) (Degrees 1824)

37   A36   UNIVERSITY OF PITTSBURGH (1908)
           Pittsburgh, Pa.
           Western University of Pennsylvania......*February 18, 1819*
           Pittsburgh, Pa.   (Pa. Laws 1818-19, p. 64)
           (Presbyterian) (Degrees 1823)

Colleges Founded (1820-1829)

38   A49   COLBY COLLEGE (1899)
           Waterville, Me.
           Colby University (1867)
           Waterville, Me.
           Waterville College (1821)
           Waterville, Me.
           Maine Literary and Theol. Institution........*June 19, 1820*
           Waterville, Me.   (Me. Laws 1820, p. 9)
           (Baptist) (Degrees 1822)

39   A38   GEORGE WASHINGTON UNIVERSITY (1904)
           Washington, D. C.
           Columbian University (1873)
           Washington, D. C.
           Columbian College.....................*February 9, 1821*
           Washington, D. C.
                  (U. S. Statutes at Large, vol. 6, p. 255)
           (Baptist) (Degrees 1824)

40   A50   UNIVERSITY OF ALABAMA.................*December 18, 1821*
           Tuscaloosa, Ala.   (Ala. Laws 1821, p. 8)[96]
           (State) (Degrees 1832)

41   A39   TRINITY COLLEGE (1845)
           Hartford, Conn.
           Washington College.......................*May 22, 1823*
           Hartford, Conn.   (Conn. Laws 1823, p. 469)
           (Episcopal) (Degrees 1827)

---

[95] Centre College was united in 1901 with Central University, a Presbyterian institution at Richmond, chartered in 1873. Each institution remained in its own location, but under the common name of Central University. In 1918, Centre College resumed its independent legal existence.

[96] An amendment to the Act of December 18, 1820.

38   *The Founding of American Colleges and Universities*

S.N.	I.N.	CHANGES IN NAME AND LOCATION	CHARTER-DEGREE DATE

42 A41 HOBART COLLEGE (1860)
        Geneva, N. Y.
        Geneva Free College (1852)
        Geneva, N. Y.
        Geneva College........................*February 8, 1825*
            Geneva, N. Y.   (By the Regents of the State of N. Y.)
        (Episcopal) (Degrees 1826)

43 A43 CENTENARY COLLEGE OF LOUISIANA (1845)[97]
        Jackson, La.
        Shreveport, La. 1908
        College of Louisiana...................*February 18, 1825*
            Jackson, La.
                        (Bullard and Curry, Digest La. Laws, p. 295)
        (Semi-State, then Methodist) (Degrees 1827)

44 A42 AMHERST COLLEGE.......................*February 21, 1825*
            Amherst, Mass.   (Mass. Law 1824-25, p. 536)
        (Congregational) (Degrees 1825)

45 A40 KENYON COLLEGE (1891)
        Gambier, O.
        Theol. Sem. of the Prot. Episc. Church....*January 24, 1826*
            Gambier, O.   (Ohio Laws 1826, p. 39)[98]
        (Episcopal) (Degrees 1829)

46 A44 WESTERN RESERVE UNIVERSITY (1884)
        Cleveland, O.
        Western Reserve College...............*February 7, 1826*
            Hudson, O.   (Ohio Laws 1825-26, p. 93)
            Cleveland, O. 1882
        (Congregational-Presbyterian) (Degrees 1830)

47 A45 LAFAYETTE COLLEGE......................*March 9, 1826*
            Easton, Pa.   (Pa. Laws 1826, p. 78)
        (Presbyterian) (Degrees 1836)

48 A46 INDIANA UNIVERSITY (1838)
        Bloomington, Ind.
        Indiana College.......................*January 24, 1828*
            Bloomington, Ind.   (Ind. Laws 1828, p. 115)
        (State) (Degrees 1830)

49 A47 GEORGETOWN COLLEGE...................*January 15, 1829*
            Georgetown, Ky.   (Ky. Laws 1829, p. 55)[99]
        (Baptist) (Degrees 1839)

[97] The Methodists founded a college by the name of Centenary College at Brandon, Mississippi, in 1839, but later gave up the enterprise and moved to Jackson, Louisiana, where they took over the old College of Louisiana, and received in 1845 a new charter for the Centenary College of Louisiana.

[98] The Act of 1826 was amendatory to the original charter of December 29, 1824.

[99] The legal name of the institution has been from the beginning, and is now, the Kentucky Baptist Education Society, but the name Georgetown College has always been used in practice. The right to grant degrees is evidently implied in the charter of 1829, as degrees were conferred beginning in 1839.

S.N.	I.N.	CHANGES IN NAME AND LOCATION	CHARTER-DEGREE DATE

Colleges Founded (1830-1839)

50   A58   RANDOLPH-MACON COLLEGE................*February 3, 1830*
      Boydton, Va.   (Va. Laws 1829-30, p. 36)
      Ashland, Va., 1868
      (Methodist) (Degrees 1835)

51   A72   MT. ST. MARY'S COLLEGE................*February 27, 1830*
      Emmitsburg, Md.   (Md. Laws 1829-30, chap. 167)
      (Catholic) (Degrees 1855)

52   A55   MISSISSIPPI COLLEGE...................*December 16, 1830*
      Clinton, Miss.   (Miss. Laws 1830-31, p. 101)
      (Semi-State, Presbyterian, then Baptist) (Degrees 1854)

53   A64   NEW YORK UNIVERSITY (1896)
      New York, N. Y.
      University of the City of New York........*April 18, 1831*
         New York, N. Y.   (N. Y. Laws 1831, p. 208)
      (Presbyterian and Others) (Degrees 1833)

54   A65   WESLEYAN UNIVERSITY......................*May 26, 1831*
      Middletown, Conn.   (Conn. Laws 1831, p. 348)
      (Methodist) (Degrees 1833)

55   A68   DENISON UNIVERSITY (1856) [100]
      Granville, O.
      Granville College (1845)
         Granville, O.
      Granville Lit. and Theol. Institution.......*February 2, 1832*
         Granville, O.   (Ohio Laws 1831-32, p. 89)
      (Baptist) (Degrees 1840)

56   A80   GETTYSBURG COLLEGE (1921)
      Gettysburg, Pa.
      Pennsylvania College of Gettysburg...........*April 7, 1832*
         Gettysburg, Pa.   (Pa. Laws 1831-32, p. 368)
      (Lutheran) (Degrees 1834)

57   A79   ST. LOUIS UNIVERSITY...................*December 28, 1832*
      St. Louis, Mo.   (Mo. Laws 1824-36, vol. 2, p. 298)
      (Catholic) (Degrees 1834)

58   A57   HANOVER COLLEGE........................*January 1, 1833*
      Hanover, Ind.   (Ind. Laws 1832-33, p. 6)
      (Presbyterian) (Degrees 1834)

59   A84   UNIVERSITY OF DELAWARE (1921)
      Newark, Del.
      Delaware College (1843)
         Newark, Del.
      Newark College ....*February 5, 1833*
         Newark, Del.   (Del. Laws 1830-35, p. 283)
      (Presbyterian, then State) (Degrees 1836)

[100] Shepardson College was affiliated with Denison University in 1900.

S.N.	I.N.	CHANGES IN NAME AND LOCATION	CHARTER-DEGREE DATE

60   A59   WABASH COLLEGE (1851)
       Crawfordsville, Ind.
       Wabash Manual Labor College...........*January 15, 1834*
          Crawfordsville, Ind.   (Ind. Laws 1833-34, p. 57)
       (Presbyterian) (Degrees 1838)

61   A71   OBERLIN COLLEGE (1850)
       Oberlin, O.
       Oberlin Collegiate Institute.............*February 28, 1834*
          Oberlin, O.   (Ohio Laws 1833, p. 226)
       (Congregational) (Degrees 1837)

62   A81   NORWICH UNIVERSITY...................*November 6, 1834*
          Norwich, Vt.   (Vt. Laws 1834, p. 66)
          Northfield, Vt., 1866
       (Universalist) (Degrees 1836)

63   A62   ILLINOIS COLLEGE........................*February 9, 1835*
          Jacksonville, Ill.   (Ill. Laws 1834-35, p. 177)
       (Congregational-Presbyterian, then Presbyterian)
                                        (Degrees 1835)

64   A67   MCKENDREE COLLEGE (1839)
       Lebanon, Ill.
       McKendrean College...................*February 9, 1835*
          Lebanon, Ill.   (Ill. Laws 1834-35, p. 177)
       (Methodist) (Degrees 1841)

65   A82   SHURTLEFF COLLEGE (1836)
       Alton, Ill.
       Alton College.........................*February 9, 1835*
          Alton, Ill.   (Ill. Laws 1834-35, p. 177)
       (Baptist) (Degrees 1837)

66   A69   MARIETTA COLLEGE.......................*February 14, 1835*
          Marietta, O.   (Ohio Laws 1834-35, p. 54)
       (Congregational) (Degrees 1838)

67   A76   OGLETHORPE UNIVERSITY (1913)
       Atlanta, Ga.
       Oglethorpe College ....*December 21, 1835*
          Milledgeville, Ga.   (Ga. Laws 1835, p. 162)
       (Presbyterian) (Degrees 1839)

68   A75   SPRING HILL COLLEGE.....................*January 9, 1836*
          Spring Hill, Ala.   (Ala. Laws 1835-36, p. 137)
       (Catholic) (Degrees 1837)

69   A96   FRANKLIN COLLEGE (1844)
       Franklin, Ind.
       Indiana Baptist Manual Labor Institute....*January 30, 1836*
          Franklin, Ind.   (Ind. Laws 1835-36, p. 109)
       (Baptist) (Degrees 1847)

S.N.	I.N.	CHANGES IN NAME AND LOCATION	CHARTER-DEGREE DATE

70 A78 EMORY UNIVERSITY (1915)
   Oxford, Ga.
   Atlanta, Ga. 1919
   Emory College...................... *December 10, 1836*
    Oxford, Ga.   (Ga. Laws 1836, p. 100)
   (Methodist) (Degrees 1841)

71 A89 WESLEYAN COLLEGE (1919)
   Macon, Ga.
   Wesleyan Female College (1843)
    Macon, Ga.
   Georgia Female College................ *December 23, 1836*
    Macon, Ga.   (Ga. Laws 1836, p. 103)
   (Methodist) (Degrees 1840)

72 A73 DePAUW UNIVERSITY (1884)
   Greencastle, Ind.
   Indiana Asbury University.............. *January 10, 1837*
    Greencastle, Ind.   (Questionnaire)
   (Methodist) (Degrees 1840)

73 A61 ST. MARY'S COLLEGE...................... *January 21, 1837*
   St. Mary's, Ky.   (Ky. Laws 1837, p. 54)
   (Catholic) (Degrees 1874)

74 A83 KNOX COLLEGE (1857)
   Galesburg, Ill.
   Knox Manual Labor College............. *February 15, 1837*
    Galesburg, Ill.   (Questionnaire)
   (Congregational-Presbyterian, then Congregational)
           (Degrees 1846)

75 A187 UNIVERSITY OF KENTUCKY (1917)
   Lexington, Ky.
   State University of Kentucky (1907)
    Lexington, Ky.
   Kentucky University (1858)
    Harrodsburg, Ky.
    Lexington, Ky. 1865
   Bacon College...................... *February 23, 1837* [101]
    Georgetown, Ky.   (Ky. Laws 1837, p. 274)
    Harrodsburg, Ky. 1839
   (Disciples, then State) (Degrees 1869)

76 A51 UNIVERSITY OF MICHIGAN................... *March 18, 1837*
   Ann Arbor, Mich.   (Mich. Laws 1837, p. 142)
   (State) (Degrees 1845)

77 A85 MUSKINGUM COLLEGE.................... *March 18, 1837* [102]
   New Concord, O. (Ohio Laws 1836-37, p. 272)
   (Presbyterian) (Degrees 1839)

[101] The same powers were granted as had been granted to Centre College.
[102] It is claimed that the Act of 1837 granted by implication the right to confer degrees.

S.N.	I.N.	CHANGES IN NAME AND LOCATION	CHARTER-DEGREE DATE

78 A74   MERCER UNIVERSITY.................... *December 22, 1837*
       Penfield, Ga.   (Ga. Laws 1837, p. 152)
       Macon, Ga. 1871
       (Baptist) (Degrees 1841)

79 A63   WAKE FOREST COLLEGE.................. *December 26, 1838*
       Wake Forest, N. C.   (N. C. Laws 1838-39, p. 107)
       (Baptist) (Degrees 1839)

80 A66   DAVIDSON COLLEGE..................... *December 28, 1838*
       Davidson, N. C.   (N. C. Laws 1838-39, p. 105)
       (Presbyterian) (Degrees 1840)

81 A88   GREENSBORO COLLEGE (1920)
       Greensboro, N. C.
       Greensboro College for Women (1913)
       Greensboro, N. C.
       Greensborough Female College.......... *December 28, 1838*
       Greensborough, N. C.   (N. C. Laws 1838-39, p. 102)
       (Methodist) (Degrees 1913)

82 A70   UNIVERSITY OF MISSOURI (1909)
       Columbia, Mo.
       University of the State of Missouri....... *February 11, 1839*
       Columbia, Mo.   (Mo. Laws 1838-39, p. 181)
       (State) (Degrees 1843)

83 A77   EMORY AND HENRY COLLEGE................. *March 25, 1839*
       Emory, Va.   (Va. Laws 1839, p. 136)
       (Methodist) (Degrees 1843)

84 A54   ADRIAN COLLEGE (1859)
       Adrian, Mich.
       Michigan Union College (——)[103]
       Marshall, Mich.
       Marshall College........................... *April 16, 1839*
       Leoni, Mich.   (Mich. Laws 1839, p. 111)
       (Presbyterian, then Methodist) (Degrees 1858)

Colleges Founded (1840-1849)

85 A101   BETHANY COLLEGE.......................... *March 2, 1840*
       Bethany, W. Va.   (Va. Laws 1839-40, p. 95)
       (Disciples) (Degrees 1844)

86 A97   UNIVERSITY OF RICHMOND (1920)
       Richmond, Va.
       Richmond College....................... *March 4, 1840*
       Richmond, Va.   (Va. Laws 1839-40, p. 92)
       (Baptist) (Degrees 1849)

[103] It has been impossible to secure from the college the legal date of the reorganization of the college under the name of Michigan Union College.

S.N.	I.N.	CHANGES IN NAME AND LOCATION	CHARTER-DEGREE DATE

87 A103 HOWARD COLLEGE......................*December 29, 1841*
    Marion, Ala.   (Catalogue and Questionnaire)
    Birmingham, Ala. 1887
    (Baptist) (Degrees 1848)

88 A111 MARYVILLE COLLEGE.....................*January 14, 1842*
    Maryville, Tenn.   (Tenn. Laws 1841-42, p. 51)
    (Presbyterian) (Degrees ——)

89 A93 UNION UNIVERSITY (1907)
    Jackson, Tenn.
    Southwestern Baptist University (1874)
    Jackson, Tenn.
    Union University ....*February 5, 1842* [104]
        Murfreesboro, Tenn.   (Tenn. Laws 1841-42, p. 111)
    (Baptist) (Degrees ——)

90 A192 ST. XAVIER COLLEGE........................*March 5, 1842*
    Cincinnati, O.   (Ohio Laws 1841-42, p. 84)
    (Catholic) (Degrees 1843)

91 A118 OHIO WESLEYAN UNIVERSITY...............*March 7, 1842* [105]
    Delaware, O.   (Ohio Laws 1841-42, p. 111)
    (Methodist) (Degrees 1846)

92 A122 CUMBERLAND UNIVERSITY.................*December 30, 1843*
    Lebanon, Tenn.   (Tenn. Laws 1843-44, p. 56)
    (Presbyterian) (Degrees 1843)

93 A105 UNIVERSITY OF NOTRE DAME................*January 15, 1844*
    Notre Dame, Ind.   (Ind. Laws 1843-44, p. 61)
    (Catholic) (Degrees 1849)

94 A114 UNIVERSITY OF MISSISSIPPI...............*February 24, 1844*
    Oxford, Miss.   (Miss. Laws 1843-44, p. 227)
    (State) (Degrees 1851)

95 A100 BAYLOR UNIVERSITY (1886)[106]
    Waco, Tex.
    Baylor University......................*February 1, 1845*
    Independence, Tex.   (Tex. Rep. Laws 1844-45, p. 86)
    (Baptist) (Degrees 1855)

96 A116 WITTENBERG COLLEGE......................*March 11, 1845*
    Springfield, O.   (Ohio Laws 1844-45, p. 376)
    (Lutheran) (Degrees 1851)

---

[104] West Tennessee College, a state institution at Jackson, chartered on January 3, 1844 (*Tenn. Laws 1843-44*, p. 76), was merged with Union University, a Baptist institution at Murfreesboro, chartered on February 5, 1842 (*Tenn. Laws 1841-42*, p. 111), to form in 1874 at Jackson the Southwestern Baptist University. This latter institution was renamed Union University in 1907.

[105] Ohio Wesleyan Female College, chartered on April 1, 1853 by filing Articles of Incorporation, was merged with Ohio Wesleyan University in 1877 by legal enactment.

[106] Waco University, chartered on December 24, 1861 (*Tex. Laws 1861*, p. 15), was merged with Baylor University in 1886 by legal enactment.

S.N.	I.N.	CHANGES IN NAME AND LOCATION	CHARTER-DEGREE DATE

97 A176 BALDWIN-WALLACE COLLEGE (1914)[107]
          Berea, O.
          Baldwin University (1854)
          Berea, O.
          Baldwin Institute . . . . *December 20, 1845* [108]
          Berea, O.   (Ohio Laws 1845-56, p. 4)
          (Methodist) (Degrees 1858)

98 A99   CARROLL COLLEGE . . . . *January 31, 1846*
          Waukesha, Wisc.   (Wisc. Laws 1845-46, p. 115)
          (Presbyterian) (Degrees 1857)

99 A102 BELOIT COLLEGE . . . . *February 2, 1846*
          Beloit, Wisc.   (Wisc. Laws 1845-46, p. 103)
          (Congregational-Presbyterian, then Congregational)
                                                      (Degrees 1851)

100 A106 BUCKNELL UNIVERSITY (1886)
          Lewisburg, Pa.
          University at Lewisburg . . . . *February 5, 1846*
          Lewisburg, Pa.   (Pa. Laws 1846, p. 34)
          (Baptist) (Degrees 1851)

101 A90   UNIVERSITY OF LOUISVILLE . . . . *February 7, 1846*
          Louisville, Ky.   (Ky. Laws 1846, p. 135)
          (Municipal) (Degrees 1908)

102 A56   COLGATE UNIVERSITY (1890)
          Hamilton, N. Y.
          Madison University . . . . *March 26, 1846*
          Hamilton, N. Y.   (N. Y. Laws, chap. 40)
          (Baptist) (Degrees 1836)[109]

103 A108 FORDHAM UNIVERSITY (1907)
          Fordham, N. Y.
          St. John's College . . . . *April 10, 1846*
          Fordham, N. Y.   (N. Y. Laws, chap. 193)
          (Catholic) (Degrees 1846)

104 A104 UNIVERSITY OF BUFFALO . . . . *May 11, 1846*
          Buffalo, N. Y.   (N. Y. Laws, chap. 193)
          (Presbyterian) (Degrees 1920)

105 A110 LAWRENCE COLLEGE (1908)
          Appleton, Wisc.
          Lawrence University (1849)
          Appleton, Wisc.
          Lawrence Institute . . . . *January 15, 1847*
          Appleton, Wisc.   (Wisc. Laws 1847, p. 6)
          (Methodist) (Degrees 1857)

---

[107] German Wallace College, established in 1863, was merged with Baldwin University in 1914, under the general name of Baldwin-Wallace College.

[108] The Act of 1845 granted by implication the right to confer degrees.

[109] From 1836 to 1846 the degrees were conferred by George Washington University (Columbian) in Washington, D. C.

S.N.	I.N.	CHANGES IN NAME AND LOCATION	CHARTER-DEGREE DATE

106 A94 TAYLOR UNIVERSITY (1893)
Upland, Ind.
Fort Wayne Methodist Episcopal College (1855)[110]
Fort Wayne, Ind.
Fort Wayne Female College.............*January 18, 1847*
Fort Wayne, Ind.   (Ind. Laws 1846-47, p. 76)
(Methodist) (Degrees ——)

107 A121 TULANE UNIVERSITY OF LOUISIANA (1884)
New Orleans, La.
University of Louisiana.................*February 16, 1847*
New Orleans, La.   (La. Laws 1846-47, p. 41)
(Semi-State) (Degrees 1857)

108 A112 ROCKFORD COLLEGE (1892)
Rockford, Ill.
Rockford Seminary (1887)
Rockford, Ill.
Rockford Female Seminary.............*February 25, 1847*
Rockford, Ill.   (Ill. Laws 1846-47, p. 124)
(Congregational-Presbyterian, then Congregational)
(Degrees 1887)[111]

109 A120 STATE UNIVERSITY OF IOWA..............*February 25, 1847*
Iowa City, Ia.   (Ia. Laws 1846-47, p. 188)
(State) (Degrees 1858)

110 A109 GRINNELL COLLEGE (1909)
Grinnell, Ia.
Iowa College.........................*June 17, 1847* [112]
Davenport, Ia.   (Articles of Incorporation)
Grinnell, Ia. 1859
(Congregational-Presbyterian, then Congregational)
(Degrees 1854)

111 A123 LAGRANGE FEMALE COLLEGE (1851)[113]
Lagrange, Ga.
Lagrange Female Institute.............*December 17, 1847*
Lagrange, Ga.   (Ga. Laws 1847, p. 121)
(Methodist) (Degrees 1848)

112 A115 AUGUSTINIAN COLLEGE OF VILLANOVA......*March 10, 1848* [114]
Villanova, Pa.   (Pa. Laws 1848, p. 134)
(Catholic) (Degrees 1855)

---

[110] Authorities differ as to whether the date of change in name was 1852 or 1855.

[111] The Catalogue of the institution states that "since 1887 the college has granted the baccalaureate degrees of A.B. and B.S." while the Questionnaire filled out by the institution for the writer states that "the first degree was given in 1882."

[112] Iowa College was incorporated under the General College Law, requiring the filing of Articles of Incorporation.

[113] The name "Lagrange College" is used in practice, but the legal name remains "Lagrange Female College."

[114] The name "Villanova College" is used in practice.

S.N.   I.N.   CHANGES IN NAME AND LOCATION   CHARTER-DEGREE DATE

113 A124 UNIVERSITY OF WISCONSIN.....................*July 26, 1848*
                 Madison, Wisc.   (Wisc. Laws 1848, p. 38)
                 (State) (Degrees 1854)

114 A127 OTTERBEIN COLLEGE (1917)
                 Westerville, Ohio
                 Otterbein University..................*February 13, 1849*
                     Westerville, Ohio   (Ohio Laws 1848-49, p. 257)
                 (United Brethren) (Degrees 1857)

115 A117 WILLIAM JEWELL COLLEGE................*February 27, 1849*
                 Liberty, Mo.   (Mo. Laws 1848-49, p. 234)
                 (Baptist) (Degrees 1855)

116 A98   AUSTIN COLLEGE.......................*November 22, 1849*
                 Huntsville, Texas   (Tex. Laws 1849-50, vol. 3, p. 4)
                 Sherman, Texas 1876
                 (Presbyterian) (Degrees 1850)

Colleges Founded (1850-1861)

117 A139 EARLHAM COLLEGE (1881)
                 Earlham, Ind.
                 Indiana Yearly Meeting...............*January 4, 1850* [115]
                     Richmond, Ind.   (Ind. Laws 1850, p. 404)
                 (Friends) (Degrees 1862)

118 A107 BUTLER UNIVERSITY (1877)
                 Indianapolis, Ind.
                 North Western Christian University.......*January 15, 1850*
                     Indianapolis, Ind.   (Ind. Laws 1849-50, p. 528)
                 (Disciples) (Degrees 1856)

119 A163 BETHEL COLLEGE.....................*February 3, 1850* [116]
                 McLemoresville, Tenn.   (Tenn. Laws 1849-50, p. 322)
                 McKenzie, Tenn. 1870
                 (Presbyterian) (Degrees 1851)

120 A175 ALBION COLLEGE (1861)
                 Albion, Mich.
                 Wesleyan Seminary and Female College (1857)
                     Albion, Mich.
                 Albion Female Collegiate Institute....*February 18, 1850* [117]
                     Albion, Mich.   (Mich. Laws 1850, p. 23)
                 (Methodist) (Degrees 1865)

[115] It is stated by the attorney of Earlham College that the Act of 1850 gave the institution, by implication, the right to confer degrees, but the catalogue of the institution states that the legislature empowered the institution to grant degrees in 1859. No legal enactment in 1859 to this effect has been found, however, by the writer, nor is there a record that Articles of Incorporation were filed in 1859 providing for the right to confer degrees, so the date 1850 is taken as definitive.

[116] An Act of December 1, 1847, to Bethel Seminary, served as a conditional charter, but as the conditions specified were not met, it was necessary to secure a new charter in 1850. This latter charter is regarded as the definitive one.

[117] Albion was not granted the right to confer degrees on men until 1861.

S.N.	I.N.	CHANGES IN NAME AND LOCATION	CHARTER-DEGREE DATE

121 A132 CAPITAL UNIVERSITY........................*March 2, 1850*
    Columbus, Ohio   (Ohio Laws 1849-50, p. 619)
    (Lutheran) (Degrees 1854)

122 A95 GENEVA COLLEGE (1883)
    Beaver Falls, Pa.
    Geneva Hall.............................*March 7, 1850*
        Northwood, Ohio [118]   (Ohio Laws 1849-50, p. 623)
        Beaver Falls, Pa. 1880
    (Presbyterian) (Degrees 1852)

123 A144 HILLSDALE COLLEGE (1855)
    Hillsdale, Mich.
    Michigan Central College..............*March 20, 1850* [119]
        Spring Arbor, Mich.   (Mich. Laws 1849-50, p. 105)
    (Baptist) (Degrees 1852)

124 A178 WAYNESBURG COLLEGE.....................*March 25, 1850*
        Waynesburg, Pa.   (Pa. Laws 1850, p. 284)
    (Presbyterian) (Degrees 1853) .

125 A189 ERSKINE COLLEGE.......................*December 20, 1850*
    Due West, S. C.   (S. C. Laws 1850, p. 43)
    (Presbyterian) (Degrees 1842)

126 A141 FURMAN UNIVERSITY....................*December 20, 1850*
    Greenville, S. C.   (S. C. Laws 1850, p. 35)
    (Baptist) (Degrees 1856)

127 A169 NORTHWESTERN UNIVERSITY (1867)[120]
    Evanston, Ill.
    North Western University................*January 28, 1851*
        Evanston, Ill.   (Ill. Laws 1850-51, p. 21)
    (Methodist) (Degrees 1867)

128 A172 RIPON COLLEGE (1864)
    Ripon, Wisc.
    Brockway College......................*January 29, 1851*
        Ripon, Wisc.   (Wisc. Laws, 1850-51, p. —)
    (Congregational-Presbyterian, then Congregational)
            (Degrees 1867)

129 A143 HEIDELBERG COLLEGE (1926)
    Tiffin, Ohio
    Heidelberg University (1890)
    Tiffin, Ohio
    Heidelberg College....................*February 13, 1851*
    Tiffin, Ohio   (Ohio Laws 1850-51, p. 123)
    (German Reformed) (Degrees 1854)

---

[118] Geneva Hall was moved from Northwood, Ohio, to Beaver Falls, Pa., in 1880, and rechartered in Pennsylvania in 1883.

[119] The Act of March 19, 1845 did not grant the power to confer degrees.

[120] The Northwestern Female College, chartered in 1857, and the Evanston College for Ladies, chartered in 1869, were merged in 1871 under the latter name. In 1874, this institution was merged with Northwestern University.

S.N.	I.N.	CHANGES IN NAME AND LOCATION	CHARTER-DEGREE DATE

130   A154   UNIVERSITY OF MINNESOTA..............*February 13, 1851*
        Minneapolis, Minn.   (Minn. Laws 1850-51, p. 142)
        (State) (Degrees 1873)

131   A155   UNIVERSITY OF ROCHESTER............*February 14, 1851* [121]
        Rochester, N. Y.   (By the Regents of the State of N. Y.)
        (Baptist) (Degrees 1851)

132   A185   LOMBARD COLLEGE (1900)
        Galesburg, Ill.
        Lombard University (1857)
        Galesburg, Ill.
        Illinois Liberal Institute.............*February 15, 1851* [122]
        Galesburg, Ill.   (Ill. Laws 1851, p. 247)
        (Universalist) (Degrees 1856)

133   A158   WESTMINSTER COLLEGE (1853)
        Fulton, Mo.
        Fulton College....................*February 18, 1851* [123]
        Fulton, Mo.   (Mo. Laws 1850, p. 358)
        (Presbyterian) (Degrees 1855)

134   A147   MILWAUKEE-DOWNER COLLEGE (1897)[124]
        Milwaukee, Wisc.
        Milwaukee College (1876)
        Milwaukee, Wisc.
        Milwaukee Female College (1853)
        Milwaukee, Wisc.
        Female Normal Institute and H. S..........*March 1, 1851*
        Milwaukee, Wisc.   (Wisc. Laws 1851, p. 109)
        (Congregational-Presbyterian, then Congregational)
                            (Degrees 1851)

135   A171   COLLEGE OF THE PACIFIC (1911)
        San Jose, Cal.
        Stockton, Cal. 1924
        University of the Pacific (1852)[125]

[121] The University of Rochester, chartered on May 8, 1846, was a separate institution which did not succeed.

[122] The Act of 1851 grants by implication the power to confer degrees. It is stated in the catalogue of the institution that college powers were granted in 1853, but no legal enactment to the effect has been found.

[123] An Act of February 23, 1852 (*Mo. Laws 1852,* p. 279) for Westminster College, states that it is amendatory to an Act of January 18, 1851 (*Mo. Laws 1850,* p. 311) creating a Female College, while the institution claims that Fulton College of February 18, 1851 (*Mo. Laws, 1850,* p. 356) was the predecessor of Westminster College of February 23, 1853, a date unconfirmed in the laws.

[124] Wisconsin Female College at Fox Lake, chartered on January 29, 1855 (*Wisc. Laws 1854-55,* p. 17) as a Baptist institution, became Downer College in 1889, and removed to Milwaukee in 1895, where it was legally merged with Milwaukee College in 1897 under the name Milwaukee-Downer College.

[125] Napa College at Napa, California, was merged with the University of the Pacific by legal enactment in 1896. The charter-degree date of Napa College has not been determined by the writer.

Santa Clara, Cal.
San Jose, Cal. 1871
California Wesleyan College . . . .*July 10, 1851* [126]
    Santa Clara, Cal.   (By the Cal. Supreme Court)
(Methodist) (Degrees 1858)

136   A182   CARSON AND NEWMAN COLLEGE (1895)
    Jefferson City, Tenn.
    Mossy Creek Baptist College (1856)
    Mossy Creek, Tenn.
    Mossy Creek Missionary Bapt. Seminary . .*December 5, 1851*
       Mossy Creek, Tenn.   (Tenn. Laws 1851-52, p. 663)
    (Baptist) (Degrees 1855)

137   A160   WOFFORD COLLEGE . . . .*December 16, 1851*
    Spartanburg, S. C.   (S. C. Laws 1851-52, p. 91)
    (Methodist) (Degrees 1856)

138   A140   ELMIRA COLLEGE (1890)
    Elmira, N. Y.
    Elmira Female College (1855)
    Elmira, N. Y.
    Elmira Collegiate Seminary (1853)
    Elmira, N. Y.
    Auburn Female University . . . .*January 29, 1852*
       Auburn, N. Y.   (N. Y. Laws 1852, chap. 3)
    (Presbyterian) (Degrees 1859)

139   A151   ST. JOSEPH'S COLLEGE . . . .*January 29, 1852* [127]
    Philadelphia, Pa.   (Pa. Laws 1852, p. 16)
    (Catholic) (Degrees 1858)

140   A153   TUFTS COLLEGE . . . .*April 21, 1852*
    Tufts College, Mass.   (Mass. Laws 1852, chap. 141)
    (Universalist) (Degrees 1857)

141   A190   WESTMINSTER COLLEGE (1897)
    New Wilmington, Pa.
    Westminster Collegiate Institute . . . .*April 27, 1852* [128]
       New Wilmington, Pa.   (Pa. Laws 1852, p. 420)
    (Presbyterian) (Degrees 1854)

142   A191   ANTIOCH COLLEGE . . . .*May 14, 1852* [129]
    Yellow Springs, O.   (Articles of Incorporation)
    (Christian) (Degrees 1857)

---

[126] The General College Law of California, of April 20, 1850, provided that colleges should be incorporated by the Supreme Court.

[127] While the Act of 1852 contains no explicit reference to the power to confer degrees, the institution states that the power was implied.

[128] The Act of April 27, 1852, Section 5, granted by implication the right to confer degrees.

[129] Antioch College was incorporated under a General College Law requiring the filing of Articles of Incorporation. New Articles were filed on April 22, 1859, when a reorganization was effected.

S.N.	I.N.	CHANGES IN NAME AND LOCATION	CHARTER-DEGREE DATE

143 A138 DUKE UNIVERSITY (1924)
Durham, N. C.
Trinity College (1859)
Randolph County, N. C.
Durham, N. C. 1892
Normal College...................... *November 21, 1852*
Randolph County, N. C.   (N. C. Laws 1852, p. 163)
(Methodist) (Degrees 1853)

144 A183 CATAWBA COLLEGE...................... *December 17, 1852*
Newton, N. C.   (N. C. Laws 1852, p. 658)
Salisbury, N. C. 1925
(German Reformed) (Degrees 1889)

145 A159 WILLAMETTE UNIVERSITY.................. *January 12, 1853*
Salem, Ore.   (Questionnaire)
(Methodist) (Degrees 1859)

146 A137 CULVER-STOCKTON COLLEGE (1917)
Canton, Mo.
Christian University...................... *January 28, 1853*
Canton, Mo.   (Mo. Laws 1852-53, p. 296)
(Disciples) (Degrees 1857)

147 A188 ILLINOIS WESLEYAN UNIVERSITY.......... *February 12, 1853*
Bloomington, Ill.   (Ill. Laws 1853, p. 325)
(Methodist) (Degrees 1853)

148 A157 WASHINGTON UNIVERSITY (1857)
St. Louis, Mo.
Eliot Seminary...................... *February 22, 1853* [130]
St. Louis, Mo.   (Mo. Laws 1852-53, p. 290)
(Unitarian) (Degrees 1862)

149 A146 LINDENWOOD FEMALE COLLEGE.......... *February 24, 1853* [131]
St. Charles, Mo.   (Mo. Laws 1852-53, p. 283)
(Presbyterian) (Degrees ——)

150 A173 ROANOKE COLLEGE........................ *March 14, 1853*
Salem, Va.   (Va. Laws 1852-53, p. 283)
(Lutheran) (Degrees 1855)

151 A194 LOUISIANA STATE UNIVERSITY (1870)
Baton Rouge, La.
Louisiana State Seminary of Learning...... *March 31, 1853*
Alexandria, La.   (La. Laws 1852-53, p. 49)
(State) (Degrees 1869)

152 A87 LOYOLA COLLEGE............................ *April 13, 1853*
Baltimore, Md.   (Md. Laws 1853, p. 163)
(Catholic) (Degrees 1853)

---

[130] The Act of February 22, 1853, granted by implication the right to confer degrees.
[131] The name Lindenwood College is used in practice. The Act of February 24, 1853, granted by implication the right to confer degrees.

S.N.	I.N.	CHANGES IN NAME AND LOCATION	CHARTER-DEGREE DATE

153 A165 CENTRAL UNIVERSITY.....................*June 3, 1853* [132]
      Pella, Ia.   (Articles of Incorporation)
      (Baptist, then German Reformed) (Degrees 1861)

154 A170 PACIFIC UNIVERSITY (1922)
      Forest Grove, Ore.
      Tualatin Academy and Pacific University...*January 13, 1854*
          Forest Grove, Ore.   (Catalogue and Letter)
      (Congregational-Presbyterian, then Congregational)
                                (Degrees 1863)

155 A136 CORNELL COLLEGE (1855)
      Mt. Vernon, Ia.
      Iowa Conference Seminary..........*February —, 1854* [133]
         Mt. Vernon, Ia.   (Articles of Incorporation)
      (Methodist) (Degrees 1858)

156 A142 HAMLINE UNIVERSITY......................*March 3, 1854*
      Red Wing, Minn.   (Minn. Laws 1854, p. 105)
      St. Paul, Minn. 1880
      (Methodist) (Degrees 1858)

157 A135 COLLEGE OF THE CITY OF NEW YORK (1866)
      New York, N. Y.
      New York Free Academy................*April 15, 1854* [134]
         New York, N. Y.   (N. Y. Laws, chap. 267)
      (Municipal) (Degrees 1854)

158 A184 COLUMBIA COLLEGE (1905)
      Columbia, S. C.
      Columbia Female College..........*December 21, 1854* [135]
         Columbia, S. C.   (S. C. Laws 1854, p. 33)
      (Methodist) (Degrees 1860)

159 A168 IOWA WESLEYAN COLLEGE (1912)
      Mt. Pleasant, Ia.
      Iowa Wesleyan University...............*January 25, 1855*
         Mt. Pleasant, Ia.   (Ia. Laws 1854-55, p. 213)
      (Methodist) (Degrees 1856)

160 A167 EUREKA COLLEGE........................*February 6, 1855*
      Eureka, Ill.   (Ill. Laws 1855, p. 542)
      (Disciples) (Degrees 1860)

---

[132] Central University was incorporated under the General College Law requiring the filing of Articles of Incorporation. The name "Central College" is used in practice, but the legal name remains Central University.

[133] Cornell College was incorporated under the General College Law requiring the filing of Articles of Incorporation. It has not been possible for the writer to determine the exact day of the month on which the Articles were filed.

[134] The Act of 1854 was amendatory to the charter of the New York Free Academy of May 7, 1847, and provided for the conferring of degrees.

[135] It is claimed that the Act of December 21, 1854, grants by implication the right to confer degrees.

S.N.	I.N.	CHANGES IN NAME AND LOCATION	CHARTER-DEGREE DATE

161   A193   KALAMAZOO COLLEGE.....................*February 10, 1855*
        Kalamazoo, Mich.   (Mich. Laws 1855, p. 138)
        (Baptist) (Degrees 1855)

162   A91   WHEATON COLLEGE (1861)
        Wheaton, Ill.
        Illinois Institute......................*February 15, 1855*
          Wheaton, Ill.   (Ill. Laws 1855, p. 508)
        (Methodist, then Congregational) (Degrees 1860)

163   A164   CENTRAL COLLEGE.......................*March 1, 1855*[136]
        Fayette, Mo.   (Mo. Laws 1855, p. 106)
        (Methodist) (Degrees 1859)

164   A195   UNIVERSITY OF CALIFORNIA (1868)
        Berkeley, Cal.
        College of California...................*April 13, 1855*[137]
          Oakland, Cal.   (By the Cal. Board of Ed.)
        (Congregational-Presbyterian, then State) (Degrees 1864)

165   A177   SANTA CLARA COLLEGE...................*April 28, 1855*[138]
        Santa Clara, Cal.   (By the Cal. Board of Ed.)
        (Catholic) (Degrees 1857)

166   A131   BIRMINGHAM-SOUTHERN COLLEGE (1918)[139]
        Birmingham, Ala.
        Southern University....................*January 25, 1856*
          Greensboro, Ala.   (Ala. Laws 1855-56, p. 221)
        (Methodist) (Degrees 1860)

167   A166   HAVERFORD COLLEGE (1875)
        Haverford, Pa.
        Haverford School Association..............*March 15, 1856*
          Haverford, Pa.   (Pa. Laws 1856, p. 123)
        (Friends) (Degrees 1856)

168   A152   ST. LAWRENCE UNIVERSITY....................*April 3, 1856*
        Canton, N. Y.   (N. Y. Laws 1856, chap. 91)
        (Universalist) (Degrees 1863)

169   A92   UPPER IOWA UNIVERSITY (1858)
        Fayette, Ia.
        Fayette Seminary......................*April 5, 1856*[140]
          Fayette, Ia.   (Articles of Incorporation)
        (Methodist) (Degrees 1858)

---

[136] Howard Female College, chartered on March 12, 1859 (*Mo. Laws 1859*, p. 60), became Howard-Payne College in 1892. The latter merged with Central College in 1922.

[137] The General College Law of California of April 20, 1850, was revised on April 13, 1855, to provide for the incorporation of colleges by the Board of Education.

[138] *Ibid.* The name "Santa Clara University" is used in practice.

[139] North Alabama Conference College at Birmingham, Ala., was chartered on December 14, 1898. It became Birmingham College in 1906. In 1918, Birmingham College and Southern University were united as Birmingham-Southern College at Birmingham.

[140] As the legality of the Articles of 1856 and 1858 was called in question, a confirmatory act was passed by the legislature on February 17, 1862.

S.N.	I.N.	CHANGES IN NAME AND LOCATION	CHARTER-DEGREE DATE

170 A174 NEWBERRY COLLEGE....................*December 20, 1856*
    Newberry, S. C.   (S. C. Laws 1856, p. 571)
    Walhalla, S. C. 1868
    Newberry, S. C. 1877
    (Lutheran) (Degrees 1869)

171 A145 LAKE FOREST UNIVERSITY (1865)[141]
    Lake Forest, Ill.
    Lind University.....................*February 13, 1857*
        Lake Forest, Ill.   (Ill. Laws 1857, p. 514)
    (Presbyterian) (Degrees 1879)

172 A149 MONMOUTH COLLEGE...................*February 16, 1857*
    Monmouth, Ill.   (Ill. Laws 1857, p. 883)
    (Presbyterian) (Degrees 1858)

173 A133 ALFRED UNIVERSITY.....................*March 28, 1857*
    Alfred, N. Y.   (N. Y. Laws, chap. 190)
    (Baptist) (Degrees 1860)

174 A179 IRVING FEMALE COLLEGE..................*March 28, 1857*
    Mechanicsburg, Pa.   (Pa. Laws 1857, p. 133)
    (Lutheran) (Degrees 1860)

175 A156 UNIVERSITY OF THE SOUTH................*January 6, 1858*
    Sewanee, Tenn.   (Tenn. Laws 1857-58, p. 38)
    (Episcopal) (Degrees 1873)

176 A150 MT. UNION COLLEGE....................*January 9, 1858* [142]
    Alliance, O.   (Articles of Incorporation)
    (Methodist) (Degrees 1858)

177 A134 BAKER UNIVERSITY.....................*February 12, 1858*
    Baldwin, Kansas   (Kan. Terr. Laws 1858, p. 71)
    (Methodist) (Degrees 1866)

178 A53 OLIVET COLLEGE.....................———— —, *1859* [143]
    Olivet, Mich.   (Articles of Incorporation)
    (Congregational) (Degrees 1860)

179 A162 ST. IGNATIUS COLLEGE...................*April 30, 1859* [144]
    San Francisco, Cal.   (By the Cal. Board of Ed.)
    (Catholic) (Degrees 1863)

180 A129 ST. STEPHEN'S COLLEGE..................*March 20, 1860*
    Annandale, N. Y.   (N. Y. Laws, chap. 89)
    (Episcopal) (Degrees 1861)

[141] The name "Lake Forest College" is used in practice, but the legal name remains "Lake Forest University."

[142] Mt. Union College was incorporated under a General College Law, requiring the filing of Articles of Incorporation. Scio College, established in 1866, was merged with Mt. Union College in 1911.

[143] Olivet was incorporated under the General College Law of 1856, requiring the filing of Articles of Incorporation. It has not been possible to secure more exact information from this college.

[144] In accordance with the General College Law of April 13, 1855. See footnotes to the College of the Pacific, the University of California, and Santa Clara College.

Chapter II

THE FOUNDING OF DENOMINATIONAL COLLEGES BEFORE THE CIVIL WAR

Colleges are Societies of Ministers for training up Persons for the Work of the Ministry.[1]
—*President Thomas Clap of Yale*—1754

The Christian College is the bulwark of the Christian Church.[2]
—*Methodist Episcopal Conference*—1824

We then proceeded in a body to the intended location in the primeval forest, and there kneeling in the snow we dedicated the grounds to the Father, the Son, and the Holy Ghost, for a Christian College.[3]
—*The Founding of Wabash College*—1833

THE RELIGIOUS CHARACTER OF THE AMERICAN COLLEGE

THE American college was founded to meet the "spiritual necessities" of a new continent. It was designed primarily as a "nursery of ministers," and was fostered as a "child of the church." The movement for the founding of colleges in America before the Civil War was identified with the rise and growth of religious denominations in this country, and thus it came to partake of the dominant religious character of the formative period of our history and reflect the motives and interests of a religious era. It is a well known fact that our colonial colleges were largely religious in origin and character, but it is not so well understood that, with the exception of a few state universities, practically all the colleges founded between the Revolution and the Civil War were organized, supported, and in most cases controlled by religious interests.[4] Thus it may be truly said that the "denominational college" was the pre-

[1] Clap, President Thomas, *The Religious Constitution of Colleges*, p. 4 (pamphlet), 1754.
[2] General Conference of the Methodist Episcopal Church, *Minutes of 1824.* Quoted in the Catalogue of Birmingham-Southern College, Alabama, for 1927-28.
[3] Quoted in Tuttle, President J. F., *The Origin and Growth of Wabash College*, p. 8 (pamphlet), 1876. (The charter of Wabash was granted in 1834.)
[4] It has not been possible to consider separately the few colleges of a more or less non-sectarian character that were founded before the Civil War, such, for example, as New York University and Washington University.

vailing American college of the middle period of our history, as it was of the colonial period.

The following contemporary statements chosen from among many similar statements testify to the essential religious character of most of the colleges founded before 1860:

> The whole number of colleges in the United States not founded by religion can be counted upon one hand.[5]

> We might go through the whole list of American Colleges, and show that, with here and there an exception, they were founded by religious men, and mainly with an eye to the interests of the Church.[6]

> Aside from state institutions, the colleges of this country may now be divided among some twenty different denominations, with whom they are either organically connected, or to the control of whose membership they are mainly subject.[7]

THE PERPETUATION OF RELIGION AND CULTURE ON THE FRONTIER

The movement for the founding of colleges before the Civil War cannot be studied, much less be appreciated at its full value, without recognizing briefly at the outset the service rendered by the denominational college in the perpetuation of culture as well as of religion on the advancing frontier of American life.[8] The leading groups that settled this new continent brought with them the cultural heritage of seventeenth century England. This heritage had from the time of the Renaissance and the Reformation been impregnated with religious dogmas and belief. It was natural, therefore, that our colonial colleges should be largely concerned with the perpetuation of a "religious culture." The achievement of a "secular culture" in Europe did not take place until well on into the eighteenth century. By that time in America the ideals of a religious culture were firmly established in our collegiate system and a beginning had been made in extending the benefits of this religious culture to the early frontier settlements in the west through the establishment of frontier colleges. Although the secular patterns of

---

[5] Magoun, President G. F., *The West: Its Culture and Its Colleges*, p. 30.
[6] *Thirteenth Report of the S.P.C.T.E.W., 1856*, pp. 20-21.
[7] *Fourteenth Report of the S.P.C.T.E.W., 1857*, p. 43.
[8] It is recognized that the points raised in this section require more adequate and extended discussion, but it was obviously impossible within the limits of this study to do more than suggest the general relation of the denominational colleges to the perpetuation of religion and culture in this country.

eighteenth century European thought received a considerable welcome in certain circles in American life during the revolutionary and
post-revolutionary eras, and were reflected in the establishment of
a few collegiate institutions during the latter part of the eighteenth
century, the forces of orthodox religion, after a temporary setback
during the Revolution, regained their ascendency over the cultural
life of this country at the turn of the century through a complex
of circumstances.[9] This ascendency was maintained in large part
up to the time of the Civil War. Thus the ideals of a religious culture continued in large part to dominate the life of our colleges during this period as they had in the past.

While it is true that the claims of a purely secular culture were
not generally admitted in the sphere of higher education before the
Civil War, it must be recognized that a significant contribution to
the general cause of culture in this country was made by the
colleges established by religious forces on the frontier lines of settlement during the middle period of our history.[10] Through the establishment of many small colleges scattered over the country, the
elements of culture as well as of religion were effectively maintained and perpetuated in a frontier society, cut off as it was per-
force in large measure from the developments that were taking
place in Europe in the early nineteenth century. It should be more
generally recognized, moreover, that the various religious denominations which developed in the United States, especially during the
early nineteenth century, were the expression, not only of the di-
verse religious interests of American life, but also of the varying
economic, social, and racial elements represented among the American people.[11] America was indeed a land with a diversified culture
during the middle period of our history, but this culture was cast
in denominational molds. Thus the denominational colleges served
not only as the strategic centers of varying religious interests but
also as radiating centers of varying cultural patterns. In the light of
these considerations, it must with justice be said that the denominational colleges in America played an important part in the for-

[9] The rise and decline of the rationalistic movement in higher education in America
during the revolutionary and post-revolutionary eras has never been adequately treated
nor has its significance been fully appreciated by students in this field.

[10] See Rusk, R. L., *The Literature of the Middle Western Frontier*, 1925, for a
description of the religious aspects of the cultural movement in the west.

[11] See Niebuhr, H. R., *The Social Sources of Denominationalism*, 1929, for a suggestive
application of the advanced theses of Weber, Tawney, and Troeltsch to the study of
American denominationalism.

mation and perpetuation of the fundamental elements of culture as well as in the propagation of religion on the wide front of an advancing population. With this background of understanding, we may turn to a consideration of the development of the movement for the founding of colleges under religious auspices in this country.

THE FOUNDING OF COLLEGES DURING THE COLONIAL ERA

1636-1769

1	Harvard	4	Princeton	7	Brown
2	William and Mary	5	Columbia	8	Rutgers
3	Yale	6	Pennsylvania	9	Dartmouth

During the early colonial era, the dominant patterns of life and thought were clearly religious, especially in New England and the Southern colonies. Under the auspices of the Congregational Church in New England and the Anglican Church in the South, the three earliest of American colleges were established. Harvard, and later Yale, were founded by Congregationalist interests in New England in direct response to the need of an educated ministry in that particular region. William and Mary was established in Virginia, about sixty years after the establishment of Harvard, to meet the somewhat less imperative needs of the Anglicans in the South for an institution of higher learning primarily devoted to the task of educating ministers.[12]

During the latter colonial period, the "Great Awakening" gave new life and strength to the religious forces in the colonies which had begun to weaken under the peculiar conditions of life on a new continent.[13] This revivalist movement, together with other factors in the general situation, created a new demand for an indigenous ministry. This demand led, either directly or indirectly, to the establishment of six other denominational colleges in the colonial period, at least four of which were definitely designed as "nurseries of ministers." The founding of Princeton by the "New Side" Presbyterians, and the founding of Dartmouth by the "New Light" Congregationalists, may be directly traced to the religious zeal

[12] One of the prominent motives present in the founding of the College of William and Mary, as of Dartmouth College and Hamilton College at a later date, was the education of Indians.

[13] An excellent general treatment of the "Great Awakening" is found in Sweet, W. W., *The Story of Religions in America*, 1930. See also "Religious History of New England," *King's Chapel Lectures*, p. 164, 1917.

engendered by the "Great Awakening." Brown was founded in
Rhode Island by one of the oppressed sects, the Baptists, who had
gained added strength from this revivalist movement.[14] Rutgers
was established in New Jersey by the Dutch Reformed Church,
which had also found fresh religious opportunities opening up for
its rather restricted constituency after the revival.[15]

In the great cities of New York and Philadelphia, the religious
influences of the time failed to exert as undisputed a sway over
men's minds as they did in other places. The colleges that were
founded in these two cities were not, therefore, so closely identified
with the narrower religious purposes of the time as were the other
colonial colleges. It is clear from a study of contemporaneous documents that Columbia and Pennsylvania were conceived on somewhat broader bases of education and culture. Nevertheless, even
these two institutions were ultimately associated in their establishment with the interests of a particular denomination, in this case
the Anglican Church, and came to be concerned in part with the
task of preparing men for the ministry.

In the light of this brief survey of the colonial period it will be
seen that all the colonial colleges were founded more or less directly
in association with religious denominations, and devoted more or
less exclusively to the perpetuation of the traditional forms of religious culture. Moreover, with the possible exception of Columbia
and Pennsylvania, all the colonial colleges were primarily designed
as institutions for the education of ministers. Nine colleges were
thus established in this early period of our national life. These
colonial institutions are particularly significant in any study of the
history of higher education in America as they furnished in large
part the patterns for our collegiate system in America before the
Civil War. The colleges that were established in the west were
modeled in many of their features on these nine colonial colleges,
particularly on Harvard, Yale, and Princeton. It was not until
after the Civil War that other institutions in the east, such as
Cornell and Johns Hopkins, arose to set up new patterns of higher
education and to challenge the influence of the older colonial colleges.[16]

[14] Bronson, W. C., *History of Brown University*, pp. 5-9, 1914.
[15] Demarest, W. H. S., *History of Rutgers College*, pp. 27-29, 1924.
[16] This discussion of the founding of the colonial colleges is abbreviated on account
of the fact that the history of their development has been more or less adequately treated
in other studies.

THE FOUNDING OF COLLEGES DURING THE
POST-REVOLUTIONARY ERA

1780-1789

10	Washington (Md.)	15	St. John's (Md.)
11	Washington and Lee	16	Georgia
12	Hampden-Sidney	17	Charleston
13	Transylvania	18	Franklin and Marshall
14	Dickinson	19	North Carolina

1790-1799

20	Vermont	23	Tusculum (Tenn.)
21	Williams	24	Tennessee
22	Bowdoin	25	Union (N. Y.)

Under the impact of the new ideas and ideals that came in with the Revolutionary era, we enter into a period when the former religious patterns of colonial times began to break down, and secular interests came to occupy a larger part of men's thoughts. The political questions of the time tended to divert the thinking of many into channels other than religious. The influence of French modes of thought served as a direct challenge to the religious ideas of colonial days. The spirit of free thought and "infidelity" permeated all ranks of society. The following contemporary statements reflect the changing character of the times:

Infidelity was rife in the State, and the College of William and Mary was regarded as the hot bed of French politics and religion. I can truly say that then and for some years after in every educated young man in Virginia whom I met I expected to find a sceptic, if not an avowed unbeliever.[17]

Yale College was in a most ungodly state. The College church was almost extinct. Most of the students were skeptical, and rowdies were plenty. Wine and liquors were kept in many rooms; intemperance, profanity, gambling, and licentiousness were common. . . . Most of the class before me were infidel, and called each other Voltaire, Rousseau, D'Alembert, etc.[18]

At this period infidelity began to obtain, in this country, an extensive currency and reception.[19]

[17] Meade, Bishop W., *Old Churches, Ministers, and Families of Virginia*, vol. 1, p. 29, 1857.
[18] Beecher, Rev. Lyman, *Autobiography*, vol. 1, p. 43, 1865.
[19] Dwight, President Timothy, *Discourse*, p. 19, 1801, quoted in Purcell, R. J., *Connecticut in Transition*, p. 9, 1918.

The religious leaders of the time were sorely distressed by these destructive forces, if such they were in whole or part. The churches were faced with a growing indifference to religious matters that was not relieved until the turn of the century. During this period, conditions were hardly propitious for a program of expansion in the field of denominational education. The denominational interests were put on the defensive. It is evident that this period was a time of contraction and consolidation for the religious forces in the more settled coastal regions, challenged as they were on every hand by the prevailing skeptical tendencies of the day. The closing years of the eighteenth century "witnessed the consolidation of the church bodies in the country, the creation of new ecclesiastical machinery where it was needed, and a fair start of the various denominations under the competitive system, which the divorce of church and state rendered inevitable." [20] Referring to the list given above of colleges founded during this period, it will be noted that in the older east, only three denominational colleges were established, viz., Washington and St. John's in Maryland, and Charleston in South Carolina, all of which were associated with the former Anglican interests on the Southern seaboard and became centers of later Episcopalian influence. [21]

On the frontier, however, there was some experimentation in the field of higher education on the part of both the church and the state. Nine denominational colleges, viz., Washington and Lee, Hampden-Sidney, Transylvania, Dickinson, Tusculum, and Union under Presbyterian auspices; [22] Franklin and Marshall under German Reformed; [23] and Williams and Bowdoin under Congregational, were founded on the frontier, where certain religious forces found an outlet for their educational activities during this period. [24] It will be noted that six of these colleges were founded by the Presbyterian Church which had emerged as the dominant church of the Revolutionary period. In some of these denominational colleges, e.g., Hampden-Sidney and Dickinson, the newer ideals of political liberty and secular culture were to some extent reflected, but in the main they

[20] *King's Chapel Lectures,* p. 54.

[21] Fuller treatment of the religious affiliation of these three colleges is given in historical references in the Bibliography.

[22] Dickinson College was taken over formally by the Methodists in 1833, while Transylvania was taken over formally by the Disciples in 1865. Union was founded as a cooperative venture under predominant Presbyterian influence.

[23] Franklin and Marshall College was founded on the basis of two separate colleges, chartered in 1787 and 1836, respectively.

[24] See Paxson, F. L., *History of the American Frontier,* p. 86, 1924.

were religious in design and purpose.[25] Four state or semi-state universities, viz., Georgia, North Carolina, Vermont, and Tennessee, were established in frontier country during this period in more direct response to the new political and secular interests of the day. These four institutions will be considered at some length in connection with a later discussion of the rise of state universities.[26] More detailed consideration of the twelve denominational colleges that were founded in this period will also be given in appropriate sections at the end of this chapter.

THE DENOMINATIONAL COLLEGE AND THE SEPARATION OF CHURCH AND STATE

During the revolutionary and post-revolutionary periods that we have been considering, the question of the complete separation of church and state became a question of immediate concern to the established religious interests in the country and to the colleges associated with them. This question also proved to be of ultimate concern to all denominational colleges, as their very existence was involved in the resolution of this question. A "standing order" in religion had been established before the Revolution in nine of the thirteen colonies, and in five of these colonies,[27] viz., Virginia, New York, Massachusetts, Connecticut, and New Hampshire, where colleges had been founded during the colonial period by church and state acting largely as one, the colleges representing the established order had maintained a privileged position in the field of higher education. The founding of rival collegiate institutions by dissenting sects had been discouraged, if not actually prevented in each of these five states. Thus we find William and Mary, Columbia, Harvard, Yale, and Dartmouth enjoying exclusive rights up to this time in their respective states. When, as a result of the new ideals of the revolutionary era, the principle of the complete separation of church and state was accepted by the states and written into the Constitution of the United States, the exclusive privileges of the Anglican colleges in Virginia and New York, and of the Congregational colleges in Massachusetts, Connecticut, and New Hampshire, were challenged.

[25] Schmidt, G. R., *The Old Time College President*, p. 24, 1930.
[26] See Chapter III.
[27] A "standing order" was not formally recognized in Pennsylvania, New Jersey, Delaware, and Rhode Island. No colleges were established during the colonial period in Maryland, North Carolina, South Carolina, and Georgia where a "standing order" existed.

In Virginia the actual separation of church and state was brought about at an early date, and as a consequence William and Mary lost its exclusive rights in the field of higher education in the state. Thus the way was opened for the founding of Washington and Lee, Hampden-Sidney, and other colleges.[28] In New York, after the principle of disestablishment was fully accepted, and the experiment of 1784 ended in failure, Columbia lost its exclusive rights, and the way was opened for the founding of Union and other colleges.[29] In Massachusetts, full religious liberty in the field of higher education was achieved at a very late date. Even after the achievement of a nominal separation of church and state in 1833, Harvard together with Williams and Amherst, which had rather reluctantly been allowed to enter the field of higher education in Massachusetts by Harvard, continued to enjoy more or less exclusive privileges until Tufts College was founded under Universalist auspices in 1852.[30] In Connecticut, the standing order in religion was not given up until 1818, and only then did Yale give way, rather reluctantly, for the establishment of Trinity and Wesleyan.[31] In New Hampshire, disestablishment took place in 1819, after which date the field was nominally open for the founding of other colleges.[32]

In the other states in the east and in the west, the principle of the separation of church and state was achieved in theory but applied in the field of higher education only with much difficulty. In a number of them, e.g., North Carolina, Georgia, Kentucky, Tennessee, Ohio, and Indiana, Presbyterian interests were able to maintain a virtual establishment and monopoly for a time in the field of higher education because of their dominance in local politics.[33] Even in states such as Pennsylvania, New Jersey, Delaware, and Rhode Island, where a measure of religious freedom had been declared in the early days of settlement, the problems connected with secular and religious relations in the field of higher education were not easily solved, and certain church groups main-

---

[28] For an extended discussion of the struggle for educational control between church and state in Virginia, see Bell, S., *The Church, the State and Education in Virginia*, chap. 6, 1930.

[29] Sherwood S., *The University of the State of New York*. U. S. Bur. of Ed. Cir. Inf., 1900, no. 3, chap. 2.

[30] Sweet, *op. cit.*, p. 275. It is to be noted that Holy Cross College was refused a charter until after the Civil War. See p. 161, footnote 74.

[31] Purcell, *op. cit.*, chap. 9.

[32] Cobb, S. H., *Rise of Religious Liberty in America*, p. 292.

[33] In Kentucky, the Disciples were able later to secure a dominant influence in higher education and in the state.

tained for a time a dominance in the state councils. When, however, the principle of the complete separation of church and state was fully accepted in the older as well as in the newer states, the way was opened for the founding of a multiplicity of colleges by the competing religious sects, most of which were eager to enter the field of higher education. An era of complete religious freedom in the establishment of these institutions, such as was not known in any other country, was thus finally ushered in by this distinctive American solution of the problem of the relation of church and state as applied in the realm of higher education.[34]

THE DENOMINATIONAL COLLEGE AND THE DARTMOUTH COLLEGE CASE

In the revolutionary and post-revolutionary eras, another question of immediate concern for the existing denominational colleges, and of ultimate concern for all colleges, presented itself in an acute form. This question was whether denominational colleges were in general to be free from interference on the part of the state. As a result of the new ideals of the time, there arose an active sentiment in favor of state-controlled institutions of higher education and an equally active sentiment against sectarian colleges. Efforts were made to ensure a measure of state representation in all the colonial colleges, except Brown, Princeton, and Rutgers. Three colonial colleges, viz., Columbia, Pennsylvania, and Dartmouth were actually taken over for a time by the states, with the approval of public opinion, and converted temporarily into state institutions, while Harvard, Yale, and William and Mary allowed for a measure of state representation.[35]

The influence of French ideals in the country during the revolutionary and post-revolutionary periods was strong, but undoubtedly the determining forces behind the agitations against sectarian colleges and in favor of state-controlled institutions were native in origin. The American people in their early enthusiasm for republican institutions, were resolved that institutions of higher education should be made more responsive to the public will, although they were not yet entirely clear as to how this result should be

---

[34] For a fuller discussion of this question, in connection with a study of state universities, see pp. 148-152.

[35] For a fuller discussion of these events, see Brown, E. E., *The Origin of American State Universities*, pp. 27-31 (pamphlet), 1903.

brought about.[36] As this early republican enthusiasm for state control of all institutions of higher education waned, however, with the passing of the revolutionary and post-revolutionary eras, and as the influence of religious interests and other forms of vested interests gained new power with the turn of the century, the supposed rights of private colleges to be free from legislative interference were eventually affirmed by the Dartmouth College Case decision of 1819.[37] Is is to be kept in mind, however, that the Dartmouth College Case decision applied only to colleges that had been or were to be chartered, without specific reservations of legislative control. Although such reservations were increasingly made after the Decision, the charters of many colleges during the pre-Civil War period did not include these reservations, largely on account of the fact that the state legislatures during this period were in general under the influence of powerful religious interests.[38] Through a legal decision of the utmost significance in the history of higher education, it became possible for the public will to be expressed in at least one of two ways, viz., either through the establishment of state institutions subject to the will of the people acting as a whole, or through the founding of private colleges subject to the will of various minority groups and generally free from public control.[39]

Until the time of the Dartmouth decision the future of denominational colleges, and private colleges in general, was in the balance.[40] There was no real assurance of immunity from state interference for private educational corporations until that time. When it was finally decided on the authority of the Supreme Court of the United States that private colleges were in general to be free from legislative control, then, and then only, was it possible for duly incorporated ventures in higher education to have this assurance. Thus the way was fully opened for the founding of a multiplicity of private and denominational colleges, as well as for the establishment of state universities in the United States. The following quo-

---

[36] See Hansen, A. O., *Liberalism and American Education in the Eighteenth Century,* 1926, for various Revolutionary proposals for higher education in this country.

[37] For an advanced interpretation of the Dartmouth College decision see Beard, C. A. and Beard, M. R., *The Rise of American Civilization,* vol. 1, pp. 818-823, 1927.

[38] Barnard, F. A. P., "On Improvements Practicable in American Colleges," *op. cit.* See also in this connection, Justice Story's opinion referred to in Bartlett, *op. cit.,* p. 29.

[39] After the Dartmouth College Case decision some legislatures in granting charters reserved certain rights.

[40] It is significant in this connection that a "College Congress" of the six Congregational colleges in New England, together with the University of Vermont, was held in Boston in 1817. See Lord, J. K., *A History of Dartmouth College,* vol. 1, p. 155, 1913.

tation suggests the significance of the Dartmouth College decision
for the small colleges of America:

Influenced by the abiding affection engendered within a comparatively
small institution, Daniel Webster won the cause essential to his Alma Mater
and benefited many another beneficent foundation by his convincing argument before the Supreme Court. *The blessing to an ever-growing population
of scattered colleges,* as radiant points of light, has seldom been better illustrated than when addressing the chief justice at the close with moving
eloquence, blanched face, brimming eyes, trembling lips, and that deep voice
faltering with suppressed emotion, he exclaimed, *"Sir, you may destroy this
little institution; it is in your hands, I know it is one of the lesser lights on
the literary horizon of our country. You may put it out. It is, as I have
said, a small college, and yet there are those who love it."* [41]

It still remained to be seen, however, whether the American
people were to choose to establish state universities, and thus give
their main support to the centralized forms of state education so
strongly advocated during the revolutionary era, or to prefer in the
next half-century to provide for themselves small denominational
colleges, widely scattered over the country, and closely fashioned
after their local and particular desires and aspirations. By the establishment of the principles of the complete separation of church
and state discussed in a previous section, and of complete immunity
for most educational corporations from legislative interference, the
opportunity for a choice of either alternative was given to the
American people. The choice that was made is now a matter of
history. The reasons that led the people of this land to choose, in
the main, at that time the latter alternative can be understood only
in the light of the religious developments that took place during
the early decades of the nineteenth century. It is to these developments that we now turn our attention.

THE "DENOMINATIONAL ERA" IN AMERICAN HIGHER
EDUCATION

At the turn of the century, the orthodox religious forces of the
country that had been so widely challenged during the revolutionary
period began, as we have seen, to regain their control of the currents of American life. The "denominational era" of our history
was ushered in with a series of revivals that spread from the settled

[41] Potter, President E. N., of Hobart College, *Church Colleges and the Church University,* p. 11 (pamphlet). Italics by the writer.

communities of the east to the pioneer settlements on the frontier. There took place a veritable "Second Awakening" throughout the land.[42]

In the early decades of the century, the older colleges in the east became the centers of a deep and fervid religious life, and the newer colleges on the frontier exhibited signs of true evangelical zeal. Revivals were frequent and prolonged. Each year students were increasingly classified by the college authorities as "hopefully pious." The menace of free thought no longer threatened the citadels of faith. The specter of infidelity no longer brooded over the sacred halls of the college. Under the leadership of President Timothy Dwight, that great champion of orthodoxy in this early period, Yale College was transformed into "a perennial fountain of orthodoxy." So great was the change in this institution that one of the students reported in a letter:

> Yale College is a little temple, prayer and praise seem to be the delight of the greater part of the students, while those who are still unfeeling are awed into respectful silence.[43]

In the colleges that were established on the frontier, likewise, the spirit of religion won out against the irreligious tendencies that had characterized the revolutionary and post-revolutionary eras. President Lindsley of the University of Nashville was able to state in 1826 that:

> Happily, the reign of atheism has passed away, and the fopperies of infidelity are no longer in fashion.[44]

The forces of irreligion, of rationalism, and of deistic thought were effectually checked on a hundred fronts; and, for better or for worse, the forces of denominational and sectarian religion gained a dominance over American life that was to remain largely unchallenged until after the Civil War. An eminent historian has well characterized the middle period of our history as "distinctly and increasingly a religious period."[45] De Tocqueville writing after a visit to the United States in 1831, testified that:

---

[42] See Sweet, *op. cit.*, pp. 322-335. See also Cleveland, C. C., *The Great Revival in the West (1797-1805)*, 1916; Elsbree, O. W., *The Rise of the Missionary Spirit in America (1790-1815)*, especially chaps. 2, 4, and 6.

[43] Quoted in Purcell, *op. cit.*, p. 29.

[44] Lindsley, Philip, *Commencement Address*, 1826, given in Halsey, *op. cit.*

[45] Fish, Carl F., *The Rise of the Common Man*, p. 179, 1927.

There is no country in the whole world in which the Christian religion retains a greater influence over the souls of men than in America. By regulating domestic life it regulates the state. Religion is the foremost of the institutions of the country.[46]

It was during this middle period that the great migrations to the west took place; and following in the wake of the westward march of population, the religious forces of the day gathered strength as they laid plans to meet the "spiritual destitution" of the new frontier settlements.

There was hope that if churches and schools kept pace with the tide of migration, and these vast solitudes were presently filled by intelligent and Christian population, our country would be a blessing to the whole earth.[47]

To plant Christianity in the West is as grand an undertaking as it was to plant it in the Roman Empire, with unspeakably greater permanence and power.[48]

The new western country became the field of "home missions," and the spiritual conquest of the continent became at once a vision and a challenge. One of the student leaders of the "Yale Band" who went out to the great west to found a college in response to this new call, made the statement that:

The present number of immortal souls within our own country living on trial for an endless destiny is deeply affecting . . . and to think of their rapid increase in a situation where little or no light shines to invite them to the world of felicity or to warn them of that dark abyss to which they rapidly hasten is truly overwhelming.[49]

In response to such sentiments, repeatedly expressed in speech and in writing at that time, a veritable campaign of evangelism was launched on all fronts, and the forces of religion as time went on were augmented by the addition of large numbers of believers. By the decade of the thirties the denominational movement in America began to assume large proportions. America indeed proved to be a virgin field for missionary activity and evangelistic endeavor. By the time of the Civil War, it was possible for Horace Mann, at that time the President of Antioch College, to say that:

[46] Quoted in Cobb, *op. cit.*, p. 525.
[47] Sturtevant, President J. M., Jr., Editor, *Autobiography of J. M. Sturtevant*, p. 134, 1896.
[48] Quoted from Rev. Lyman Beecher in Nichols, R. H., *The Growth of the Christian Church*, vol. 2, p. 179, 1914.
[49] Quoted in Rammelkamp, *op. cit.*, p. 22.

The great West has been conquered, religiously speaking, from Black Hawk to John Calvin.[50]

THE GROWTH AND EXPANSION OF RELIGIOUS DENOMINATIONS IN AMERICA

The religious conquest of the continent was the goal of a militant and aggressive Christianity. By the time of the Civil War, the forces of denominationalism were able to win such a large number of adherents, scattered far and wide across the country, that the claim could seriously be made that the advance of the Church had kept up with the advance of population and territory. The numerical strength of the more important religious bodies in 1860 is indicated in the following statistics. According to the Census of 1860, 54,745 churches had been built up during this era of sectarian effort, and accommodations for 18,958,686 persons out of a total population of 31,040,840, were provided in these churches.

TABLE V

RELIGIOUS AND EDUCATIONAL STATISTICS FOR 1860 [51]

DENOMINATIONAL GROUP	NUMBER OF CHURCHES	SEATING ACCOMMODATIONS	PERMANENT COLLEGES [52]
1. METHODIST	19,816	6,238,014	34
2. BAPTIST	12,139	4,039,928	25
3. PRESBYTERIAN	6,379	2,555,299	49
4. CATHOLIC	2,442	1,314,462	14
5. CONGREGATIONAL	2,230	955,626	21
6. EPISCOPAL	2,129	837,596	11
7. LUTHERAN	2,123	755,637	6
8. CHRISTIAN (DISCIPLES)	2.066	680,666	5
9. GERMAN REFORMED	676	273,697	4
10. FRIENDS	725	268,734	2
11. UNIVERSALIST	664	235,219	4
12. DUTCH REFORMED	440	211,068	1
13. UNITARIAN	263	137,213	2
14. OTHER GROUPS [53]	2,653	455,527	2
TOTALS	54,745	18,958,686	180

[50] Mann, Mrs. Mary, *Life and Works of Horace Mann*, p. 514, 1865, quoting letter to Mr. May. It should be noted that Horace Mann, a Unitarian, in making this statement, was deprecating the fact that Calvinism had won out so completely.

[51] *United States Census, Vol. for 1860.* The actual membership of each denomination was, of course, much smaller than the figures for the seating accommodations.

[52] These figures are taken, not from the Census returns, but from the researches made in connection with this study. The total figure includes duplicates. See p. 90.

[53] The minor denominations represented in this group were many, but only the United

With this background of denominational achievement, it is possible to appreciate more fully the reasons for the multiplication of denominational colleges during the middle period of our history. In the larger strategy of the campaign of evangelism, initiated and carried on by various religious sects during this period of expansion, the "Christian College" came to play an important and significant rôle. It is to the gradual development of a large scale movement for the founding of denominational colleges during this period that we now turn our attention.

THE FOUNDING OF COLLEGES DURING THE EARLY DENOMINATIONAL ERA

1800-1809

26	Middlebury		29	South Carolina
27	Ohio		30	Miami
28	Washington and Jefferson			

1810-1819

31	Hamilton		35	Allegheny
32	Maryland		36	Centre
33	Georgetown (D. C.)		37	Pittsburgh
34	Virginia			

1820-1829

38	Colby		44	Amherst
39	George Washington		45	Kenyon
40	Alabama		46	Western Reserve
41	Trinity		47	Lafayette
42	Hobart		48	Indiana
43	Centenary		49	Georgetown (Ky.)

While the movement for the founding of denominational colleges did not begin to assume large proportions or take on real significance until the decade of the thirties, seventeen denominational institutions, out of a total of twenty-four institutions of higher education, were established on a permanent basis during the first thirty

Brethren and the Christian denominations were able to establish permanent colleges before the Civil War.

years of the century. Seven state or semi-state institutions were established, viz., Ohio, South Carolina, Miami, Maryland, Virginia, Alabama, and Indiana. These institutions will be considered in another connection.[54] The seventeen denominational colleges were divided as follows: Washington and Jefferson, Hamilton, Allegheny, Centre, Pittsburgh, Western Reserve, and Lafayette under Presbyterian auspices, making a total of fourteen colleges established by the Presbyterians up to this time.[55] Middlebury and Amherst in New England were founded during this period under Congregational auspices, making a total of seven colleges in all established up to this time by the Congregationalists in New England. Georgetown (D. C.) was founded under Catholic auspices during this period. Colby, George Washington, and Georgetown (Ky.) were founded under Baptist auspices. Trinity, Hobart, and Kenyon were founded under Episcopal auspices. Centenary College in Louisiana was founded in this period under state auspices, but was taken over by the Methodists in 1845.

It will be noted that the Presbyterian Church was again the most active denomination in the founding of colleges during the early decades of the century. The Congregational Church continued to confine its activities in college-building to New England, although there was a large measure of coöperation between Congregationalists and Presbyterians in the founding of Hamilton and Western Reserve on the western frontier, as there had been in the previous founding of Union. The Catholic Church established its first permanent college in the decade of the teens. The Baptist Church entered the field of higher education in the decade of the twenties, not having established any permanent college since the founding of Brown in the colonial period. The Episcopal Church founded three colleges in the decade of the twenties, having become less closely affiliated with the interests of six previous institutions founded more or less directly under the auspices of the church, viz., William and Mary, Columbia, Pennsylvania, Washington, St. John's, and Charleston. The Methodist Church did not establish any permanent college until the decade of the thirties. Of the seventeen de-

[54] See Chapter III.

[55] Allegheny College in Pennsylvania, while founded largely under Presbyterian auspices, was taken over by the Methodists in 1833. In 1834 another college previously founded by Presbyterians—Dickinson College—was taken over by the Methodists. It is to be noted that Washington and Jefferson College was the result of the union of two separate institutions founded in 1806 and 1802, respectively. Congregational interests were equally represented in the founding of Western Reserve.

nominational colleges considered above, however, all but five, viz.,
Amherst, Lafayette, Georgetown, George Washington, and Trinity,
were founded on the frontier, indicating that the westward movement had begun in earnest.

COLLEGES AS THE AGENTS OF A HOME MISSIONARY PROGRAM DURING THE LATER DENOMINATIONAL PERIOD

By the decade of the thirties, the religious forces of the country
were ready to engage on a large scale in the spiritual conquest of
the continent, and it was clear that a new day had dawned for the
churches in America.[56] In the great stretches of the western country,
the denominational college was now destined to play an even more
significant rôle. A number of factors combined to accelerate the
movement for the founding of colleges in this later denominational
era. The one hundred and thirty-three colleges that were founded
on a permanent basis between the years 1830 and 1861, practically
all of which were associated with sectarian interests, bear witness to
the new strength of the denominational college movement.[57] These
institutions came to serve as one of the most effective agencies
of the rapidly increasing religious forces in the country. During
this period the founding of "Christian Colleges" came to be
clearly identified with the work of Home Missions. It was urged
that:

> The very same reasonings which led to the founding of Yale and Harvard
> amid the primeval forests of New England will lead the Christian missionary,
> who goes forth to any other wilderness as an apostle of the same faith and
> the same Christian civilization, to lay foundations for Christian learning at
> the very beginning of his labors. And this will not take place at one or a few
> points, but it will take place wherever enlightened Christian men go to lay
> the foundations of Christian society in the wilderness.[58]

Such denominational organizations as the American Education
Society, the American Home Missionary Society, and later the
Society for the Promotion of Collegiate and Theological Education

[56] See Thompson, R. E., *History of the Presbyterian Church in the United States,* p. 95, 1895.
[57] These colleges are not listed in this place on account of their number, but in the general list of colleges given at the end of Chap. I.
[58] Sturtevant, President J. M., *Address in Behalf of the S.P.C.T.E.W.,* p. 11, 1853 (pamphlet).

at the West, came to exert a powerful influence on the development of higher education on the part of the various denominations.[59] It is to be recalled that the American Home Missionary Association was represented in 1855 by one thousand and thirty-two missionaries on the frontier.[60] Many of these missionaries were leaders in the movement for the founding of colleges. The Rev. Edward Beecher, in speaking before the Society for the Promotion of Collegiate and Theological Education at the West on the need for the founding of denominational colleges in the west, expressed the prevailing sentiment of Christian leaders of the time in the following words:

> Most deeply am I persuaded that among all the enterprises now commanding the attention of the church, with reference to the conversion of the World, there are few which involve so much of the instrumentality essential to that end, as this enterprise for securing Puritan Educational Institutions for the West.[61]

Colleges were to serve as the outposts of an army of occupation of the advancing forces of religion that now arrayed themselves in deadly warfare against the forces of evil that were felt to be incarnate in the rude frontier population. The relation of the denominational colleges to the general movement of a militant Christianity engaged in the work of Home Missions is well portrayed in the following contemporary statements:

> It is therefore an effort of present and most urgent necessity, to raise up Institutions to do for the mighty West what Yale, and Dartmouth, and Williams, and Amherst have done for New England; to call forth from the bosom of the Western church a learned and pious ministry; to send life, and health, and vigor through the whole system of popular education, and to erect there fortresses of evangelical truth which may be expected to arrest the fatal progress of Popery and Infidelity, and found society on the lasting basis of religious freedom and evangelical truth. The sun shines not on such another missionary field as the valley of the Mississippi.[62]

> The grand duty and accomplishment of Western Colleges is the introduction of Christianity into Western civilization. . . . In order to discharge this obligation in respect to the infusion of Christianity into Western civil-

---

[59] For a discussion of the work of one of these organizations see p. 11.
[60] Sweet, *op. cit.*, p. 362.
[61] Beecher, Edward, "Address," *Third Report of the S.P.C.T.E.W.*, 1846, p. 34.
[62] Sturtevant, President, J. M., "Discourse before the S.P.C.T.E.W.," *Fourth Report of the S.P.C.T.E.W., 1847*, p. 48.

ization, Western Colleges, without squeamishness, concealment, or fear, are avowed and known to be places for the diligent inculcation of spiritual Christianity, as well as the truths of science and the grace of literature.[63]

Not dark or doubtful is the relation sustained by such Colleges to Christianity. It finds in every one of them, and more and more as they more fully complete the office foreshadowed in their structure . . . an institution which is to it as the very Citadel of Jerusalem, the tower of David, builded for an armory. The past and the present combine to declare this. The very structure of Christianity is vocal with its proofs. The College is its magazine, the depot of troops, its arsenal and its fortress, combined in one.[64]

THE CHALLENGE OF FOREIGN IMMIGRATION AND CATHOLICISM

Added impetus and motive were given to the cause of founding denominational colleges by the challenge presented in the large immigration from foreign countries that took place during the latter decades of the period under consideration. Among the new peoples that entered the country at that time were many that were without faith, or with what was regarded in that day with even greater foreboding, a faith in Roman Catholicism.[65] Appeals were made to the Protestant forces to redouble their efforts in the face of these "twin menaces" to society, Infidelity and Roman Catholicism. The following quotations indicate the nature of the appeals that were made at that time:

Europe is pouring into this fairest portion of our earth a flood of rationalism. It can only be met by the united efforts of enlightened Christians. Here is the battleground. The hour of conflict is now upon us. The hosts of Satan are marching upon us in three distinct divisions—the Papal—the Rational—and the Sensual. Who will furnish the munitions of war for the conflict? The majestic west must be educated. If Christianity does not do it through her literary institutions, Infidelity will.[66]

If the disciples of Christ are not sufficiently enlightened and benevolent to provide Christian Colleges, then the world will take to itself infidel

---

[63] White, C., "Address before the S.P.C.T.E.W.," *Fifth Report of the S.P.C.T.E.W., 1848*, pp. 49-50.

[64] Storrs, R. S., *Colleges, a Power in Civilization to Be Used for Christ*, p. 20 (pamphlet), 1856.

[65] From 1845-1855 more than one million Irish Catholics came to the United States. Erbacher, S. A., *Catholic Higher Education for Men in the United States, 1850-1866*, p. 1, 1931.

[66] Smith, R., *Importance and Claims of the Lawrence University of Wisconsin*, p. 13 (pamphlet), 1866.

Colleges; and then we shall have a godless society, for it is indisputably certain that the Christian college is indispensable to the perpetuity of Christian civilization.[67]

In particular, the "peril" of the Jesuit movement for the founding of colleges in different parts of the country aroused tremendous feeling and led to vivid forebodings of the extinction of "our Protestant civilization." [68] Many quotations might be brought forward, giving evidence of the general feeling of Protestant leaders in regard to this particular "menace" to the collegiate system that had been built up by the religious forces in this country, but the following statement, not more extreme than many others, will suffice for our purpose in this connection:

> But the main consideration to excite our fears, is not the transient phases of an immigrant society, nor the rush of adventurers to rich lands and gold regions; it is not the rude chartism of one country, or the beer-befogged skepticism of another; it is the calm, shrewd, steady, systematic movement of the Jesuit order now attempting to do in California and in the Mississippi valley what it once did in Austria; by the unobtrusive, unobserved power of the College, to subvert the principles of the Reformation, and to crush the spirit of liberty. There, Brethren, there our great battle with the Jesuit, on Western soil, is to be waged. We must build college against college. If the musty atmosphere of a Jesuit School suits the freeborn Western child of the prairies, then we may fail in the contest. But all experience has confirmed our anticipation, that America is a field on which the open, manly, Christian discipline of a Protestant College must annihilate the rival system of Jesuitical instruction.[69]

COMPETITION IN COLLEGE-BUILDING AMONG RELIGIOUS DENOMINATIONS

The spirit of competition in college-building was not confined to the efforts of the Protestants to combat the activity of the Catholics in the field of higher education. In the decades of the thirties and forties and fifties, the various Protestant denominations entered into a period of excessive rivalry and competition among them-

[67] Kirk, E. N., *Discourse before the S.P.C.T.E.W.*, p. 20 (pamphlet), 1856.
[68] A most illuminating document, widely circulated by the S.P.C.T.E.W., was written by Noah Porter and entitled *The Educational Systems of the Puritans and Jesuits Compared*, (pamphlet), 1852. For an excellent treatment of the founding of Jesuit colleges, see Erbacher, *op. cit.* See also Williams, M., *The Shadow of The Pope*, pp. 73, 80, 1932, which treats of the rise of the Native American and Know-Nothing parties in 1835 and 1852, respectively.
[69] Kirk, *op. cit.*, pp. 28-29.

selves in the college field. The following contemporary statement, chosen from a large number of similar statements, points to the existence of a strong competitive spirit among the denominations, particularly during the latter denominational era that we are considering:

> There has arisen, within a few years, an earnest, not to say violent, competition among several religious denominations in respect to their educational arrangements. Each denomination seems anxious to outdo the others in the number of its Colleges and Schools. This spirit of rivalry has proved itself contagious, as well as debilitating.[70]

Colleges came in many cases to be regarded as the agents of a type of denominational imperialism, and as a means of sectarian aggrandizement and aggression. There arose an inordinate desire for possessing the promised land. The fear of losing out in this competitive struggle for new territory led many leaders to resort to policies difficult to justify in the light of ethical principles. Many examples of the adoption of aggressive policies on the part of certain sections of the denominational forces might be cited, but references to a few particular instances will be sufficient for our purposes. In Illinois, for example, during the decade of the thirties, there arose a widespread conflict between the Congregationalists and Presbyterians in the field of higher education. The rising forces of Congregationalism demanded, in this case, a larger share in the control of Illinois College and Knox College, institutions founded on a coöperative basis by the Presbyterians and Congregationalists. Much acrimonious debate followed over the respective claims of the two churches in the founding of these two colleges, and for a long period these two institutions were the bone of contention between them.[71] Wheaton College was later established by a certain disaffected element in the Congregational ranks, as a protest against what was felt to be Presbyterian domination at Illinois and Knox.[72] In Kentucky, to give another example, a strong spirit of competition developed between the Presbyterians and the Disciples. The Presbyterian stronghold of Transylvania was eventually surrendered to the Disciples, Centre College was founded as a protest and designed as a more effective Presbyterian outpost, while Bacon College, later

[70] Peters, A., "Address before the S.P.C.T.E.W.," *Fifteenth Report of the S.P.C.T.E.W., 1858*, p. 45.
[71] See references in Bibliography A under Knox College.
[72] See references in Bibliography A under Knox College.

known as Kentucky University, was built by the Disciples as another rival institution.[73] In like manner one might go through the history of denominational higher education in most of the states and find evidences of a strong competitive spirit at work in the field of college building.

There were, however, leaders among the various denominations who deplored and protested against these tendencies toward aggressive sectarian tactics in the realm of higher education. One of the most notable advocates of a more reasonable spirit was President J. M. Sturtevant, who actively pleaded for coöperative endeavor, and boldly denounced the policy of using colleges as means for mere sectarian aggrandizement. In an able speech before the Society for the Promotion of Collegiate and Theological Education at the West in 1853, President Sturtevant deprecated the prevailing tendencies toward denominational rivalry in the field of higher education.[74] A still stronger case was made by him against purely sectarian colleges in an article in the *New Englander* in 1860, from which the following quotation is taken:

> The very spirit and principle of Denominationalism must be abjured in our Colleges. We must found them upon a broad and comprehensive platform of Evangelical Faith. We must cooperate in sustaining them as Christians, and not as Sectarians. . . . We must esteem them as precious, not as instruments of aggrandizing our Denomination, but as blessings to our country, to mankind, and to the distant future.[75]

The Society for the Promotion of Collegiate and Theological Education at the West acted as a powerful restraining influence on excessive denominational zeal. In 1858 a Committee of Ten was appointed by the Society to study the particular problem of denominational policy in higher education. The report of this Committee, written by the Rev. Absalom Peters, is a valuable document in this connection.[76] It was not until after the Civil War that the evils of sectarianism came to attract wide public attention, and call forth effective criticism both within and without the circle of the church.[77] The founding of heavily endowed independent colleges,

[73] Breckinridge, W. C. P., *Address before Alumni Association of Centre College, 1885,* p. 7 (pamphlet).
[74] Sturtevant, J. M., *An Address in behalf of the S.P.C.T.E.W., 1853,* p. 25 (pamphlet).
[75] Sturtevant, J. M., "Denominational Colleges," *New Englander,* February, 1860.
[76] Peters, Rev. Absalom, *Address before the S.P.C.T.E.W., 1858.*
[77] President Andrew D. White of Cornell was one of the most active opponents of sectarian colleges. See his *Autobiography,* and also his article in the *N.E.A. Proceedings*

such as Cornell and Johns Hopkins, and the expansion of the state
university program under the impetus of the Morrill Act, coming
soon after the Civil War, mark the rise of new tendencies in higher
education and the wane of the distinctive denominational era in
higher education.

THE NEED FOR AN EDUCATED MINISTRY

In the founding of denominational colleges in America, the primary purpose in most cases was that of providing the churches on
the frontier with a succession of learned and devoted ministers of
the gospel. This purpose was as impelling in the founding of the
colleges established on the successive lines of frontier settlement
across the continent as it was in the case of the earlier colleges
established on the eastern seaboard. It was a realization of the
"painful destitution of ministers" on the ever advancing frontiers
of American life that led directly to the creation of institutions of
higher education at strategic centers of denominational influence.
In the light of the picture that has been drawn in the preceding
sections of the magnitude and power of the denominational movement in the country at large, it is only natural to expect that most
of the colleges established before the Civil War should have been
devoted primarily to the raising up of leaders for the church.[78]
    The need for an educated ministry was recognized from the very
beginning by certain denominations and met directly by them
through the institution of colleges. Sooner or later practically all
sects came to recognize that the establishment of colleges as "nurseries of ministers" was the chief desideratum of a sound policy
of denominational advance.[79] As theological seminaries and departments of theology came to be founded to meet the specific needs
for ministerial education, the religious colleges were left free to
devote themselves more definitely to the broader program of the
cultivation and the perpetuation of a denominational constituency.[80]

for 1874 on "Advanced Education: The Relations of the National and State Governments
to Advanced Education."

    [78] The position taken by President A. Meiklejohn in his *Liberal College*, pp. 17-23, 1920,
that the colonial colleges were not professional schools for ministers, is in the main a
dialectical position, intended to emphasize the point that the early colleges were liberal
rather than mere professional institutions for the education of ministers.

    [79] For a discussion of the varying emphases of the different denominations on minis-
terial training, see pp. 89-91.

    [80] The movement for the founding of separate theological seminaries and departments
followed in general the movement for the founding of colleges—exceptions in point are

In the beginnings of practically all colleges established before the Civil War, however, the achievement of these broader denominational purposes was seen to be dependent upon a prior attention to the specific ends of ministerial education.[81] Furthermore, it is to be noted that the more general purposes of higher education, such as the advancement of learning, the diffusion of culture, the enlargement of the boundaries of knowledge, the training of republican citizens, the pursuit of practical and utilitarian ends, and the promotion of the interests of the state, although undoubtedly present and active in the minds of the founders in many instances, were in the nature of the situation forced to occupy a position of secondary importance in the early years of most colleges founded before 1861.

In the pre-Civil War period, institutions founded primarily on principles other than religion generally suffered for want of support, or failed to survive. The difficulties met by the state universities that were founded during this period are fully discussed in another chapter of this study. Among the many private colleges that died in this country were a considerable number that were founded on non-religious principles. Contemporary sources testify to the sad fate of non-religious institutions of higher education in the pre-Civil War period.

The following quotations reflect the situation which prevailed during that era.

Those colleges in the United States that have been conducted by, or under the patronage of, some prominent Christian sect have been more flourishing in their operations, and more useful in their influence, than others that have not had these advantages.[82]

It seems to be decided by experience, that all literary institutions must be controlled by some sects, and efforts to prevent this have blasted their usefulness.[83]

Kenyon in Ohio, Maryville in Tennessee, and Gettysburg in Pennsylvania. It is recognized that any comprehensive study of the development of colleges in this early period of our national life would necessarily involve a careful study of the correlative development of theological institutions. See Bibliography for references on theological seminaries.

[81] The colleges established by the Society of Friends, viz., Earlham and Haverford, are exceptions in point. See p. 132. The women's colleges that were established were also exceptions in point. Before the Civil War the following ten permanent women's colleges were founded: Wesleyan (Ga.), Greensboro (N. C.), Irving (Pa.), Rockford (Ill.), Elmira (N. Y.), Lagrange (Ga.), Lindenwood (Mo.), Columbia (S. C.), Milwaukee-Downer (Wis.) and Vassar (N. Y.).

[82] Himes, C. F., *A Sketch of Dickinson College*, p. 56, 1879.

[83] Smith, Rev. Reeder, *Importance and Claims of the Lawrence University of Wisconsin*, p. 5, 1860.

A recent author, who has given special attention to the subject, says that of the first one hundred and nineteen colleges established, "one hundred and four are under decided evangelical and orthodox influence." Those established by worldly men for mere worldly objects, have not prospered. Some that were founded by infidelity it has been found necessary to transfer to the hands of religious guardians and teachers, to save them from utter extinction.[84]

It is only within the present generation that any systematic attempts have been made to establish the higher institutions of learning without the church,—and these attempts have generally been failures.[85]

The evidences that tend to substantiate the position taken in the preceding paragraphs are to be found not only in the contemporary sources that reveal the dominating motives of the pre-Civil War period, but also in the contemporary sources dealing with the founding of the individual colleges. This material is largely found in pamphlet form, and is not only extensive in nature but often difficult of access. A survey of representative sections of this source material has, however, given the writer added evidence of the soundness of the position advanced relative to the primary motive for the founding of denominational colleges. In the course of this survey, it was discovered that it was not in the formal preambles of college charters, nor in the printed announcements of the early colleges, nor even in the petitions made to the legislatures for a charter, that trustworthy evidence was to be found, but rather in the materials relating to individual institutions found in the candid statements of contemporary religious leaders, in the revealing reports and journals of educational societies and denominational organizations, and in the illuminating records of denominational history. From these latter sources it was possible to reconstruct the general situation that confronted the religious leaders of the day, and to see that the problem of providing for a "trained leadership" for the churches on the ever-advancing frontier was uppermost in their minds. It was realized at that time that this problem of denominational leadership was to be met largely through the establishment of "Schools of the Prophets." There was a general agreement on the part of the older denominations, and eventually on the part of practically all denominations, that:

---

[84] *Thirteenth Report of the S.P.C.T.E.W., 1856*, pp. 20-21.
[85] Stowe, C. E., "Address," *Ninth Report of the S.P.C.T.E.W., 1852*, p. 55.

The Ministry is God's instrumentality for the conversion of the world. Colleges and Seminaries are God's means for training up a learned and efficient Ministry.[86]

Colleges, therefore, are a necessity to the church. . . . To our colleges the churches look for their future teachers and guides. The destitute and opening fields on the frontiers of civilization on our own continent look to our colleges, and wait for our young men, to bring them the words of life.[87]

While it is obviously impossible within the limits of this study to present full evidence of the primary motives of the founders of each of the denominational colleges established before the Civil War, a number of illustrative statements from various contemporary sources are given in this place. These statements indicate the primary reasons involved in the founding of a number of more or less representative institutions founded before the Civil War. The motives for the founding of the three earliest of American colleges—Harvard, William and Mary, and Yale—need, however, to be taken up first, and in some detail, as these have often been misinterpreted.

The statement that Harvard was founded in order to "advance learning and perpetuate it to Posterity" has often been quoted to indicate that Harvard was established in the interests of general learning, but it is to be noted that the remainder of the quotation reads as follows: "dreading to leave an illiterate ministry to the churches when our present ministers shall lie in the Dust." President Josiah Quincy stated, moreover, in no uncertain terms that Harvard had fulfilled the design of its founders in that, during the years from 1636 to 1692, the college had been "conducted as a theological institution."[88] Further testimony as to the real purpose of the founding of Harvard is given by Cotton Mather in the following words: "Our fathers saw that without a College to train an able and learned ministry, the church in New England must have been less than a business of one age, and soon have come to nothing."[89]

In the charter of William and Mary we find a full and candid statement of the motives for the founding of the college. There

---

[86] Quoted in *Sixth Report of the S.P.C.T.E.W.*, *1849*, p. 17.
[87] Kendall, H., *The College and Christian Missions*, p. 28, 1862.
[88] Quoted in Quincy, Josiah, *The History of Harvard University*, vol. 1, p. 3, 1840.
[89] Quoted in *Third Report of the S.P.C.T.E.W.*, *1846*, p. 13. See also testimony given in Eliot, S. A., *A Sketch of the History of Harvard College*, p. 5, 1848.

was no need in this early charter to conceal the real intentions of the founders, as the institution was to be an instrument of the Established Church of England in an Anglican colony, and the charter itself was granted by the sovereign heads of this very Church of England. Thus, while a number of general purposes are stated in the Preamble, among which the oft-quoted statement, that "the youth may be piously educated in good letters and manners," was included, the first motive assigned was undoubtedly primary in the establishment of this institution, a fact which is clear as well from an abundance of corroborative evidence. As stated this was: "That the Church in Virginia may be furnished with a seminary of ministers of the Gospel." [90]

In the case of the founding of Yale, it has often been emphasized that this institution was established that young men might be "fitted for public employment both in Church and Civil State," indicating that general purposes were dominant in the undertaking. While undoubtedly the preparing of young men for service in the state, as well as in the church, was involved in the undertaking, particularly as Yale was to be established in a theocratic state in which church and state were one, nevertheless the primary expectation in the founding of Yale, as evidenced by the omitted section of the quotation from the charter referred to above, as well as by a large number of contemporary statements that might be cited, was that orthodox ministers would be provided for the churches in Connecticut, which had separated themselves from their sister churches in Massachusetts and were therefore no longer able to look to Harvard for their supply of ministers.[91] The omitted section of the above quotation from the Yale charter reads as follows: "whereas several well disposed and publick spirited Persons, of their sincere regard to, and zeal for the upholding and propagating of the Christian protestant Religion by a succession of Learned and Orthodox men. . . ."[92] The following statement of President Thomas Clap gives added evidence of the primary motive in the founding of Yale: "The great design of founding this School was to Educate Ministers in our Own Way."[93]

[90] Given in Parsons, E. C., *Educational Legislation and Administration of the Colonial Governments*, p. 136, 1899.

[91] See Dexter, F. B., *A Selection from the Miscellaneous Historical Papers of Fifty Years*, pp. 76-79, 1918, for arguments intended to prove that Yale was not founded primarily for ministerial education.

[92] Quoted from the charter of 1701 given in full in Dexter, F. B., Editor, *Documentary History of Yale University*, pp. 16-18, 1916.

[93] Clap, President Thomas, *op. cit.*, p. 15.

In the quotations that follow, the primary motives of the founders of a number of other more or less representative institutions are set forth. These institutions may be regarded as representative only in the sense that they were situated in different parts of the country, were founded at different times during the period under consideration, and were associated with a number of different denominations. In reading the following statements one is led to appreciate more fully what seems to have been the common purpose that dominated the minds of the founders of most of our early ventures in higher education:

Western Reserve University, established by Presbyterians and Congregationalists in Ohio in 1826, was founded as an "instrument for providing an able, learned, and pious ministry for the infant churches which pious missionaries were gathering and nurturing with untiring zeal and energy. It was a missionary establishment for planting the Gospel upon a new field. Nearly all the ministers who coöperated in establishing it, were missionaries from the Connecticut Missionary Society. They were not mindful of the benefits that would result from a College with professional departments, to the state and the country, but their first object was to prepare the men who should feed the flock of God." [94]

The founders of Davidson College, established by Presbyterians in North Carolina in 1838, stated in a leading memorandum that "the great and leading object shall be the education of young men for the gospel ministry." [95]

Marietta College, established by Congregationalists in Ohio in 1835, was founded mainly to meet the demands for competent teachers and ministers of the Gospel. [96]

Pacific University, established by Congregationalists in Oregon in 1854, was founded "chiefly to acquire and perpetuate a strong religious influence by educating those who will become ministers and missionaries of the Cross." [97]

Lafayette College, established by Presbyterians in Pennsylvania in 1826, was founded by one whose "ruling motive was to help educate young men for the gospel ministry." [98]

Of Colgate University, established by Baptists, in New York in 1846, it was said that "the idea of ministerial education long continued to dominate the policy of the institution." [99]

[94] Pierce, President G. E., "Sketch of Western Reserve College," *Fifth Report of the S.P.C.T.E.W., 1848,* p. 31.
[95] Quoted in Shaw, C. R., *History of Davidson College,* p. 14, 1923.
[96] *Seventh Report of the S.P.C.T.E.W., 1850,* p. 61.
[97] Quoted in *Ninth Report of the S.P.C.T.E.W., 1852,* p. 12.
[98] Quoted in White, H. A., *Lafayette College,* p. 116.
[99] Newman, A. H., *A History of the Baptist Churches in the United States,* p. 410, 1894.

Wabash College, established by Presbyterians in Indiana in 1834, was founded in response to "the painful destitution of educated ministers in the state." [100]

Kenyon College, established by Episcopalians in Ohio in 1826, was "not founded for the spread of mere secular knowledge or even of general Christianity, but with the object of raising up college men to minister to the flock of Christ in the remote West." [101]

Of Hanover College, established by Presbyterians in Indiana in 1833, it was said that "at first the great and ultimate object of the founder was the education of young men for the gospel ministry." [102]

The original purpose of Westminster College, established by the Presbyterians in Missouri in 1851, is stated in the following terms: "The beginning of Westminster College was a great adventure in faith. Resources in money and constituency were scant. The daring and the heroism that moved the men of that day set an example to us for all time. They had a great vision of a Christian College to be located on the highway towards the West, and from the halls of which trained Christian leaders might go out, east and west, north and south, in the service of our Lord and His Christ." [103]

The founder of Maryville College, established in 1842 in Tennessee, said that "if any one passion has governed me more than another it is to have qualified, devoted Presbyterian ministers greatly multiplied." [104]

It was said of the founders of Washington and Jefferson College, established in 1802 in Pennsylvania, that "their ultimate purpose was to fit some of them (sons of the pioneers) to become ministers and missionaries." [105]

THE APPEAL OF A MINISTERIAL CAREER

During the period before the Civil War, the number of college graduates entering the ministry is truly impressive. It was stated in 1855 that approximately 10,000 of the 40,000 graduates of American colleges whose records had been studied, had become ministers. This statement reveals in a striking fashion the dominant theological character of our pre-Civil War college education. [106] The minis-

---

[100] *Seventh Report of the S.P.C.T.E.W., 1850*, p. 12.
[101] Chase, Bishop Philander, *Reminiscences*, p. 216.
[102] Millis, President W. A., *History of Hanover College*, p. 142, 1927.
[103] "Historical Statement," *Catalogue of Westminster College, 1927-28.*
[104] Quoted in Merriam, L. S., *Higher Education in Tennessee*, U. S. Bur. of Ed., Cir. Inf., 1895, no. 5, p. 234.
[105] Moffat, President J. D., *Historical Sketch of Washington and Jefferson College*, p. 2 (pamphlet), 1890.
[106] Magoun, President G. F., *The West: Its Culture and Its Colleges*, p. 30 (pamphlet), 1855. It must be recognized that such a general figure includes the graduates of institutions of varying ages many of which had changed their original ministerial design, and is thus a much diluted figure. See also pp. 48, 100.

terial career obviously made a powerful and an intrinsic appeal to the young men of that era. The church in that day was an active force in society, and under the leadership of able men it took a prominent part in the social, political, and intellectual interests of the day.[107] The minister was generally looked up to, even as late as the Civil War, as the leader in the cultural as well as in the religious life of the time. Moreover, the increasing importance of the church as a civilizing force in the great west caught the imagination of young men in college ready to start out on their lifework. A ministerial or missionary career on the frontier held for many the attraction of a life of individual achievement, and even of adventure, in the service of a great cause.[108] Thus the varied aspects of Christian service in that day made a compelling appeal to college men, and colleges devoted themselves, with a zeal that is often difficult for persons in this day and generation to comprehend, to the task of preparing leaders for the church, particularly among the frontier communities.

It would obviously be impossible without extensive research to give complete data on the occupational destinies of the early graduates of all the one hundred and eighty-two permanent colleges which were established before the Civil War. The general proportion of graduates that entered the ministry may, however, be deduced from general statements given in contemporary sources, such as the one referred to above, and from particular statements from various sources giving the proportion of graduates entering the ministry from a number of more or less representative colleges, such as those quoted below.[109] At least two considerations should be kept in mind in attempting to interpret these statements. First, it is the proportion of graduates of the early graduating classes who became ministers that is significant as evidence, for, as the dominant purposes of many colleges changed, the proportion of graduates who became ministers fell off accordingly. Second, the proportion of graduates who became ministers need not be high in order to be significant, for even proportions under one half may indicate a plurality of graduates going into the

---

[107] A wealth of contemporary material corroborates this statement. The relation of the church to the slavery question is an example in point.

[108] In this connection, see *Quarterly Register*, November 1835, "An Appeal to Pious Young Men on the Subject of Devoting Themselves to the Work of the Ministry."

[109] A tabulation of the number of graduates entering the ministry from twelve eastern institutions was made in 1852. See Hitchcock, E., *Reminiscences of Amherst College* pp. 189 ff., 1863.

ministry. In the light of these considerations, the following statements seem most significant:

More than half of the graduates of *Harvard*, for the first sixty years of its existence, became ministers of the Gospel. Nearly three-fourths of the graduates of *Yale* for the first twelve years, entered the ministry, and a trifle less than one-half during the first thiry years.[110]

About seven out of ten of the graduates of *Marietta* have become professional teachers or preachers of the Gospel.[111]

Of the eight hundred graduates of *Middlebury*, nearly one-half have devoted themselves to the ministry.[112]

Of the first 65 graduates of *Wabash*, 45, or more than two-thirds have devoted themselves to the Christian Ministry.[113]

Of the first 94 graduates of *Illinois*, 45 have devoted themselves to the work of the ministry.[114]

Of *Knox* in 1850 it was stated that "of 25 alumni, 11 have devoted themselves to the work of the ministry."[115]

Dartmouth gave from her first ten classes of 99 graduates, 46 to the ministry.[116]

Amherst gave "from its first six classes of 106 gradutes, 68, or 15 more than one-half of the entire number to the ministry."[117]

Of *Western Reserve* in 1849 it was stated that "of its 153 graduates, about one-half of those living are either in the ministry or in actual preparation for it."[118]

In a statement issued in 1847, it was said that "Since its charter, ninety-two students have graduated from *Hanover;* of these forty-seven are now preachers of the gospel."[119]

As late as 1923, it is stated of *Davidson* that "among the graduates the number of ministers ranks highest."[120]

Of *Hampden-Sidney* in 1916 it could be said that "fifty per cent of all its graduates have entered the ministry of the Gospel. This record cannot be matched by any other college in America."[121]

[110] *Third Report of the S.P.C.T.E.W., 1846,* p. 15. These figures correspond with those given in the Alumni records of Harvard and Yale.
[111] *Ibid.,* p. 26.
[112] Beeman, N. S. S., *Collegiate and Theological Education at the West,* p. 23 (pamphlet), 1847.
[113] *Seventh Report of the S.P.C.T.E.W., 1850,* p. 12.
[114] *Ibid.*
[115] *Ibid.,* p. 13.
[116] Whiting, L., *Address before the S.P.C.T.E.W., 1855,* p. 19, footnote (pamphlet). See *Centennial Celebration of Dartmouth College,* p. 93, for confirmation of this statement.
[117] *Ibid.,* p. 19, footnote.
[118] Quoted in the *Sixth Report of the S.P.C.T.E.W., 1849,* p. 17.
[119] Millis, *op. cit.,* p. 142.
[120] Shaw, *op. cit.,* p. 264.
[121] Heatwole, C. J., *History of Education in Virginia,* p. 144, 1916.

It was said that *Washington and Jefferson* "from 1802 to 1865 contributed to the ministry an average of 45 per cent of their graduates." [122]

It is said today of the total alumni of *Monmouth* that "almost 40% have entered the ministry." [123]

It was said of *Erskine,* as late as 1888, that "one-fourth of its graduates up to 1880" were ministers.[124]

THE PROBLEM OF MINISTERIAL SUPPLY AND DEMAND

The problem of supply and demand in the ministerial profession was a serious one at each stage of frontier settlement across the continent. From the earliest days of settlement on the eastern seaboard to the days when the western coast became the scene of new religious communities, the advancing religious population tended to lose touch with its base of supply. It was recognized that "the greatest obstacle to the work of Evangelization and Church Extension at the West is the want of Competent ministers of the gospel." [125] Viewed from the standpoint of denominational strategy, this situation was disastrous. Unless the eastern colleges and seminaries could supply the needs of the western country for ministers, it was only by the building up of institutions for the training of local ministers that the increasing demands for Christian leadership in the west could be met. It was seen that as Harvard and Yale were built up in the early days of colonial settlement in order to minister to the needs of communities cut off in those days from the sources of European supply, so must colleges be built up all along the line of western migration to meet the demands for ministers of the new communities on the advancing frontier, cut off in each case from the eastern sources of supply. It was recognized that:

Western Colleges are hereafter to be the chief sources of a Western ministry. The ministers, sent from the East to the West, are not one twenty-fifth of the numbers which are immediately needed. . . . We at the West shall never be completely supplied from Eastern Churches. Western Colleges, as sources of supply, are wholly indispensable.[126]

---

[122] Moffat, *op. cit.,* p. 27.
[123] "Historical Statement," *Catalogue of Monmouth College, 1927-28.*
[124] Meriwether, C., "History of Higher Education in South Carolina," U. S. Bur. of Ed., Cir. Inf., 1888, no. 3, p. 90.
[125] *Home Missionary,* September, 1851.
[126] White, Rev. Charles, "Address before the S.P.C.T.E.W.," *Fifth Report of the S.P.C.T.E.W., 1848,* pp. 50, 51. See also similar statements quoted in Wilson, S. T., *A Century of Maryville College,* p. 38, 1916; and in Millis, *op. cit.,* pp. 11-12, 1927.

As Christian settlements extended themselves to California, the need for trained leadership in that remote state became imperative. The leaders in California, while pleading for help from the east, recognized that:

> California must shortly educate her own ministry. For the present work the churches must send along with that great emigration an already trained band of ministers and teachers. But our land lies many days' journey to the west. The ministers and teachers must not always be transported so far. Besides, we may find among our many thousands of pious young men, talent enough to educate on our own soil, without drawing from other fields.[127]

Many arguments lent force to the position that local colleges were necessary for meeting the need for ministers on the frontier. The practical impossibility of securing a sufficient number from the eastern colleges and seminaries was recognized; the difficulty, on account of distance, expense, and risk, of sending western youth to the east for ministerial education was pointed out; local pride was appealed to; economy of management in local colleges was claimed; and finally the greater adaptability of native talent, "sons of the soil," raised and educated in frontier surroundings, was repeatedly argued. The following contemporary statements bear testimony to the need for local institutions:

> Those who are trained on the spot, other things being equal, are best adapted to the country, and most likely to be useful. They grow up in sympathy with the people, know their circumstances, and can appreciate their difficulties; are familiar with their modes of thought, and feeling, and action, and can throw their influence through numerous channels which would be closed to those who were trained elsewhere.[128]

> Unless we can have some little means of educating our pious young men *here,* and *here* being secure of their affections, station them in the woods and among our scattered people, to gather in and nourish our wandering lambs, we have no reason to hope in the continuance of the Church in the West.[129]

> For Men of the West, educated in the West, will be best suited to work for the West.[130]

In the fullness of time, the problem of the sources of ministerial supply on the frontier was successfully met by the advancing re-

---

[127] Brayton, Rev. J. J., "Address before the S.P.C.T.E.W.," *Eleventh Report of the S.P.C.T.E.W., 1854,* p. 6.

[128] *Fifth Report of the S.P.C.T.E.W., 1848,* p. 28.

[129] Smythe, G. F., *Kenyon College,* p. 16, italics in original.

[130] Chapin, President A. L., of Beloit, given in *Twentieth Report of S.P.C.T.E.W., 1863,* p. 12.

ligious forces of the country through the establishment of a large number of small colleges on each of the far-flung battle-lines of Christianity. In addition to meeting the urgent demands of the frontier communities for an educated ministry, these colleges served as the instruments for the building up of the various denominational constituencies, and in general as the agents for the cultural and religious advancement of a frontier civilization. These denominational colleges, built up on the successive lines of western migration, were able to uphold "the ideals of an educated ministry" on a wide front, to train some ten thousand ministers for the "Christian Cause," to recruit countless numbers of the youth of the land "for Christ and His Church," and withal to extend the benefits, if such they were in whole or part, of a "religious culture" to the remotest settlements of a vast and mighty continent.[131]

CONTRASTING DENOMINATIONAL ATTITUDES TOWARD THE FOUNDING OF COLLEGES

The fifteen religious denominations of this country at work in the field of higher education during the pre-Civil War period were divided into two general groups. One group, being thoroughly convinced of the desirability of an educated ministry, was active from the beginning in promoting colleges designed primarily for ministerial education. The other group, being opposed at the outset to the ideal of an educated ministry, was late in initiating a movement for the founding of colleges. Among the denominations that stood for an educated ministry and were very early in the field of higher education were the Congregationalists, Presbyterians, Episcopalians, Catholics, Lutherans, German Reformed, Dutch Reformed, and the Unitarians. In the case of these denominations, a tradition of ministerial learning and culture was inherited either directly or indirectly from Europe. This tradition of learning was maintained, in the face of many difficulties, and even at the cost of schism, on the new continent through the instrumentality of colleges. The influence of frontier conditions tended inevitably to lower the standards of ministerial education,[132] and it was only by the most strenuous efforts that these denominations upheld on

[131] It was estimated that 70,000 students had been graduated from American colleges by 1859. *Sixteenth Report of the S.P.C.T.E.W., 1859*, p. 31.
[132] See Sweet, *op. cit.*, for an extended discussion of the points raised in this section.

TABLE VI

SUMMARY TABLE OF PERMANENT COLLEGES AND UNIVERSITIES FOUNDED
BEFORE THE CIVIL WAR ARRANGED ACCORDING TO DENOMINATIONAL
AND OTHER ASSOCIATION

S.N.	DENOMINATIONAL AND OTHER ASSOCIATION	TOTAL PERMANENT COLLEGES	COLLEGES DUPLICATED OR TRIPLICATED
1	PRESBYTERIAN	49	17
2	METHODIST	34	5
3	BAPTIST	25	2
4	CONGREGATIONAL	21	12
5	CATHOLIC	14	—
6	EPISCOPAL	11	2
7	LUTHERAN	6	—
8	DISCIPLES	5	1
9	GERMAN REFORMED	4	1
10	UNIVERSALIST	4	—
11	FRIENDS	2	—
12	UNITARIAN	2	1
13	CHRISTIAN	1	—
14	DUTCH REFORMED	1	—
15	UNITED BRETHREN	1	—
16	SEMI-STATE *	3	2
17	MUNICIPAL **	3	1
18	STATE ***	21	4
	TOTAL COLLEGES LISTED	207 less	48 — 23 = 182

* Tulane (La.), Mississippi (Miss.), and Centenary (La.).
** College of Charleston (S. C.), University of Louisville (Ky.), and College of the City of New York (N. Y.).
*** See Table XXII on pp. 167-168.

the wide front of denominational advance the ideals of an educated leadership.

Among the denominations that were opposed to the ideal of a highly educated ministry during the early years of their history, and were late in the field of higher education, were the Methodists, Baptists, Disciples, Friends, United Brethren, Christians, and Universalists. In the cases of these denominations, evangelical fervor was more highly regarded than learning or scholarship. Thus the main incentive for a program of college-building was absent. An active prejudice existed, moreover, among the denominations against colleges and collegiate training. This attitude was in general the reflection of the interests of a membership drawn largely from the ranks of a frontier society.[133] Owing to the rapid growth in member-

[133] See Niebuhr, *op. cit.*, for an excellent treatment of the social origins of the various denominations.

ship of these denominations, particularly the Methodists, Baptists, and the Disciples, the standards of ministerial training were allowed to fall lamentably low. It was not until late in the period before the Civil War that they began to appreciate the necessity of higher standards for the ministry and to establish colleges designed to accomplish this purpose. In the following sections, a survey of the work of four denominations in the field of higher education is given, viz., the Presbyterians, Methodists, Baptists, and Congregationalists. Lists of all the permanent colleges that were established by the fifteen denominations that eventually entered the field of higher education in the period before the Civil War are also included in the following pages. A summary table of all these colleges (Table VI) appears on the preceding page.

THE FOUNDING OF PERMANENT COLLEGES BEFORE THE CIVIL WAR IN ASSOCIATION WITH PRESBYTERIAN INTERESTS

The Presbyterian Church was more closely identified with the development of institutions of higher education in America than any other church in the period before the Civil War. One of the most pronounced characteristics of this church was "its uniform and ardent zeal in behalf of an educated ministry." [134] This ideal of a highly educated ministry formed a part of its Calvinistic heritage from Europe. With such a zeal for ministerial training and with such a heritage of culture, it was natural that the Presbyterian Church should concern itself from the outset with the establishment of colleges designed primarily for the education of ministers. By the time of the Civil War, forty-nine permanent colleges had been founded in association with the church in various parts of the country.

The rigor of its faith in higher education is evidenced by the founding of the early "Log Colleges" on the frontiers of Presbyterian settlement. At the time of the Great Awakening the need for ministers on the frontier became insistent, and there arose a demand for institutions designed specifically for the training of a native ministry. The Log College at Neshaminy, Pennsylvania, established by the Rev. William Tennent, proved to be one of the

[134] Patton, J. H., *A Popular History of the Presbyterian Church in the United States of America*, p. 127, 1900. See also Laws, S. S., *An Address in Behalf of Westminster College, 1857*, p. 31 (pamphlet).

most significant ventures of this type.[135] The founding of Princeton College by the "New Side" Presbyterians, who had sponsored
the Log College movement, was an achievement of the greatest
import for the Presbyterian Church, initiating as it did a new and
higher standard for ministerial training. Princeton became "the
mother of colleges" within the denomination, and, throughout the
period under consideration, exerted a powerful influence over the
whole field of Presbyterian activity in higher education.[136]

From the earliest days of Scotch-Irish settlement the Presbyterian Church in this country took on the character of a frontier
church.[137] When the Presbyterian settlers entered this country by
way of the Middle Atlantic states, they found most of the territory
along the coast already occupied, and so were forced to establish
themselves on the frontier back from the more settled tide water
sections. These frontier settlements were in the course of time extended to the west, and the Presbyterian Church became one of
the most active churches on the western frontier. A large number
of colleges were built up along the successive lines of Presbyterian
settlement under the guiding hand of the clergy.[138] These institutions were primarily designed to serve the need of the churches for
consecrated and educated leadership. As the denomination grew
in numbers and in power, it came to exercise a dominating influence
on the development of higher education in this country. As early as
1831, it was stated that "of all the colleges in the United States they
[the Presbyterians] have possession of a large majority."[139] In
1851 it was affirmed that "two-thirds of the colleges in the land
were directly or indirectly under the control of the Presbyterian
Church."[140] It is clear from the researches made in connection with
this study that more colleges were established before the Civil War
in association with Presbyterian interests than with any other denomination at work in the field of higher education. The names of
forty-nine colleges founded in association with the Presbyterian
Church on a permanent basis before 1861 are given in Table VII
which follows.

[135] Alexander, A., *Biographical Studies of the Founder and Principal Alumni of the Log College*, 1845. See also Gilbert Tennent's letter on ministerial standards, quoted in Ford, H. J., *The Scotch-Irish in America*, p. 415, 1915.

[136] Patton, *op. cit.*, p. 119.

[137] Niebuhr, *op. cit.*, p. 157.

[138] Smith, J., *History of Jefferson College*, 1857, p. 27 (pamphlet), footnote indicates influence of clergy in the founding of frontier colleges.

[139] Durbin, Rev. John P., quoted in *Quarterly Register*, August 1831, p. 13.

[140] Quoted in Snow. M. S., "Higher Education in Missouri," U. S. Bur. of Ed. Cir. Inf., 1888, no. 2, p. 93.

TABLE VII

FORTY-NINE PERMANENT COLLEGES FOUNDED IN ASSOCIATION WITH PRESBYTERIAN INTERESTS BEFORE THE CIVIL WAR

S.N.	I.N.	PRESENT NAME AND LOCATION	CHARTER-DEGREE DATE
1	A4	PRINCETON UNIVERSITY Princeton, N. J.	October 22, 1746
2	A32	WASHINGTON AND LEE UNIVERSITY Lexington, Va.	October —, 1782
3	A24	TRANSYLVANIA COLLEGE Lexington, Ky.	May 5, 1783
4	A11	HAMPDEN-SIDNEY COLLEGE Hampden-Sidney, Va.	May —, 1783
5	A12	DICKINSON COLLEGE * Carlisle, Pa.	September 9, 1783
6	A6	UNIVERSITY OF PENNSYLVANIA * Philadelphia, Pa.	June 16, 1755 (1791)**
7	A21	TUSCULUM COLLEGE Greeneville. Tenn.	September 3, 1794
8	A22	UNIVERSITY OF TENNESSEE *** Knoxville, Tenn.	September 10, 1794
9	A23	UNION UNIVERSITY Schenectady, N. Y.	February 25, 1795
10	A27	WASHINGTON AND JEFFERSON COLLEGE Washington, Pa.	January 15, 1802
11	A31	HAMILTON COLLEGE Clinton, N. Y.	May 26, 1812
12	A34	ALLEGHENY COLLEGE * Meadville, Pa.	March 24, 1817
13	A35	CENTRE COLLEGE Danville, Ky.	January 21, 1819
14	A36	UNIVERSITY OF PITTSBURGH Pittsburgh, Pa.	February 18, 1819
15	A44	WESTERN RESERVE UNIVERSITY * Cleveland, O.	February 7, 1826
16	A45	LAFAYETTE COLLEGE Easton, Pa.	March 9, 1826
17	A64	NEW YORK UNIVERSITY New York, N. Y.	April 18, 1831
18	A57	HANOVER COLLEGE Hanover, Ind.	January 1, 1833
19	A84	UNIVERSITY OF DELAWARE *** Newark, Del.	February 5, 1833
20	A59	WABASH COLLEGE Crawfordsville, Ind.	January 15, 1834
21	A62	ILLINOIS COLLEGE * Jacksonville, Ill.	February 9, 1835

S.N.	I.N.	PRESENT NAME AND LOCATION	CHARTER-DEGREE DATE
22	A76	OGLETHORPE UNIVERSITY Atlanta, Ga.	December 21, 1835
23	A83	MUSKINGUM COLLEGE New Concord, O.	March 18, 1837
24	A83	KNOX COLLEGE * Galesburg, Ill.	February 15, 1837
25	A66	DAVIDSON COLLEGE Davidson, N. C.	December 28, 1838
26	A54	ADRIAN COLLEGE * Adrian, Mich.	April 16, 1839
27	A111	MARYVILLE COLLEGE Maryville, Tenn.	January 14, 1842
28	A55	MISSISSIPPI COLLEGE * Clinton, Miss.	December 16, 1830 (1842)**
29	A122	CUMBERLAND UNIVERSITY Lebanon, Tenn.	December 30, 1843
30	A99	CARROLL COLLEGE Waukesha, Wisc.	January 31, 1846
31	A102	BELOIT COLLEGE * Beloit, Wisc.	February 2, 1846
32	A104	UNIVERSITY OF BUFFALO Buffalo, N. Y.	May 11, 1846
33	A112	ROCKFORD COLLEGE * Rockford, Ill.	February 25, 1847
34	A109	GRINNELL COLLEGE * Grinnell, Ia.	June 17, 1847
35	A98	AUSTIN COLLEGE Sherman, Tex.	November 22, 1849
36	A163	BETHEL COLLEGE McKenzie, Tenn.	February 3, 1850
37	A95	GENEVA COLLEGE Beaver Falls, Pa.	March 7, 1850
38	A178	WAYNESBURG COLLEGE Waynesburg, Pa.	March 25, 1850
39	A189	ERSKINE COLLEGE Due West, S. C.	December 20, 1850
40	A172	RIPON COLLEGE * Ripon, Wisc.	January 29, 1851
41	A158	WESTMINSTER COLLEGE Fulton, Mo.	February 18, 1851
42	A147	MILWAUKEE-DOWNER COLLEGE * Milwaukee, Wisc.	March 1, 1851
43	A140	ELMIRA COLLEGE Elmira, N. Y.	January 29, 1852
44	A190	WESTMINSTER COLLEGE New Wilmington, Pa.	April 27, 1852

S.N.	I.N.	PRESENT NAME AND LOCATION	CHARTER-DEGREE DATE
45	A146	LINDENWOOD FEMALE COLLEGE St. Charles, Mo.	February 24, 1853
46	A170	PACIFIC UNIVERSITY * Forest Grove, Ore.	January 13, 1854
47	A195	UNIVERSITY OF CALIFORNIA * and *** Berkeley, Cal.	April 13, 1855
48	A145	LAKE FOREST UNIVERSITY Lake Forest, Ill.	February 13, 1857
49	A149	MONMOUTH COLLEGE Monmouth, Ill.	February 16, 1857

* The 15 colleges duplicated on other denominational lists are indicated by an asterisk.
** The date on which the institution became more closely associated with Presbyterian interests is indicated in parentheses.
*** Tennessee, Delaware, California also duplicated on state university lists.

Of the forty-nine colleges listed above, twenty-five remain to-day more or less closely associated with some branch of the Presbyterian Church, as indicated by the fact that they are included in the lists of associated colleges published in 1927-28 by the various Presbyterian Boards of Education, while twenty-four are not so included.[141] Consideration will first be given to the twenty-four colleges that became, in the course of time, less closely associated with the church. Three of the colleges listed, viz., Tennessee, Delaware, and California, after brief careers as Presbyterian colleges, became the state universities of Tennessee, Delaware, and California, respectively.[142] Three colleges, viz., Allegheny, Dickinson, and Adrian, after brief careers as Presbyterian institutions, were taken over by the Methodists and are listed today as colleges associated with the Methodist Church. One college, viz., University of Pennsylvania, after a brief career as an institution associated with the Anglican Church, became associated with the Presbyterian Church, but later became an independent institution. One college, viz., Transylvania, after a brief career as a Presbyterian college, was successively associated with a number of denominations, but in the course of time became more closely associated with the Disciples, and is listed today as an associated college of the Disciples Church. Another college, viz., Mississippi, after a brief career

[141] Consult the *Christian Education Handbook* for 1928, published by the Council of Church Boards of Education.
[142] Blount College was founded under Presbyterian auspices and later was taken over and merged into the University of Tennessee, while California College was founded on a coöperative basis by Presbyterians and Congregationalists and later taken over and merged with the University of California. See Chapter III on "The Founding of State Universities."

as a semi-state institution, became associated with Presbyterian interests in 1842, but became more closely associated with the Baptists in 1850, and is listed today as an associated college of the Baptist Church. Seven colleges,[143] viz., Knox, Beloit, Grinnell, Rockford, Ripon, Milwaukee-Downer, and Pacific University, founded on a coöperative basis by Presbyterians and Congregationalists under the Plan of Union of 1801, became more closely associated with the Congregationalists than with the Presbyterians, and are listed today as associated colleges of the Congregational Church.[144] Eight colleges, viz., Princeton, Pittsburgh, Buffalo, Washington and Lee, Oglethorpe, Western Reserve, Union, and New York, are not included on the 1927-28 list of the various Presbyterian Boards of Education, on the ground that they have become in recent years less closely associated with Presbyterian interests.[145] The remaining twenty-five colleges founded in association with Presbyterian interests before the Civil War are today regarded as associated colleges of the church.

Among the total number of forty-nine Presbyterian colleges established on a permanent basis before the Civil War will be found a number that have been associated at different times with various divisions of the Presbyterian Church. The story of the schisms within the church is closely bound up with the history of certain Presbyterian colleges. The initial division of the church into "New Side" and "Old Side" Presbyterians, following the Great Awakening, resulted in the founding of Princeton College. The New Side party, rejecting the stern standards of ministerial training of the more conservative Old Side party, initiated the Log College movement for the training of native ministers, and, with the help of the Presbyterian elements that had become dissatisfied with the "Old Light" stand of Yale, ultimately brought about the founding of Princeton.[146] It has been said, not without a touch of malice, that the founding of Princeton was "a sort of Providential rebuke to the

[143] These seven plus Western Reserve, Illinois, and California were the ten permanent colleges founded on a coöperative basis by Presbyterians and Congregationalists before the Civil War.

[144] Illinois College has remained a coöperative undertaking of Presbyterians and Congregationalists, with the Presbyterian element predominant in control. It is listed today as an associated college of both Congregational and Presbyterian Churches.

[145] Western Reserve University was founded on a coöperative basis by Presbyterians and Congregationalists under the Plan of Union, but on its removal to Cleveland, it became less closely associated with both groups.

[146] Alexander, *op. cit.*, p. 78.

cold, intellectually proud old Sisters." [147] With the coming of the Revolutionary War and the rise of a new generation of church leaders sympathetic with the position of the New Side party, this schism within the church was brought to an end.

At the time of the Great Awakening the Reformed and Associate Reformed divisions of the Presbyterian Church, representing the so-called "Covenanter" branch of the church, began their work in this country. For a considerable period they depended largely upon Europe for their ministerial supply, but later they were able to establish five colleges on a permanent basis, viz., Muskingum, Erskine, Westminster, Monmouth, and Geneva. In 1858, the two Reformed Churches joined under the name of the United Presbyterian Church, and of the five colleges mentioned above, all except Geneva and Erskine, which remain as associated colleges of an independent branch of the former Associate Reformed Church, are listed as associated colleges of the United Presbyterian Church.[148]

One of the most important schisms that took place within the church in the early 19th century was that of the Cumberland Presbyterian Church. This schism of 1810 was in large part the result of a difference of opinion on the question of the licensing of ministers who lacked the required educational qualifications of the Presbyterian ministry.[149] The force of frontier conditions tended to lead this branch of the church to reject the high standards of ministerial training upheld by the main body of Presbyterians. It was not until some time later that the Cumberland Presbyterians gave up to a large degree their objection to an educated ministry and set about to establish colleges of their own. Three colleges were founded on a permanent basis by the Cumberland Presbyterians before the Civil War, viz., Cumberland, Waynesburg, and Bethel, the first two of which are listed today as associated colleges of the Presbyterian Church, North, the branch of the church with which most of the Cumberland Presbyterian Churches united in 1905, while Bethel remains an associated college of an independent branch of the former Cumberland Presbyterian Church.[150]

The breach between the "Old School" and "New School" parties

[147] Funk, H. D., "Influence of the Presbyterian Church in Early American History," *Journal of the Presbyterian Historical Society*, p. 177, April 1925.
[148] Geneva and Erskine are not listed in the *Christian Education Handbook* for 1928, but are listed in the publications of the Associate Reformed Church.
[149] Sweet, *op. cit.*, p. 335.
[150] Bethel College is not listed in the *Christian Education Handbook* for 1928 but is listed in the publications of the Cumberland Presbyterian Church.

within the Presbyterian Church that took place in 1837 was far-reaching in its effects on the colleges of the church. The New School party, partly because of its theology and polity, and partly because of its concentration in the north, where the Plan of Union was in force, coöperated with the Congregationalists in the work of higher education more fully than the Old School party. The Old School party, which was represented largely by the colleges in the southern states, was also associated with a few colleges such as Hanover in Indiana and Westminster in Missouri. In a number of institutions, the conflict between the Old School and New School groups was a striking feature of their history.[151] In 1869 the breach between the two groups in the church was ended. The Presbyterian Church did not divide, as did the Methodist and Baptist Churches, into northern and southern branches, until after the Civil War, although to some extent the breach between the Old School and the New School parties represented such a division turning on the question of slavery.

At the present time the twenty-five Presbyterian colleges that were founded before the Civil War, and which remain more or less closely associated with the church, are divided into five groups: the fourteen that are listed today as associated colleges of the Presbyterian Church, North; the three, viz., Austin, Davidson, Hampden-Sidney, that are listed today as associated colleges of the Presbyterian Church, South; the two, viz., Centre in Kentucky and Westminster in Missouri, that are listed today by both the Presbyterian Church, North, and the Presbyterian Church, South; the three, viz., Monmouth, Michigan, and Westminster (Pa.), that are listed as associated colleges of the United Presbyterian Church; and finally the three, viz., Geneva, Erskine, and Bethel, that are regarded today as associated colleges of independent branches of the Associate Reformed Presbyterian Church and the Cumberland Presbyterian Church, respectively. These twenty-five colleges founded before 1861 constitute about one-third of the sixty-eight colleges listed as associated colleges of the Presbyterian Churches today.

It will be observed by reference to the accompanying map that the forty-nine permanent Presbyterian colleges founded before the Civil War were widely scattered over the country, indicat-

---

[151] At Tusculum such a conflict was severe and prolonged. Illinois College was also affected by this conflict.

MAP 11

FORTY-NINE PERMANENT COLLEGES FOUNDED IN ASSO-
CIATION WITH PRESBYTERIAN INTERESTS BEFORE THE
CIVIL WAR

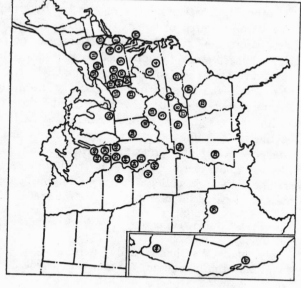

Donald G. Tewksbury

MAP 10

PRESBYTERIAN CHURCHES, 1860

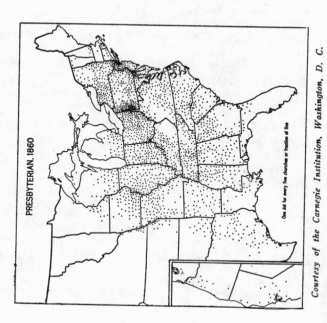

Courtesy of the Carnegie Institution, Washington, D. C.

ing on the one hand the wide extent of the Scotch-Irish migrations, and on the other, the national scope of the Presbyterian Church. These colleges were located in twenty-one of the thirty-four states of the Union before the Civil War. In thirteen states no permanent Presbyterian colleges were founded before that date. In sixteen of the twenty-five states east of the Mississippi River, forty-three colleges were establishd on a permanent basis, while in nine states no permanent Presbyterian colleges were founded before 1861. New England, with its six states, was not represented by a Presbyterian college, as the closely allied Congregational Church maintained a virtual monopoly over higher education in that region. Florida and Alabama were without permanent Presbyterian colleges before the Civil War. The forty-three colleges that were established east of the Mississippi were located in the following sixteen states: [152]

1. *New York:* Union, Hamilton, New York, Elmira, Buffalo
2. *New Jersey:* Princeton
3. *Pennsylvania:* Washington and Jefferson, Allegheny, Dickinson, Lafayette, Pittsburgh, Westminster, Waynesburg, Geneva, Pennsylvania
4. *Delaware:* University of Delaware
5. *Ohio:* Western Reserve, Muskingum
6. *Indiana:* Hanover, Wabash
7. *Illinois:* Illinois, Knox, Rockford, Lake Forest, Monmouth
8. *Michigan:* Adrian
9. *Wisconsin:* Beloit, Carroll, Ripon, Milwaukee-Downer
10. *Kentucky:* Centre, Transylvania
11. *Tennessee:* Tusculum, Cumberland, University of Tennessee, Maryville, Bethel
12. *Virginia:* Washington and Lee, Hampden-Sidney
13. *North Carolina:* Davidson
14. *South Carolina:* Erskine
15. *Georgia:* Oglethorpe
16. *Mississippi:* Mississippi

In glancing over the list of colleges given above, it will be noted that the early center of Presbyterian influence in higher education was located in New Jersey, with Princeton as the mother of Presbyterian colleges. More colleges were associated with Presbyterian

[152] Colleges, such as Washington and Jefferson, and Milwaukee-Downer, which were founded as two separate institutions and later merged, are counted here and elsewhere as one institution.

interests in Pennsylvania than in any other state. In New York, on the border line between Congregationalism and Presbyterianism, the colleges that were established were less exclusively Presbyterian in character, yet were an integral part of the general Presbyterian program of higher education. In the states of the Northwest Territory, the colleges were in a similar way generally coöperative ventures of Congregationalists and Presbyterians working under the Plan of Union of 1801. Muskingum, Hanover, Lake Forest, Monmouth, and Carroll do not fall within this category, however, being distinctly Presbyterian ventures. In the border states of Kentucky and Tennessee, Presbyterian influences were strong from the early days of frontier settlement. In Virginia, two colleges were founded in the western part of the state, which became the center of Presbyterian influence for the piedmont region. Davidson in North Carolina, Erskine in South Carolina, and Oglethorpe in Georgia later served the interests of the Presbyterian Church in their respective states, while Mississippi College in the distant state of Mississippi was for a time associated with the church.

In five of the nine states west of the Mississippi River, six permanent colleges were founded in association with the Presbyterian Church before the Civil War. Minnesota, Kansas, Arkansas, and Louisiana were not represented by permanent Presbyterian colleges before 1861, the six colleges that were established west of the Mississippi being in the following five states:

1. *Iowa:* Grinnell
2. *Missouri:* Westminster, Lindenwood
3. *Texas:* Austin
4. *Oregon:* Pacific
5. *California:* University of California

It is to be noted that the extension of Presbyterian influence west of the Mississippi took place in conjunction with the Congregational program for higher education, especially in the states of Iowa, Oregon, and California. Later events led the Presbyterians, however, to transfer their interests to colleges more directly under their own control. In Missouri, the Presbyterian Church was directly associated with Westminister and with Lindenwood, a college for women, while in Texas, Presbyterianism was represented by Austin College.

Summarizing the more important features of the movement for the founding of Presbyterian colleges before the Civil War, as revealed by this study, we find that:

1. The Presbyterian Church, with its traditional emphasis on an educated ministry, became a powerful influence in the development of higher education in this country. Forty-nine permanent colleges were established in the period before the Civil War. This number was larger than that of any other church.

2. While the Presbyterian Church was essentially a frontier church, it was able to maintain throughout its history high standards of ministerial training, through the establishment of colleges on the successive lines of Presbyterian settlement across the continent. The Log College movement and the founding of Princeton testify to the zeal of the early fathers for an educated ministry in this country.

3. The church maintained its high standards of ministerial training on the frontier even at the cost of schism. Such events as the division of the church into New Side and Old Side adherents, and the later division into New School and Old School parties, the separation of the Cumberland Presbyterians and Disciples groups from the main body of Presbyterians, and the independent action of the Reformed Churches, were not allowed to interfere appreciably with the church program of higher education.

4. Of the forty-nine permanent colleges established in association with the Presbyterian Church before the Civil War, twenty-five remain more or less closely associated with the church. This number constitutes about one-third of the sixty-eight colleges listed today as associated colleges of the church.

5. Of the forty-nine permanent colleges established in association with the Presbyterian Church, twenty-four have either become more closely associated with other churches, or have become more or less independent enterprises.

6. The Presbyterians coöperated with the Congregationalists in establishing ten permanent colleges, viz., Illinois, Western Reserve, Beloit, California, Knox, Rockford, Ripon, Grinnell, Milwaukee-Downer and Pacific. Of this group Illinois alone maintains today a primary association with the Presbyterian Church.

7. The Presbyterian movement in higher education was of national scope and significance. Permanent colleges were established in twenty-one of the thirty-four states of the Union before the

Civil War. Of these twenty-one states, sixteen were east of the Mississippi, and five west of the Mississippi.

THE FOUNDING OF PERMANENT COLLEGES BEFORE THE CIVIL WAR IN ASSOCIATION WITH METHODIST INTERESTS

Although the Methodist Church "took its rise, received its name, and began its conquests in the University of Oxford," the circumstances of its rapid development in this country, together with the basic evangelical emphasis of its message, tended to preclude the rise of a movement within its membership in favor of colleges designed for the higher education of ministers. In fact a strong prejudice against ministerial education, and higher education in general, was a prominent characteristic of the development of Methodism during the early part of its history in this country. The Methodists came to be regarded by many as "the enemies of learning." [153] In the Book of Discipline of 1784, it was stated that "gaining knowledge is a good thing, but saving souls is better." [154] With such an intense faith in personal salvation, and a distrust of learning, it was natural that higher education should become a matter of little concern to the church at large.

Following the Great Awakening in the eighteenth century, the church received considerable accessions to its membership, while, as a result of the Second Awakening at the turn of the century, a very rapid increase in membership took place. With this rapid acceleration in membership, particularly among the underprivileged classes in the east, and the rank and file on the frontier, the church came increasingly to count on the ministry of lay preachers, organized on the basis of itinerancy and circuit-riding.[155] It was not until the decade of the thirties that higher standards for the ministry were advocated to any significant extent by the leaders of the church. A general movement was initiated at that time for the founding of colleges designed primarily for the education of ministers. Although late in entering the field of higher education, the Methodist Church was able to build up in the short space of three decades thirty-four permanent colleges distributed widely over the

[153] Quoted in Bangs, N., *A History of the Methodist Episcopal Church*, vol. 2, pp. 318-321, 1838-41.

[154] Quoted in Moats, F. I., *The Educational Policy of the Methodist Episcopal Church Prior to 1860*. Unpublished manuscript in the Library of the State University of Iowa, p. 184.

[155] Niebuhr, *op. cit.*, p. 170.

country to serve its constituency of over a million members. These colleges are listed in Table VIII.

TABLE VIII

THIRTY-FOUR PERMANENT COLLEGES FOUNDED IN ASSOCIATION WITH METHODIST INTERESTS BEFORE THE CIVIL WAR

S.N.	I.N.	PRESENT NAME AND LOCATION	CHARTER-DEGREE DATE
1	A58	RANDOLPH-MACON COLLEGE Ashland, Va.	February 3, 1830
2	A65	WESLEYAN UNIVERSITY Middletown, Conn.	May 26, 1831
3	A34	ALLEGHENY COLLEGE * Meadville, Pa.	March 24, 1817 (1833)**
4	A12	DICKINSON COLLEGE * Carlisle, Pa.	September 9, 1783 (1834)**
5	A67	McKENDREE COLLEGE Lebanon, Ill.	February 9, 1835
6	A78	EMORY UNIVERSITY Atlanta, Ga.	December 10, 1836
7	A89	WESLEYAN COLLEGE Macon, Ga.	December 23, 1836
8	A73	DePAUW UNIVERSITY Greencastle, Ind.	January 10, 1837
9	A88	GREENSBORO COLLEGE Greensboro, N. C.	December 28, 1838
10	A77	EMORY AND HENRY COLLEGE Emory, Va.	March 25, 1839
11	A118	OHIO WESLEYAN UNIVERSITY Delaware, O.	March 7, 1842
12	A43	CENTENARY COLLEGE OF LOUISIANA Shreveport, La.	February 18, 1825 (1845)**
13	A176	BALDWIN-WALLACE COLLEGE Berea, O.	December 20, 1845
14	A110	LAWRENCE COLLEGE Appleton, Wisc.	January 15, 1847
15	A94	TAYLOR UNIVERSITY Upland Ind.	January 18, 1847
16	A123	LAGRANGE FEMALE COLLEGE Lagrange, Ga.	December 17, 1847
17	A175	ALBION COLLEGE Albion, Mich.	February 18, 1850
18	A169	NORTHWESTERN UNIVERSITY Evanston, Ill.	January 28, 1851
19	A171	COLLEGE OF THE PACIFIC Stockton, Cal.	July 10, 1857

S.N.	I.N.	PRESENT NAME AND LOCATION	CHARTER-DEGREE DATE
20	A160	WOFFORD COLLEGE Spartanburg, S. C.	December 16, 1851
21	A138	DUKE UNIVERSITY Durham, N. C.	November 21, 1852
22	A159	WILLAMETTE UNIVERSITY Salem, Ore.	January 12, 1853
23	A188	ILLINOIS WESLEYAN UNIVERSITY Bloomington, Ill.	February 12, 1853
24	A136	CORNELL COLLEGE Mt. Vernon, Ia.	February —, 1854
25	A142	HAMLINE UNIVERSITY St. Paul, Minn.	March 3, 1854
26	A184	COLUMBIA COLLEGE Columbia, S. C.	December 21, 1854
27	A168	IOWA WESLEYAN COLLEGE Mt. Pleasant, Ia.	January 25, 1855
28	A91	WHEATON COLLEGE * Wheaton, Ill.	February 15, 1855
29	A164	CENTRAL COLLEGE Fayette, Mo.	March 1, 1855
30	A54	ADRIAN COLLEGE * Adrian, Mich.	April 16, 1839 (1855)**
31	A131	BIRMINGHAM-SOUTHERN UNIVERSITY Birmingham, Ala.	January 25, 1856
32	A92	UPPER IOWA UNIVERSITY Fayette, Ia.	April 5, 1856
33	A150	MT. UNION COLLEGE Alliance, O.	January 9, 1858
34	A134	BAKER UNIVERSITY Baldwin, Kan.	February 12, 1858

* The 4 colleges duplicated on other denominational lists are indicated by an asterisk, viz., Allegheny (Presb.), Dickinson (Presb.), Wheaton (Cong.), and Adrian (Presb.).
** The date on which the institution became more closely associated with Methodist interests is indicated in parentheses.

The geographical distribution of the thirty-four colleges listed above is indicated on the accompanying map. It will be observed that Methodist colleges were as widely distributed over the country as were the Presbyterian and Baptist. These institutions were located in nineteen of the thirty-four states of the Union before the Civil War. In fifteen states, no permanent Methodist colleges were established before 1861. In twelve of the states east of the Mississippi River twenty-five were founded, while in thirteen of the states east of the Mississippi River, viz., Maine, New Hampshire, Vermont, Massachusetts, Rhode Island, New York, New Jersey,

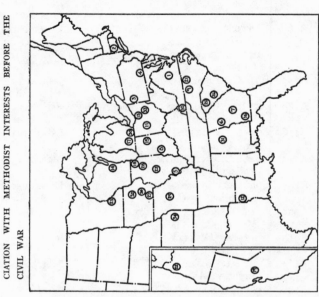

MAP 13

THIRTY-FOUR PERMANENT COLLEGES FOUNDED IN ASSO-
CIATION WITH METHODIST INTERESTS BEFORE THE
CIVIL WAR

Donald G. Tewksbury

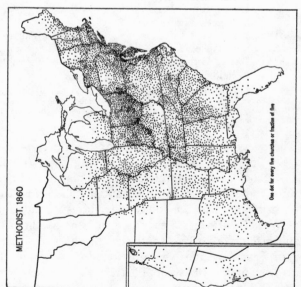

MAP 12

METHODIST CHURCHES, 1860

Courtesy of the Carnegie Institution, Washington, D. C.

Delaware, Maryland, Kentucky, Tennessee, Florida, and Mississippi, no permanent Methodist institutions were established. In seven of the states west of the Mississippi River, nine were founded, while in two of the states west of the Mississippi River, viz., Arkansas and Texas, no permanent Methodist institutions were established. The thirty-four Methodist colleges founded in this country before the Civil War are arranged according to states in the following list:

Twenty-five Methodist Colleges in Twelve States East of the
Mississippi River

1. *Connecticut:* Wesleyan
2. *Pennsylvania:* Allegheny, Dickinson
3. *Virginia:* Randolph-Macon, Emory and Henry
4. *North Carolina:* Duke, Greensboro
5. *South Carolina:* Columbia, Wofford
6. *Georgia:* Emory, Lagrange, Wesleyan
7. *Alabama:* Birmingham-Southern
8. *Ohio:* Ohio Wesleyan, Baldwin-Wallace, Mt. Union
9. *Indiana:* DePauw, Taylor
10. *Illinois:* Wheaton, Northwestern, Illinois Wesleyan, McKendree
11. *Michigan:* Albion, Adrian
12. *Wisconsin:* Lawrence

Nine Methodist Colleges in Seven States West of the
Mississippi River

1. *Minnesota:* Hamline
2. *Iowa:* Iowa Wesleyan, Cornell, Upper Iowa
3. *Missouri:* Central
4. *Kansas:* Baker
5. *Louisiana:* Centenary
6. *Oregon:* Willamette
7. *California:* College of the Pacific

The movement for the founding of Methodist colleges was slow in getting under way. At the time of the reorganization of this church on a national basis following the Revolution, a number of attempts were made to organize such a movement, but it was in large part abortive.[156] A number of ill-fated institutions were founded

---

[156] Duvall, S. M., *The Methodist Episcopal Church and Education up to 1869*, pp. 27-36, 1928.

during this early period, among which the more prominent were Cokesbury College and Asbury College, both in Maryland. It was evident that the constituency of the church was not ready at that time to support a general movement for the establishment of denominational colleges. For a period of more than a quarter of a century the Methodist Church, although increasing rapidly in membership, remained outside the general movement for the founding of colleges in this country. Meanwhile such denominations as the Presbyterian and Congregational were growing more powerful and influential in the field of higher education.

With the decade of the thirties, however, a widespread interest in higher education manifested itself within the denomination in sufficient force to lead to the founding of a number of successful colleges. A variety of circumstances combined to bring about this change of policy on the part of the church. The wealth of its membership had increased and a measure of social stability and influence had been achieved. The competition of other denominations which had built up colleges of their own began to be keenly felt in the struggle to recruit young men for the ministry and the church, while the criticisms to which the ministers of the Methodist Church were increasingly subjected by the more highly educated clergy of other churches led in time to much searching of heart and mind. In the following statements made in 1831 and 1839, some of these considerations are reflected:

These young men, generally the most promising of our best families, will be educated somewhere. If there be not proper and elevated institutions under our own patronage, they will be sent to others. What is the consequence? Many of them return with prejudice against the religious opinions and practices of their parents; not only injured themselves, as we think, but prove a great mortification to their parents. They frequently forsake our assemblies, and become able and efficient supporters of other people. Let me ask you, my brethren, if these things ought to be so? Think of our immense loss in this way, and then think of the means to remedy it. An active, unanimous effort throughout the connection would set this matter right in less than ten years.[157]

Those of our youth who were in pursuit of an education were obliged to seek it in institutions under the influence and control of other denominations. As might be expected, many became alienated, or were drawn from us. The ranks of our ministry were often impoverished by young men of piety and promise going out among others to seek literary advantages which

[157] Durbin, Rev. John, Quoted in *Quarterly Register,* August 1831, p. 16.

we could not give them, and finally connecting themselves with other ecclesiastical bodies. . . . To see our young men drawn away from us in this way—young men for whom we had labored and prayed, and over whom we had rejoiced as children born into our spiritual household—was by no means agreeable.[158]

In the founding of Randolph-Macon College in Virginia in 1830 and of Wesleyan University in Connecticut in 1831, the movement for the founding of Methodist colleges was successfully initiated. These two colleges, one in the north and the other in the south, became the parent institutions of the church. During the succeeding decades before the Civil War, a large number of frontier colleges were built up on the wide front of Methodist settlement. In a number of cases, institutions formerly held by other interests were taken over by the Methodists. Allegheny College and Dickinson College in Pennsylvania, having suffered a decline due in part to the withdrawal of the Presbyterian support, were given a new lease on life in 1833 under the Methodists. Centenary College in Louisiana, founded as a semi-state institution, was taken over by the Methodist Church in 1845. Adrian College in Michigan was taken over by the Methodists from the Presbyterians in 1855.

By the decade of the forties the movement for the founding of Methodist colleges had achieved large proportions. In the decade of the fifties, the peak of the movement was reached. Those that had already been established had proved their worth and value to the denomination, especially in the direction of providing a better educated and more able body of ministers. A church once largely indifferent to the need for ministerial education now gave its full support to a program for college-building. The following statement made in 1852 indicates the great change that had taken place in the policy of the church:

The Methodists at first had no colleges—why? Because the Methodists in England under Wesley were not a church—did not profess to be a church—they were simply a society for the promotion of a revival of religion in the church of England, and the educational institutions of the national church were their educational institutions. In this country, from the necessity of the case, they became a church by themselves; and though they endeavored to live here as they had done in England, they soon found it absolutely impossible—to maintain their church existence and influence, they saw that they must maintain colleges, and they do. What denomination

[158] *Methodist Magazine*, July 1839, p. 272; quoted in Duvall, *op. cit.*, p. 76.

is now establishing colleges with such rapidity and in such numbers? So now in the West, the Cumberland Presbyterians, the Campbellites, the New Lights, the United Brethren, are all establishing colleges; for they see that they cannot live as churches, and have influence with men without them.[159]

The colleges that were founded in association with Methodist interests before the Civil War came to be associated in practically all cases with either the northern or the southern branch of the church, after the Great Schism of 1844. Only three are not listed today as associated colleges of these two main branches of the church. Adrian College in Michigan was associated for a time with the Wesleyan Methodist Church, and then with the Methodist Protestant Church, with which it is still associated today. Wheaton College in Illinois was associated with the Wesleyan Methodist Church until 1861, when it was taken over by the Congregationalists. Taylor University in Indiana gradually became associated with special Methodist interests and is regarded as a more or less independent Methodist institution. Of the remaining thirty-one permanent colleges founded before the Civil War, nineteen became associated with the northern branch of the Methodist Church, while twelve became associated with the southern branch of the church, viz., Randolph-Macon (Va.), Emory (Ga.), Wesleyan (Ga.), Greensboro (N. C.), Emory and Henry (Va.), Centenary (La.), Lagrange (Ga.), Wofford (S. C.), Duke (N. C.), Columbia (S. C.), Central (Mo.), and Birmingham-Southern (Ala.).

Summarizing the more important facts relating to the movement for the founding of Methodist colleges before the Civil War, as revealed by this study, we find that:

1. The Methodist Church, with its traditional emphasis upon evangelical doctrines, and its reliance upon a lay ministry, was late in initiating a movement for the founding of colleges designed primarily for the higher education of ministers. It was not until the decade of the thirties that the church was led to recognize the necessity for colleges of its own. Once convinced of this necessity, however, the Methodist Church within a short space of time, built up thirty-four permanent colleges in different parts of the country.

2. The Methodist Church was essentially a frontier church, like the Baptist Church. Its membership was largely recruited in the early years from the underprivileged classes in the east and from

[159] Stowe, Calvin E., "Address," *Ninth Annual Report of S.P.C.T.E.W., 1852*, pp. 53-4.

the rank and file on the western frontier. The denominational membership reached a total of over a million persons by the time of the Civil War, a membership approximated only by the Baptist Church.

3. The movement for the founding of Methodist colleges, although late in starting, eventually assumed as extensive a character as that of the Presbyterian and Baptist Churches. Permanent colleges were established in nineteen of the thirty-four states composing the Union before the Civil War. Of these states, twelve were east and seven west of the Mississippi River.

4. During the course of the development of this movement, the Methodist Church took over four colleges originally associated with other interests, viz., Allegheny, Dickinson, Centenary, and Adrian. Only one college, viz., Wheaton College, has been lost to the Methodist cause by a transfer to some other denomination. Two colleges, viz., Adrian College and Taylor University, are associated today with separate Methodist interests. Adrian College is listed today as an associated institution of the Methodist Protestant Church. Taylor University is regarded today as a more or less independent Methodist institution. Of the thirty-one remaining Methodist institutions, nineteen are at present listed as associated colleges of the Methodist Church, North, and twelve as associated colleges of the Methodist Church, South.

THE FOUNDING OF PERMANENT COLLEGES BEFORE THE CIVIL WAR IN ASSOCIATION WITH BAPTIST INTERESTS

Unlike a number of other denominational groups, such as the Presbyterians and Congregationalists, the Baptists in America did not inherit from Europe a tradition of an educated ministry. In fact, throughout the greater part of the history of the Baptist Church in this country before the Civil War, there existed among the larger portion of its membership a deep-seated and active prejudice against the education of ministers.[160] The ranks of the church were for long recruited from the poorer and less educated classes who naturally tended to favor the "lowly ministry of uneducated men." The rapid spread and growth of the denomination, especially among the underprivileged classes, following the Great

[160] Newman, A. H., *A History of the Baptist Churches in the United States*, pp. 336-380, 1894.

Awakening during the eighteenth century and the Second Awakening at the turn of the century, taken together with the strong evangelistic character of the doctrines of the church, tended to preclude, or at least to retard, the development of a sentiment in favor of an educated ministry.[161] Meanwhile other denominations were building up colleges designed primarily for ministerial training in various parts of the country. As the Baptist denomination, however, achieved a measure of stability and wealth in the decade of the twenties, and as the competition of other denominations holding higher educational standards became a matter of concern, a program for the building up of institutions of higher learning was finally initiated and carried through with considerable success. By the time of the Civil War, twenty-four permanent colleges had been established in association with Baptist interests in different parts of the country to serve a constituency of over a million members.

While the establishment of Brown University in the early days of colonial settlement was "an event of primary importance in the history of the American Baptists," it did not lead directly to the founding of other colleges on the frontiers of Baptist settlement.[162] Its successful establishment in this early period of Baptist history is to be explained largely by the action of local forces in the State of Rhode Island, supported by prominent Baptist interests in Philadelphia, rather than by any general denominational concern for higher education or devotion to ministerial education. The Baptist community in Rhode Island had come to occupy for all practical purposes the position of an established sect in the state, with a social, economic, and cultural status which set it off in a marked way from other Baptist communities in the country. It is natural, therefore, that the efforts made toward the establishment of an institution of higher education in Rhode Island, initiated and reinforced as they were by a small group of Philadelphia Baptists, should prove successful in this state. Significant, therefore, as was the establishment of Brown University, it was not until some sixty years later that another permanent Baptist college was founded in the country.

The general movement for the founding of colleges on the part

<hr />

[161] See Sweet, W. W., *Religion on the American Frontier—the Baptists*, p. 75, 1931, and Niebuhr, *op. cit.*, pp. 167-170.

[162] Newman, *op. cit.*, p. 418.

of the denomination was not initiated until the Second Triennial Baptist Convention held in Washington in 1817.[163] The denominational membership had increased, meanwhile, until it numbered 200,000 persons.[164] At this Convention, an active campaign was launched by certain groups within the denomination that had come to realize the important relation which colleges bore to the problem of ministerial supply, particularly on the home and foreign missionary field. Under the leadership of Luther Rice, and others, such as Going, Peck, and Furman, steps were taken in various parts of the country toward the founding of denominational colleges. The first one to be organized was the institution in Washington, D. C., which later came to be known as George Washington College.[165] With this institution as the real parent institution of the Church, the movement for the founding of colleges spread over the country.

The motto of "every state its own Baptist college" soon became the watchword of the college movement.[166] The identification of home and foreign missions with the college movement was complete, since colleges came to be regarded as essential to an effective missionary program. The work of setting up colleges among the widespread Baptist communities, however, proceeded against great odds. The prejudices against ministerial education were only gradually removed, and then only in certain regions. The rise of the "anti-mission" Baptists on the frontier was a constant challenge to the work of college-building as well as to missionary work, with which it was so closely identified.[167] Considering these opposing forces, it is truly remarkable that the Baptist Church was able to accomplish as much as it did in the field of higher education before 1861. In Table IX the names of the twenty-five permanent colleges that were established in association with Baptist interests before the Civil War are given.

The geographical distribution of these twenty-five Baptist colleges is indicated on the accompanying map. It will be observed that the Baptist institutions were widely scattered over the country —as widely scattered, in fact, as the more numerous colleges of the Presbyterian and Methodist denominations. They were located in nineteen of the thirty-four states of the Union before the Civil War,

[163] Sweet, W. W., *The Story of Religions in America*, p. 358.
[164] Newman, *op. cit.*, p. 379, gives the figures for 1812 as 172,972.
[165] Colby College in Maine was actually chartered before George Washington College.
[166] Newman, *op. cit.*, p. 418.
[167] *Ibid.*, p. 433.

MAP 15

TWENTY-FIVE PERMANENT COLLEGES FOUNDED IN ASSO-
CIATION WITH BAPTIST INTERESTS BEFORE THE CIVIL
WAR

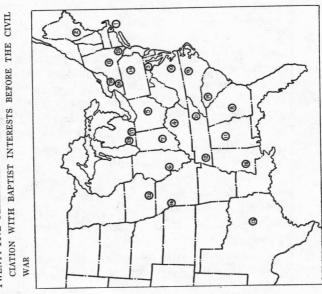

Donald G. Tewksbury

MAP 14

BAPTIST CHURCHES, 1860

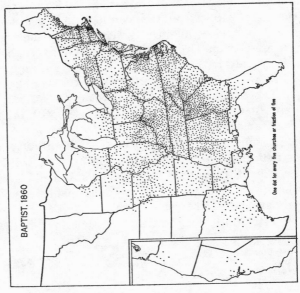

BAPTIST. 1860

One dot for every five churches or fraction of five

Courtesy of the Carnegie Institution, Washington, D. C.

TABLE IX

TWENTY-FIVE PERMANENT COLLEGES FOUNDED IN ASSOCIATION WITH
BAPTIST INTERESTS BEFORE THE CIVIL WAR

S.N.	I.N.	PRESENT NAME AND LOCATION	CHARTER-DEGREE DATE
1	A7	BROWN UNIVERSITY Providence, R. I.	October 24, 1765
2	A49	COLBY COLLEGE Waterville, Me.	June 19, 1820
3	A38	GEORGE WASHINGTON UNIVERSITY Washington, D. C.	February 9, 1821
4	A47	GEORGETOWN COLLEGE Georgetown, Ky.	January 15, 1829
5	A68	DENISON UNIVERSITY Granville, O.	February 2, 1832
6	A82	SHURTLEFF COLLEGE Alton, Ill.	February 9, 1835
7	A96	FRANKLIN COLLEGE Franklin, Ind.	January 30, 1836
8	A74	MERCER UNIVERSITY Macon, Ga.	December 22, 1837
9	A63	WAKE FOREST COLLEGE Wake Forest, N. C.	December 26, 1838
10	A97	UNIVERSITY OF RICHMOND Richmond, Va.	March 4, 1840
11	A103	HOWARD COLLEGE Birmingham, Ala.	December 29, 1841
12	A93	UNION UNIVERSITY Jackson, Tenn.	February 5, 1842
13	A100	BAYLOR UNIVERSITY Waco, Tex.	February 1, 1845
14	A106	BUCKNELL UNIVERSITY Lewisburg, Pa.	February 5, 1846
15	A56	COLGATE UNIVERSITY Hamilton, N. Y.	March 26, 1846
16	A117	WILLIAM JEWELL COLLEGE Liberty, Mo.	February 27, 1849
17	A144	HILLSDALE COLLEGE Hillsdale, Mich.	March 20, 1850
18	A55	MISSISSIPPI COLLEGE * Clinton, Miss.	December 16, 1830 (1850)**
19	A141	FURMAN UNIVERSITY Greenville, S. C.	December 20, 1850
20	A155	UNIVERSITY OF ROCHESTER Rochester, N. Y.	February 14, 1851
21	A182	CARSON AND NEWMAN COLLEGE Jefferson City, Tenn.	December 5, 1851

TABLE IX—*Continued*

S.N.	I.N.	PRESENT NAME AND LOCATION	CHARTER-DEGREE DATE
22	A165	CENTRAL UNIVERSITY * Pella, Ia.	June 3, 1853
23	A193	KALAMAZOO COLLEGE Kalamazoo, Mich.	February 10, 1855
24	A133	ALFRED UNIVERSITY Alfred, N. Y.	March 28, 1857
25	A130	VASSAR COLLEGE Poughkeepsie, N. Y.	January 18, 1861

* The 2 colleges duplicated on other denominational lists are indicated by an asterisk, viz., Mississippi (Presb.), and Central (German Ref.).

** The date on which the institution became more closely associated with Baptist interests is indicated in parentheses.

and in Washington, D. C. In fifteen states, no permanent Baptist colleges were established before 1861. In sixteen of the states east of the Mississippi River, and in Washington, D. C., twenty-two were founded, while in nine of the states east of the Mississippi River no permanent Baptist institutions were established, viz., New Hampshire, Vermont, Massachusetts, Connecticut, New Jersey, Delaware, Maryland, Florida, and Wisconsin. In three of the states west of the Mississippi River, three were founded, while in six of the states west of the Mississippi River, viz., Minnesota, Kansas, Arkansas, Louisiana, Oregon, and California, no permanent Methodist institutions were established. The twenty-five Baptist colleges founded in this country before the Civil War are arranged according to states in the following list:

Twenty-two Baptist Colleges in Sixteen States East of the Mississippi River

1. *Maine:* Colby
2. *Rhode Island:* Brown
3. *New York:* Colgate, Rochester, Alfred, Vassar
4. *Pennsylvania:* Bucknell
5. *Virginia:* Richmond
6. *North Carolina:* Wake Forest
7. *South Carolina:* Furman
8. *Georgia:* Mercer
9. *Alabama:* Howard
10. *Mississippi:* Mississippi
11. *Kentucky:* Georgetown
12. *Tennessee:* Carson and Newman, Union
13. *Ohio:* Denison

14. *Indiana:* Franklin
15. *Michigan:* Hillsdale, Kalamazoo
16. *Illinois:* Shurtleff
   (*Washington, D. C.:* George Washington)

Three Baptist Colleges in Three States West of the Mississippi River

1. *Iowa:* Central
2. *Missouri:* William Jewell
3. *Texas:* Baylor

The colleges that were founded in association with Baptist interests before the Civil War were associated in all but two cases, viz., Hillsdale and Alfred, with the main body of Baptists in this country. The Free-Will Baptists were a small frontier sect that was organized at the time of the Great Awakening. It was composed not only of those that held distinctive theological beliefs, but also of those that tended to be even more opposed to an educated ministry than were the regular Baptists themselves.[168] It was not until 1839 that a general movement for the founding of colleges was initiated by certain leaders in that branch of the church. In Michigan where the Free-Will Baptists were strongly represented, a charter was secured in 1850 for Hillsdale College, an institution designed to serve the newly recognized needs of this sect for a better educated ministry. In Maine, another state where the Free-Will Baptists had from the beginning been well represented, an institution—Bates College—was organized before 1861, but did not receive its charter until after the War.[169] The Free-Will Baptists united with the Northern Baptist Church in 1911, hence Hillsdale College and Bates College are listed today as associated colleges of that division of the main body of Baptists. The Seventh Day Baptists founded a number of churches in Rhode Island at an early date but did not achieve a general ecclesiastical organization until 1818.[170] The need for an educated ministry was not recognized by this group for a considerable time. Alfred University was founded in New York in 1857 to meet the needs for ministerial education that this branch of the church finally came to recognize. This in-

---

[168] Niebuhr, *op. cit.,* p. 170; and Newman, *op. cit.,* p. 498.
[169] The regular Baptists were represented in the two states of Michigan and Maine by Kalamazoo College and Colby College, respectively.
[170] Newman, *op. cit.,* pp. 484-486.

stitution remains at the present time an associated college of the Seventh Day Baptist Church.[171]

During the early part of the nineteenth century, the Baptist Church on the frontier suffered a great loss in membership from the defection of the Disciples. Much strife between the Baptists and Disciples in the field of higher education resulted from this situation. Georgetown College, for example, was for long a bone of contention between the two groups of interests. The situation was largely relieved when the Disciples set about to establish colleges of their own. In 1844, the Great Schism divided the Baptist Church into northern and southern branches. The various Baptist colleges lined themselves up with one or the other branch of the church. Of the twenty-one that remain today as associated colleges of the Baptist Church, ten are listed as associated colleges of the northern branch, while ten are listed as associated colleges of the southern branch, viz., Georgetown (Ky.), Mercer (Ga.), Wake Forest (N. C.), Mississippi (Miss.), Carson and Newman (Tenn.), Union (Tenn.), Howard (Ala.), Furman (S. C.), Richmond (Va.), Baylor (Tex.). William Jewell College in Missouri is listed by both branches of the church as an associated college. Alfred University in New York is listed today as an associated college of the Seventh Day Baptists. Three colleges are not listed today as associated colleges of the church, viz., George Washington (D. C.), Central (Ia.), and Vassar (N. Y.). Central University in Iowa was taken over by the German Reformed Church in 1916.

Summarizing the more important facts relating to the movement for the founding of Baptist colleges before the Civil War, as revealed by this study, we find that:

1. The Baptist Church, with its strong evangelistic message, and its traditional opposition to an educated ministry, was slow in initiating a general movement for the founding of colleges. Once convinced of the necessity of church institutions, however, the leaders of the denomination set in motion a powerful movement for the building up of colleges. By the time of the Civil War, twenty-five permanent colleges were founded in association with Baptist interests.

2. The Baptist Church, like the Methodist, was essentially a frontier church organization, ministering to the underprivileged

---

[171] *Christian Education Handbook* for 1928.

classes in the east and the masses on the western frontier. By 1861, the Baptist Church was able to recruit a membership of over a million persons, a number approximated only by the Methodist.

3. The movement for the founding of Baptist colleges, although late in starting, was widespread in character. Baptist colleges were established in nineteen of the thirty-four states composing the Union before the Civil War, thus being as widely distributed as the more numerous institutions of the Presbyterian and Methodist Churches. Of these nineteen states, sixteen were situated east of the Mississippi River and three west of the Mississippi River.

4. The Baptist Church was subjected to a number of minor schisms. These were closely related to the general college movement. The Free-Will Baptists, while not strong in numbers, were able in 1850 to bring about the establishment of a permanent institution in Michigan by the name of Hillsdale College. This institution became an associated college of the Baptist Church, North, when in 1911 the Free-Will Baptists united with that branch of the Church. The Seventh Day Baptists, another small group of separatists, were able to establish just before the time of the Civil War a permanent college in New York, by the name of Alfred University. This institution is still associated with this separate division of the Baptist Church.

5. As a result of the Great Schism of 1844, the Baptist Church was divided into northern and southern branches. Of the twenty-five Baptist colleges founded before the Civil War, twenty-one are listed today as associated colleges of one or the other, or both, of these branches. In the course of time three colleges, viz., George Washington (D. C.), Central (Ia.), and Vassar (N. Y.), have become less closely associated with the Baptist Church. Alfred University remains an associated college of the Seventh Day Baptists.

THE FOUNDING OF PERMANENT COLLEGES BEFORE THE CIVIL WAR IN ASSOCIATION WITH CONGREGATIONAL INTERESTS

The history of the Congregational Church in this country reveals a consistent regard for the need for higher education. From the earliest days of colonial settlement, a definite policy of linking church and college in a program of advancement for the church was followed. By the time of the Civil War, twenty-one permanent colleges were established in association with Congregational interests. In the founding of Harvard College in 1636, the early Puritan fathers expressed their faith in higher education as the means of training up ministers for the church. This faith in higher education was based in part on the Calvinistic tradition of an educated ministry, and in part on the Anglican tradition of ministerial learning and culture.[172] Many of the church leaders of the Massachusetts Bay Colony, moreover, were graduates of English universities, and were regarded as "the peers in learning and ability of any in the Puritan wing of the Church of England." [173] It was natural, therefore, that, at the very beginning of the Congregational Church in this country, attention should have been given to laying securely the foundations of an educational program for the church.

The establishment of Yale in 1701, following the defection of Harvard from the paths of orthodox Congregationalism, proved to be a most significant event in the history of the church. Yale became the "mother of colleges" within the denomination, exerting throughout the pre-Civil War period a far-reaching influence on the development of Congregational institutions of higher education.[174] At first the colleges that were founded under the auspices of the Congregational Church were confined within the limits of New England. With the expansion of New England westward, however, and the gradual spread of Congregational polity to the settlements on the Western Reserve, the Mississippi Valley, and the Pacific Coast, the need for western colleges patterned on the model of Yale became imperative. The demand for ministers on the western frontiers of Congregational settlement became as urgent as had been the demand for ministers in the early days of colonial settlement in New England. Thus it came about that a line of colleges was built up across the continent, designed for the education of ministers and the development of a devoted constituency. In Table X the names of twenty-one permanent colleges founded in association with Congregational interests before the Civil War are given in order of their founding.

[172] It is to be recalled that the settlers of the Massachusetts Bay Colony, unlike the settlers of the colony of Plymouth, remained to a large extent within the Anglican tradition, holding that they did "not go to New England as separatists from the Church of England." Quoted in "Religious History of New England," in *King's Chapel Lectures*, p. 10, 1917.

[173] See Walker, Williston, *A History of the Congregational Churches in the United States*, p. 98, 1894.

[174] In the *Yale Alumni Weekly* for October 18, 1929, will be found a list of sixteen colleges established before the Civil War by Yale men. Because of the change in the religious constitution of Harvard, it did not, like Yale, reproduce itself in the West, and thus could not be called, in the same sense at least, the "mother of colleges." See Rusk, *op. cit.*, p. 64.

TABLE X

TWENTY-ONE PERMANENT COLLEGES FOUNDED IN ASSOCIATION WITH
CONGREGATIONAL INTERESTS BEFORE THE CIVIL WAR

S.N.	I.N.	PRESENT NAME AND LOCATION	CHARTER-DEGREE DATE
1	A1	HARVARD UNIVERSITY * Cambridge, Mass.	October 28, 1636
2	A3	YALE UNIVERSITY New Haven, Conn.	October 16, 1701
3	A9	DARTMOUTH COLLEGE Hanover, N. H.	December 13, 1769
4	A19	WILLIAMS COLLEGE Williamstown, Mass.	June 22, 1793
5	A20	BOWDOIN COLLEGE Brunswick, Me.	June 24, 1794
6	A25	MIDDLEBURY COLLEGE Middlebury, Vt.	November 1, 1800
7	A42	AMHERST COLLEGE Amherst, Mass.	February 21, 1825
8	A44	WESTERN RESERVE UNIVERSITY * Cleveland, O.	February 7, 1826
9	A71	OBERLIN COLLEGE Oberlin, O.	February 28, 1834
10	A62	ILLINOIS COLLEGE * Jacksonville, Ill.	February 9, 1835
11	A69	MARIETTA COLLEGE Marietta, O.	February 14, 1835
12	A83	KNOX COLLEGE * Galesburg, Ill.	February 15, 1837
13	A102	BELOIT COLLEGE Beloit, Wisc.	February 2, 1846
14	A112	ROCKFORD COLLEGE * Rockford, Ill.	February 25, 1847
15	A109	GRINNELL COLLEGE * Grinnell, Ia.	June 17, 1847
16	A172	RIPON COLLEGE * Ripon, Wisc.	January 29, 1851
17	A147	MILWAUKEE-DOWNER COLLEGE * Milwaukee, Wisc.	March 1, 1851
18	A170	PACIFIC UNIVERSITY * Forest Grove, Ore.	January 13, 1854

* The twelve colleges duplicated on other denominational lists are indicated by an asterisk. Of these, ten were founded on a coöperative basis by the Presbyterians and Congregationalists. Harvard is duplicated on the Unitarian list, and Wheaton on the Methodist list.

** The date on which the institution became more closely associated with Congregational interests is indicated in parentheses.

*** California also duplicated on state university list.

TABLE X—*Continued*

S.N.	I.N.	PRESENT NAME AND LOCATION	CHARTER-DEGREE DATE
19	A195	UNIVERSITY OF CALIFORNIA * and *** Berkeley, Cal.	April 13, 1855
20	A53	OLIVET COLLEGE Olivet, Mich.	——— —, 1859
21	A91	WHEATON COLLEGE * Wheaton, Ill.	February 15, 1855 (1861)**

Note: *, **, and ***, see footnotes p. 121.

The geographical distribution of the colleges listed above is indicated on the accompanying map. It will be observed that the first seven colleges to be founded in association with Congregational interests were located in New England itself. These institutions were all founded during the period of the "establishment" in New England, a period which was only finally brought to a close in Vermont in 1807, in Connecticut in 1818, in New Hampshire in 1819, in Maine in 1820, and in Massachusetts in 1833. Harvard, Williams, and Amherst were established in Massachusetts, Yale in Connecticut, Dartmouth in New Hampshire, Middlebury in Vermont, and Bowdoin in Maine. Rhode Island alone of the New England states was unrepresented by a Congregational college. It was to be expected, however, that the dissenters from the "standing order," who had found a refuge in Rhode Island, should feel little need for a Congregational college in their midst. In this state, where a large measure of religious freedom was early attained, Brown University was established with the Baptist elements in the population largely in control.[175] After a period of comparative toleration in religion was brought about in the rest of New England, five other permanent colleges were founded in association with other denominations, viz., Colby with the Baptists in Maine, Trinity with the Episcopalians and Wesleyan with the Methodists in Connecticut, Norwich and Tufts with the Universalists in Vermont and Massachusetts, respectively.[176] These colleges were not established, however, without opposition on the part of Congregational interests, and even after their establishment the original seven Congregational colleges con-

[175] In this connection it is well to recall the peculiar circumstances surrounding the drawing up of the charter of Brown University, when the Congregational interests in the state all but succeeded in gaining a position of significant influence in this Baptist venture. See Bronson, W. C., *History of Brown University*, pp. 14-26.

[176] In Vermont, a state university had been founded in 1791. This institution was initiated in large part by Congregational interests. After the founding of Middlebury College, an institution more directly under the control of the church, the state university lost a large measure of its support. See Wheeler, John, *A Historical Address on the University of Vermont*, pp. 16-17 (pamphlet), 1854.

MAP 17

TWENTY-ONE PERMANENT COLLEGES FOUNDED IN ASSO-
CIATION WITH CONGREGATIONAL INTERESTS BEFORE
THE CIVIL WAR

Donald G. Tewksbury

MAP 16

CONGREGATIONAL CHURCHES, 1860

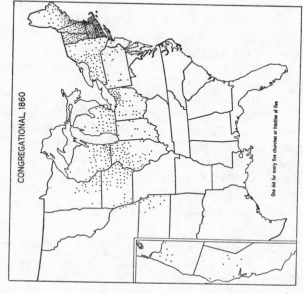

CONGREGATIONAL, 1860

One dot for every five churches or fraction of five

Courtesy of the Carnegie Institution, Washington, D. C.

tinued to exercise a dominance in the field of higher education in New England up to the time of the Civil War. Of the seven original Congregational colleges founded in New England, all except Harvard and Yale are listed today by the Congregational Education Society as associated colleges of the church.[177]

In the expansion of New England population to the west during the early part of the nineteenth century, the Western Reserve and its adjacent territory became the first area of more or less permanent Congregational settlement and of Congregational initiative in college building. It is rather significant that no Congregational colleges were established in the state of New York, which lay directly in the path of migration. This was largely because of the fact that the New England settlers, in the early days of westward expansion, tended to merge their interests with those of the Presbyterian Church under the Plan of Union of 1801, thus leaving their Congregationalism at home.[178] It was felt at that time that Congregationalism was unsuited to pioneer communities, and that "a church westward of the Hudson ought to be Presbyterian, as surely as one east of that dividing stream should be Congregational."[179] The needs of the New England settlers in New York state for higher education were met by Union College at Schenectady and Hamilton College at Clinton, institutions established under Presbyterian auspices but in coöperation with Congregational interests, as well as by the New England colleges which were not too far distant. It was in the state of Ohio, and particularly in the Western Reserve, that the Congregational Church began to take a more active part in the work of founding colleges. Three were established in this region during the period between 1826 and 1835, viz., Western Reserve, Oberlin, and Marietta. At a later date, Olivet was founded in the adjacent state of Michigan, on a plan similar to that of Oberlin. Of these four, Oberlin, Marietta, and Olivet were distinctively Congregational ventures, while Western Reserve was a coöperative undertaking of the Congregationalists and Presbyterians working under the Plan of Union. All four of these institutions were built up primarily as agencies for the preparation of ministers to meet

---

[177] *Christian Education Handbook* for 1928.

[178] The Plan of Union of 1801 was an agreement between Congregational and Presbyterian interests relative to coöperation in missionary work on the frontiers. In the actual working out of the Plan, the Presbyterian Church gained at the expense of the Congregational Church. See Sweet, *op. cit.,* pp. 306-309.

[179] Walker, *op. cit.,* p. 370.

the needs of the churches for leadership in this frontier region, which in time came to be regarded as a second New England. Western Reserve College, on its removal to Cleveland, became less closely associated with both Congregational and Presbyterian interests, and is not listed at the present time as an associated college of either of the two Congregational or Presbyterian Churches.[180]

While the foundations of higher education were being laid in this region, the New England settlers were making their way still further westward to the Mississippi Valley. For a number of reasons the state of Indiana did not prove a permanent place of settlement for the Congregationalists, or a promising field for college-building. The state was early dominated by the southern element in the population.[181] The Presbyterian interests in the state had taken the initiative in higher education by associating themselves with the state university, which for a considerable period exercised more or less of a monopoly in the college field. When denominational colleges came onto the scene in the thirties, the Plan of Union was beginning to weaken, and Wabash College, in which the Congregationalists had at first an interest, became increasingly Presbyterian in character.[182] It is a noteworthy fact, moreover, that comparatively few Congregational Churches were established in Indiana, and to this day Congregationalism is weak in the state.[183] The Indiana State Association of Congregational Churches was not organized until 1858, some fourteen years after an association had been formed in Illinois.[184] In the light of these factors in the situation, it was natural that little was effected in the way of college building on the part of the Congregationalists in Indiana.

It was in the upper Mississippi Valley that the Congregationalists decided to establish another New England. The Congregational Church in the east had become fully aroused to the need of an active home missionary program. Its rising denominational spirit came to regard northern Illinois, southern Wisconsin, and eastern Iowa as its own special sphere of missionary influence in the west. In this general region eight colleges were established on a permanent basis before the Civil War, viz., Illinois, Knox, Beloit, Grinnell, Rockford, Ripon, Milwaukee-Downer, and Wheaton. All

[180] *Christian Education Handbook* for 1928.
[181] See *Twelfth Report of the S.P.C.T.E.W.*, 1855, p. 40.
[182] Dunning, A. E., *Congregationalists in America*, pp. 141-142.
[183] For a study of the development of higher education in Indiana, see Boone, R. G., *A History of Education in Indiana*, 1892.
[184] Walker, *op. cit.*, p. 371.

these colleges except the women's colleges of Rockford and Milwaukee-Downer were founded primarily in response to the need for educated ministers in this frontier region. In the establishment of all these institutions except Wheaton there was a measure of coöperation between the Congregationalists and the Presbyterians under the Plan of Union of 1801, which, although already beginning to weaken, had not yet been repudiated.[185] The decades of the thirties and the forties proved to be a period of rivalry and jealousy between the two denominations. While Illinois College was able to maintain in large measure its original basis of coöperation between them, and is today listed as an associated college of both, but under predominant Presbyterian control, Knox, Beloit, Grinnell, Rockford, Milwaukee-Downer, and Ripon came in time to associate themselves more closely with the Congregational Church and are today listed as associated colleges of the Congregational Church.[186] Wheaton was established in 1855 as a Methodist venture, but was refounded under the auspices of the Congregational Church in 1861. It remains today as an associated college of the Congregational Church, and is listed as such by the Congregational Education Society.

In the distant territory bordering upon the Pacific Ocean, the Congregational Church was instrumental, in coöperation with the Presbyterian, in establishing two colleges, viz., Pacific University and California College, later known as the University of California. Although the Plan of Union had been officially given up in 1852, the home missionary activity of the two denominations was carried on for a time in Oregon and California in a coöperative spirit. It was the urgent need for educated ministers on this distant frontier that led to the founding of these two colleges. Pacific University later came to be more Congregational than Presbyterian in character, and is today listed as an associated college of the Congregational Church. After the Civil War, California College became a state institution under the name of the University of California. Of the twenty-one colleges originally founded in association with Congregational interests, seventeen are listed today by the Congregational Education Society as associated colleges of the church, while four, viz., Harvard, Yale, Western Reserve, and California, are not so listed. These seventeen colleges constitute about one-half

---

[185] The Plan of Union was officially repudiated at the Albany Convention of Congregational Churches in 1852. Sweet, *op. cit.,* p. 487.
[186] *Christian Education Handbook* for 1928.

of the thirty-five colleges listed today as associated colleges of the Congregational Education Society.[187]

This brief survey of the influence of Congregationalism in the field of college-building before the Civil War reveals the fact that the Congregational Church was not national in its territorial scope as were some of the other denominations. The distribution of colleges associated with other denominations, such as the Presbyterian, the Methodist, and the Baptist, as indicated on the maps given on previous pages, tends to confirm this statement. Colleges were founded in association with Congregational interests in only twelve of the thirty-four states admitted before the Civil War, while twenty-two states were entirely unrepresented. No Congregational colleges were founded in Rhode Island or in Indiana; in the Middle Atlantic states of New York, New Jersey, or Pennsylvania; in the border states of Kentucky or Tennessee; in the Southern states of Delaware, Maryland, Virginia, North Carolina, South Carolina, Georgia, Florida, Alabama, or Mississippi; in the states west of the Mississippi River of Minnesota, Missouri, Arkansas, Louisiana, Kansas, or Texas. The statistics of Congregational Church membership for 1863 give added evidence of the limited territorial scope of the church. Out of a total of 250,657, New England was represented by 178,020 members, New York state by 17,885 members, the Northwest Territory by 43,477 members, Iowa by 5,515 members, Oregon by 229 members, and California by 838 members, leaving 4,693 for all the other states of the Union.[188] The distribution of colleges follows in general this distribution of church population.

The Congregational Church, being distinctively a New England product, elected at first to stay within its own narrow confines under the more or less direct protection of a theocratic government. Following the Revolution, and after the last steps in disestablishment were taken, Congregationalism began to realize that it was now but one of a number of rival denominations in the country at large, destined not only to struggle for its own corporate life as a church in New England but also to engage in the sectarian strife that was already assuming large proportions in the effort to possess the promised land in the west. After a considerable period of hesitation the Congregational Church ventured westward in the wake of

[187] This number does not include the Negro colleges associated with the church. See *Christian Education Handbook* for 1928.

[188] Dunning, *op. cit.*, pp. 411-412.

New England expansion,[189] in coöperation with the Presbyterian Church under the Plan of Union. With the rise of a more independent spirit on the part of the Congregationalists, particularly in the western country, hesitation gave way to an active and even aggressive denominational campaign. The Plan of Union was eventually repudiated, and the colleges that had been built up in coöperation with the Presbyterian Church became, in most cases, increasingly Congregational in character. At the time of the Civil War, Congregational New England had reproduced itself in at least three definite areas in the west. For long the Congregational Church remained almost exclusively a religious faith and polity held by a group of people of upper middle class lineage living either within the bounds of New England or of the New England settlements in the west.[190] The colleges that were established under the auspices of the Congregational Church, both in the east and in the west, although ministering to a limited denominational group, took their place from the start in the forefront of the institutions of higher education in this country.

Summarizing the more important features of the movement for the founding of Congregational colleges before the Civil War, as revealed by this study, we find that:

1. The Congregational Church, from the earliest days of colonial settlement, maintained a consistent policy of linking church and college in a program of advancement for the church. This policy was based on Calvinistic precedent and Anglican tradition in the field of higher education, and it was directed primarily to the work of ministerial education. Twenty-one permanent colleges were established in association with Congregational interests in the country before the Civil War.

2. The movement for the founding of Congregational colleges followed in general the course of New England expansion across the continent along the lines of parallel latitude. At first, the church confined its activities to New England, where seven colleges were established in all. Of these, Yale came to exercise a dominating influence on the development of higher education under the auspices of the church. After the rise of an active missionary spirit on the part of the Congregational Church in the decade of the thirties,

---

[189] See the excellent maps of the expansion of New England population in Matthews, L. K., *The Expansion of New England*, 1909.
[190] See Niebuhr, *op. cit.*, pp. 147-154.

institutions were built up on the western frontier. Before the Civil War, fourteen permanent colleges were established along the lines of the westward expansion of New England population. At the time of the Civil War, twelve of the thirty-four states in the Union were represented by Congregational colleges.

3. The Congregational Church coöperated with the Presbyterian under the Plan of Union in the establishment of ten colleges, viz., Western Reserve, Illinois, Beloit, Rockford, Milwaukee-Downer, Knox, Ripon, Grinnell, Pacific, and California. Of these, eight are listed today as associated colleges of the Congregational Church, while two, viz., Western Reserve and California, are no longer listed by the church. The most serious schism within the Congregational Church was that of the breaking away of the Unitarian churches.

4. Of the twenty-one permanent colleges founded before the Civil War, seventeen are listed today as associated colleges of the Congregational Church, while four, viz., Harvard, Yale, Western Reserve, and California, are no longer listed by the Church. The former group of seventeen colleges constitutes about one-half of the thirty-five colleges listed today as associated colleges of the Congregational Church.

THE FOUNDING OF PERMANENT COLLEGES BEFORE THE CIVIL WAR IN ASSOCIATION WITH ELEVEN OTHER DENOMINATIONAL INTERESTS

The limitations of this study preclude the possibility of even surveying the work of the eleven other denominations at work in the field of higher education before the Civil War. In Tables XI to XXI, inclusive, however, lists are given of the permanent colleges founded in association with each of these denominations.

TABLE XI

FOURTEEN PERMANENT COLLEGES FOUNDED IN ASSOCIATION WITH CATHOLIC INTERESTS BEFORE THE CIVIL WAR

S.N.	I.N.	PRESENT NAME AND LOCATION	CHARTER-DEGREE DATE
1	A33	GEORGETOWN COLLEGE Washington, D. C.	March 1, 1815
2	A72	MT. ST. MARY'S COLLEGE Emmitsburg, Md.	February 27, 1830
3	A79	ST. LOUIS UNIVERSITY St. Louis, Mo.	December 28, 1832

TABLE XI—*Continued*

S.N.	I.N.	PRESENT NAME AND LOCATION	CHARTER-DEGREE DATE
4	A75	SPRING HILL COLLEGE Spring Hill, Ala.	January 9, 1836
5	A61	ST. MARY'S COLLEGE St. Mary's, Ky.	January 21, 1837
6	A192	ST. XAVIER COLLEGE Cincinnati, O.	March 5, 1842
7	A105	UNIVERSITY OF NOTRE DAME Notre Dame, Ind.	January 15, 1844
8	A108	FORDHAM UNIVERSITY Fordham, N. Y.	April 10, 1846
9	A115	AUGUSTINIAN COLLEGE OF VILLANOVA Villanova, Pa.	March 10, 1848
10	A151	ST. JOSEPH'S COLLEGE Philadelphia, Pa.	January 29, 1852
11	A87	LOYOLA COLLEGE Baltimore, Md.	April 13, 1853
12	A177	SANTA CLARA COLLEGE Santa Clara, Cal.	April 28, 1855
13	A162	ST. IGNATIUS COLLEGE San Francisco, Cal.	April 30, 1859
14	A52	SETON HALL COLLEGE South Orange, N. J.	March 8, 1861

TABLE XII

ELEVEN PERMANENT COLLEGES FOUNDED IN ASSOCIATION WITH EPISCOPAL INTERESTS BEFORE THE CIVIL WAR

1	A2	COLLEGE OF WILLIAM AND MARY Williamsburg, Va.	February 8, 1693
2	A5	COLUMBIA UNIVERSITY New York, N. Y.	October 31, 1754
3	A6	UNIVERSITY OF PENNSYLVANIA Philadelphia, Pa.	June 16, 1755
4	A10	WASHINGTON COLLEGE Chestertown, Md.	April —, 1782
5	A13	ST. JOHN'S COLLEGE Annapolis, Md.	November —, 1784
6	A15	COLLEGE OF CHARLESTON Charleston, S. C. (Episcopalian to Municipal in 1838)	March 19, 1785
7	A39	TRINITY COLLEGE Hartford, Conn.	May 22, 1823
8	A41	HOBART COLLEGE Geneva, N. Y.	February 8, 1825
9	A40	KENYON COLLEGE Gambier, O.	January 24, 1826

TABLE XII—*Continued*

S.N.	I.N.	PRESENT NAME AND LOCATION	CHARTER-DEGREE DATE
10	A156	UNIVERSITY OF THE SOUTH Sewanee, Tenn.	January 6, 1858
11	A129	ST. STEPHEN'S COLLEGE Annandale, N. Y.	March 20, 1860

TABLE XIII

SIX PERMANENT COLLEGES FOUNDED IN ASSOCIATION WITH LUTHERAN INTERESTS BEFORE THE CIVIL WAR

1	A80	GETTYSBURG COLLEGE Gettysburg, Pa.	April 7, 1832
2	A116	WITTENBERG COLLEGE Springfield, O.	March 11, 1845
3	A132	CAPITAL UNIVERSITY Columbus, O.	March 2, 1850
4	A173	ROANOKE COLLEGE Salem, Va.	March 14, 1853
5	A174	NEWBERRY COLLEGE Newberry, S. C.	December 20, 1856
6	A179	IRVING FEMALE COLLEGE Mechanicsburg, Pa.	March 28, 1857

TABLE XIV

FIVE PERMANENT COLLEGES FOUNDED IN ASSOCIATION WITH DISCIPLES INTERESTS BEFORE THE CIVIL WAR

1	A187	UNIVERSITY OF KENTUCKY Georgetown, Ky.	February 23, 1837
2	A101	BETHANY COLLEGE Bethany, W. Va.	March 2, 1840
3	A107	BUTLER UNIVERSITY Indianapolis, Ind.	January 15, 1850
4	A137	CULVER-STOCKTON COLLEGE Canton, Mo.	January 28, 1853
5	A167	EUREKA COLLEGE Eureka, Ill.	February 6, 1855

TABLE XV

FOUR PERMANENT COLLEGES FOUNDED IN ASSOCIATION WITH GERMAN REFORMED INTERESTS BEFORE THE CIVIL WAR

1	A16	FRANKLIN AND MARSHALL COLLEGE Lancaster, Pa.	March 10, 1787
2	A143	HEIDELBERG COLLEGE Tiffin, O.	February 13, 1851
3	A183	CATAWBA COLLEGE Salisbury, N. C.	December 17, 1852
4	A165	CENTRAL UNIVERSITY Pella, Ia. (Baptist to German Reformed in 1916)	June 3, 1853

TABLE XVI

FOUR PERMANENT COLLEGES FOUNDED IN ASSOCIATION WITH UNIVERSALIST
INTERESTS BEFORE THE CIVIL WAR

S.N.	I.N.	PRESENT NAME AND LOCATION	CHARTER-DEGREE DATE
1	A81	NORWICH UNIVERSITY Northfield, Vt.	November 6, 1834
2	A185	LOMBARD COLLEGE Galesburg, Ill.	February 15, 1851
3	A153	TUFTS COLLEGE Tufts College, Mass.	April 21, 1852
4	A152	ST. LAWRENCE UNIVERSITY Canton, N. Y.	April 3, 1856

TABLE XVII

TWO PERMANENT COLLEGES FOUNDED IN ASSOCIATION WITH FRIENDS
INTERESTS BEFORE THE CIVIL WAR

1	A139	EARLHAM COLLEGE Earlham, Ind.	January 4, 1850
2	A166	HAVERFORD COLLEGE Haverford, Pa.	March 15, 1856

TABLE XVIII

TWO PERMANENT COLLEGES FOUNDED IN ASSOCIATION WITH UNITARIAN
INTERESTS BEFORE THE CIVIL WAR

1	A1	HARVARD UNIVERSITY Cambridge, Mass. (Congregational to Unitarian in 1805)	October 28, 1636
2	A157	WASHINGTON UNIVERSITY St. Louis, Mo.	February 22, 1853

TABLE XIX

ONE PERMANENT COLLEGE FOUNDED IN ASSOCIATION WITH CHRISTIAN
INTERESTS BEFORE THE CIVIL WAR

1	A191	ANTIOCH COLLEGE Yellow Springs, O.	May 14, 1852

TABLE XX

ONE PERMANENT COLLEGE FOUNDED IN ASSOCIATION WITH DUTCH
REFORMED INTERESTS BEFORE THE CIVIL WAR

1	A8	RUTGERS UNIVERSITY New Brunswick, N. J.	November 10, 1766

TABLE XXI

ONE PERMANENT COLLEGE FOUNDED IN ASSOCIATION WITH UNITED
BRETHREN INTERESTS BEFORE THE CIVIL WAR

1	A127	OTTERBEIN COLLEGE Westerville, O.	February 13, 1849

Chapter III

THE FOUNDING OF STATE UNIVERSITIES BEFORE THE CIVIL WAR

I would first establish it as a Truth, that Societies have an indisputable Right to direct the Education of their youthful Members.[1]
    —*The Independent Reflector—William Livingston.*

Thomas Jefferson, author of the Declaration of American Independence, of the Statute of Virginia for Religious Freedom, and Father of the University of Virginia.[2]
    —*An Inscription on the Monument to Thomas Jefferson.*

Two complete townships to be given perpetually for the purposes of an University . . . to be applied to the intended object by the legislature of the state.[3]
    —*The Congressional Land Grant to the Ohio Company.*

THE GENERAL MOVEMENT FOR THE FOUNDING OF STATE UNIVERSITIES

THE forces that were largely instrumental in creating and shaping the twenty-one state universities established in this country before the Civil War were in the final analysis native and indigenous in character. While European conceptions of state education were indeed influential at various times in the development of state universities in this country, the evidence is convincing that the dominating influences in this development were largely those that arose from the democratic impulses and aspirations of the American people. During the Revolutionary period, when state universities were first established in this country, these native influences were clearly directed toward an ideal of higher

[1] Livingston, Wm., "The Independent Reflector," April 12, 1753. Pratt, D. J., *Annals of Public Education in the State of New York*, p. 207. Reprinted from the Proceedings of the University Convocation held at Albany, New York, July 29, 30, and 31, 1873.
[2] Inscription on the Monument over the Grave of Thomas Jefferson. Given in Adams, H. B., *Thomas Jefferson and the University of Virginia*, U. S. Bur. of Ed., Cir. Inf., 1888, no. 1, p. 148.
[3] "Sale of Land in the Western Territory," July 23, 1787, *Journal of Congress*, vol. 4, Appendix, p. 17. This sale of land to the Ohio Company was authorized by the Continental Congress ten days after the passing of the Northwest Ordinance of July 13, 1787.

education which contrasted sharply with that of the colonial era.[4] The state university movement initiated during this period was motivated in large part by the new social and political doctrines of the day. While this movement was short-lived, it was unusually successful while it lasted.

At the turn of the century there arose a renewed sentiment in favor of church-controlled institutions of higher education, and a strong prejudice against state-controlled institutions. In spite of this fact, however, the state university movement in the eastern states continued to receive the support of an active minority during the middle period of our history, and state universities were founded in the western states during this period under the stimulus of land grants from the national government. This latter movement was at first more or less indefinite in character and uncertain in its action, but in time it came to assume significant proportions and to achieve substantial results even in a religious era. By the time of the Civil War there finally developed a rather widespread and popular demand throughout the country for institutions of higher education that should be more completely responsive to the public will and more directly related to the needs of the people. Thus, after a somewhat long period of trial and experimentation, the state university emerged after the Civil War as a distinctive and recognized type of institution in this country, destined to supplement, but not to supersede, the denominational college which had for so long maintained special privileges in the field of higher education.[5]

In reviewing, in larger outline, the development of the movement for the founding of state universities in this country, it will be seen that during the colonial period, under the influence of English patterns of thought, the preferences of the early settlers were clearly in line with the theory that control over institutions of higher education should be exercised by the church. In those colonies where an established religion prevailed, it was assumed that the state should be allied in some measure with the church in the control of higher education. This alliance in no case, however, implied that the state was primarily responsible for higher educa-

---

[4] See Hansen, A. O., *Liberalism and American Education in the Eighteenth Century*, 1926, for evidences of a new ideal of higher education.

[5] Following the Civil War the state universities of the country entered into a period of significant influence, supported as they were in most cases by the provisions of the Morrill Land Grant Act, and by the industrial forces that now became dominant in American society.

tion or for the control and support of the institutions that were established.[6] Only in the latter part of the colonial period, with the growth of secular and republican sentiments, did there appear a theory of control that urged the establishment of institutions sponsored primarily by the state rather than by the church. With the coming of the Revolution, and the spread of French ideals in higher education, this theory came to be rather widely adopted, and a movement was begun for the founding of institutions which should be primarily civil rather than religious in character.

This revolutionary movement in higher education, while successful for a time and definitely prophetic in its emphasis, was in a very real sense premature, as the discussion in following sections will reveal. With the wane of the early secular and republican enthusiasm of the Revolutionary era, there was a revival of church interests in the country at large. While the state universities that were established in the east were indeed able in large part to maintain their identity as state institutions during the middle period of our history, they were nevertheless fated to undergo a long period of disfavor and neglect. Moreover, the state universities that were established in the west largely through the munificence of the national government, although able to achieve a measure of success, were also obliged to pass through a long period of opposition and criticism.[7] It was apparent that a new era of religious influence in higher education which was to prove unfavorable to the development of state universities both in the east and in the west had been ushered in at the turn of the century. It was during these years that the "American college" was evolved to meet the needs of a religious era and an advancing people. This institution was sponsored by the rapidly developing and expanding denominational forces of the country, and came to be preferred to the state universities by the mass of the people.

It was evident that the state university had yet to make its case with the American people, and that the "revolutionary" theory of state control of higher education had yet to become an accepted theory in this country. Eventually, however, as it became clearer

<hr />

[6] See Sears, J. B., *Philanthropy in the History of American Higher Education*. U. S. Bur. of Ed. Bulletin, 1922, no. 26, pp. 31-32.

[7] German influences became dominant in certain state universities in the west, and served further to alienate these institutions from the sympathies of the people. For a discussion of German influences at the University of Michigan, see McLaughlin, A. C., *History of Higher Education in Michigan*, U. S. Bur. of Ed. Cir. Inf., 1891, no. 4, p. 35.

that in most cases the denominational colleges were not prepared to meet the new needs of American society which arose at the end of the middle period, and which became insistent in the period following the Civil War, large sections of the American public turned to the state as the instrument for furthering the work of higher education.[8] Thus, we find that it was not until after the Civil War that the state university finally came into its own as an institution peculiarly adapted to meet the developing needs and new aspirations of the American people, and well fitted to take its place alongside the American college as one of the truly indigenous institutions of this country.

COLONIAL PRECEDENTS FOR THE STATE CONTROL AND SUPPORT OF HIGHER EDUCATION

While the church was generally assumed to be responsible for higher education during the colonial period, the state was associated with the church in the control and support of higher education in most of the colonies where an established religion prevailed. In nine of the thirteen colonies a standing order in religion was legally recognized.[9] The colonial governments of the three colonies of Massachusetts, Connecticut, and New Hampshire were identified with the interests of the Puritan Church, and three colleges were founded in these colonies; while the colonial governments of the six colonies of Virginia, New York, Maryland, North Carolina, South Carolina, and Georgia were identified with the interests of the Anglican Church, and two colleges were founded in these colonies. In most of these colonies where colleges were founded, the state was associated in a substantial way with the church in the control and support of higher education. In the four colonies of Rhode Island, Pennsylvania, New Jersey, and Delaware, however, the interests of the church and state were more or less separate, and consequently the colonial governments exercised little or no control, and provided little or no support for the four colleges that were founded within their territory. The relationship which the colonial governments bore to each of the nine colonial colleges will

[8] See Nevins, A., *Illinois*, pp. 12-29, 1917, for an excellent discussion of the popular demands for a new type of higher institution in this country at the end of the middle period.

[9] See Cobb, S. H., *The Rise of Religious Liberty in America*, 1902. See also footnote 59 on New York, p. 155 of this study.

now be taken up in detail, in order to discover what precedents, if any, were established during the colonial era for the state control and support of higher education.

In each of the three Puritan colonies an institution of higher education was established during the colonial period. *Harvard University*,[10] the first of the Puritan colleges to be founded, was created by the General Court of Massachusetts in 1636. A charter was not granted to the institution, however, until 1650.[11] The college received some measure of support from the colony throughout the colonial period. Representatives of the colony shared, by legal stipulation, with the leaders of the church in the control of the college through the board of overseers. The general direction of the development of the college, however, was clearly toward placing the primary responsibility for the control and support of the institution upon the church. Thus while Harvard may be regarded as more definitely a state college or university than some of the other colonial colleges, owing to the fact that the state took a more active part in its control and support than in any other college, it may be regarded as a state institution only in a limited sense, and as one that falls far short of the conception of a state university that came to prevail in certain quarters during the Revolutionary era. *Yale University*, the second of the Puritan colleges to be founded, was created by the General Court of Connecticut in 1701, but did not receive its charter until 1745.[12] While the colony granted aid to the college at various times, and looked upon the institution as one whose interests were largely identical with its own, it turned over from the very beginning the entire control of the institution to a self-perpetuating board on which the colony was not officially represented.[13] Thus while Yale truly reflected the interests of a Puritan state over a long period of time, it was actually less directly allied with the state in an official capacity than was Harvard, and thus may with still less propriety be regarded as a state college or university in the "revolutionary" sense of the term. *Dartmouth College*, the third of the Puritan colleges to be founded, received a

[10] Throughout this study, the present name of an institution is used in order to avoid the necessity of referring in every case to the changes in name of an institution. For these changes, see the general list of colleges at the end of Chapter I.

[11] The charter of 1850 is given in full in Parsons, E. C., *Educational Legislation and Administration of the Colonial Governments*, 1899.

[12] The charter of 1745 is given in full in Parsons, *op. cit.*

[13] During the post-Revolutionary period state representation on the board was provided for by legal enactment. See p. 144.

royal charter from the Governor of New Hampshire in 1769. The colonial government granted some aid to the college from time to time, but it was even more definitely assumed in this case than in the case of Harvard and Yale that the support of the institution was to come from private sources. The control of the college was turned over at the outset to a self-perpetuating board on which the colony was by charter stipulation represented only by its Governor acting ex-officio.[14] In the light of these considerations, therefore, it is clear that Dartmouth College during the colonial period may be regarded as a state college or university only in a very limited sense of the term.

In the six Anglican colonies, institutions of higher education were established during the colonial period only in Virginia and New York. The *College of William and Mary*, the first of the Anglican colleges to be founded, was the creation of church and state acting as one, as had been the case at Harvard. The college received its royal charter in 1693. Liberal aid was given by the colony to the institution in the beginning and at subsequent periods. Representatives of the colony took a prominent part in the establishment of the college. By mutual agreement the colony was given fourteen out of eighteen seats on the early Board of Trustees which was delegated to establish the college. In 1729 the institution was turned over to a corporation of the "President and Masters, or Professors" and a Board of "Visitors and Governors," both of which were self-perpetuating bodies, with no obligations to provide for state representation. In these circumstances, the primary responsibility for the control and the support of the institution came to rest finally with the Anglican Church rather than with the colony. Thus although William and Mary may with some propriety be regarded as a state college or university, yet it was a type of state college or university which differed quite radically from the type that was later advocated during the Revolutionary period. In the colony of New York a royal charter was granted by the Governor in 1754 to *Columbia University*, the second of the Anglican colleges to be founded. This charter was secured only after considerable acrimonious discussion had taken place over the desirability of establishing a church college in the colony. Proposals had already

[14] By mutual agreement, four state officials, in addition to the Governor acting ex-officio, were made members of the first Board of Trustees. See Smith, B. P., *The History of Dartmouth College*, p. 46, 1878.

been made in the colony for an institution that was to be free from the control of the church and primarily under the control of the state.[15] In the light of this situation, it was natural that difficulties should have arisen at the time of the granting of the charter and that a system of control which was distinctive in nature should have been finally evolved for Columbia University. The colony was strongly represented on the Board in an ex-officio capacity, and other churches than the Anglican were given a measure of representation, but yet the primary responsibility for control rested with the Anglican Church.[16] The colony granted aid to the institution only reluctantly on account of the opposition to the college in the colony, so that the institution was obliged to depend largely upon private philanthropy for its support. In the light of these conditions, it is apparent that Columbia University may be regarded as a state college or university only in a very restricted sense of the term. In the Anglican colonies of Maryland, North Carolina, South Carolina, and Georgia, no institutions of higher education were established during the colonial period either by the church or the state.

It remains to consider the relation of the colonial governments to the four colleges founded in Rhode Island, New York, Delaware, and Pennsylvania, where the church was not established. As no colleges were founded during the colonial period in Delaware, it is not necessary to discuss the situation in this colony. In Rhode Island, *Brown University* received a royal charter from the Governor in 1765. The colonial government was not officially represented in the control of the institution.[17] The management of the institution was turned over to the Baptist Church, which at that time was the leading church in the colony. The support of the college was derived from private sources, as the colony in the circumstances felt no obligation to undertake even the partial support of the institution. While it is undoubtedly true that the interests of the institution were regarded as being more or less identical with the interests of the state, it is clear that Brown University was in only the widest interpretation of the term a state university. In New Jersey, *Princeton University* was granted a royal charter by the Governor in 1746.[18] This charter was never officially recorded, and a second

---

[15] For a discussion of the early proposals for a state college in New York, see Moore, N. F., *An Historical Sketch of Columbia College*, pp. 9-12, 1846.

[16] *Ibid.*, p. 22.

[17] Bronson, W. C., *The History of Brown University*, p. 32, 1914.

[18] The charter of 1746 was the first royal charter granted to a dissenting institution. Harvard and Yale received their charters from the legislature.

charter with slight changes was secured in 1748.[19] The control of
the college was vested by the second charter in a self-perpetuating
board made up largely of Presbyterian ministers, with the Governor
of the colony acting as ex-officio member. No state representation
was provided for in the original charter. A later proposal for the
ex-officio representation of four other members of the colonial
government was not embodied in the second charter, but four
representatives were, however, appointed for the time being to the
first board, in addition to the Governor acting ex-officio.[20] With
little direct share in the control of the college, the colony felt slight
obligation to support it. The only aid rendered the college by the
colony during the colonial era was the authorization of a lottery
for the institution. It is apparent, therefore, that Princeton University, situated in a colony with a diversity of religious sects and
official sympathies with the Anglican Church, but controlled by a
dissenting church, cannot in any sense be regarded as a state college
or university. In the same state of New Jersey, another institution
of higher education was established, in this case, under the auspices
of the Dutch Reformed Church. *Rutgers University* was granted a
royal charter by the Governor of New Jersey in 1766. This original
charter, like that of Princeton, was never officially recorded, but
another charter was secured in 1770.[21] The control of the institution
was turned over by legal stipulation in both charters to a large
board, on which the colonial government was represented by four
members acting ex-officio. This state representation proved to be
largely formal in nature, and the colonial government assumed
little or no responsibility for the control of the college, and at no
time granted aid to the institution. It is apparent, therefore, that
Rutgers University was in no sense a state institution. In Pennsylvania, the *University of Pennsylvania* was granted a college
charter in 1755 by the Lieutenant Governor in the name of the
Proprietors. The colony, however, exercised no control over the
institution through legal representation on the Board of Trustees.
The college was turned over to a board composed of leading citizens
of the colony.[22] In the institution the Anglican Church was able to

[19] Collins, V. L., *Princeton*, pp. 11-14, 1914.
[20] Collins, *op. cit.*, pp. 14, 24, 29.
[21] Demarest, W. H. S., *A History of Rutgers College*, p. 57, 1924.
[22] Thorpe, F. N., *Benjamin Franklin and the University of Pennsylvania*, U. S. Bur.
of Ed. Cir. Inf., 1892, no. 2, pp. 71-77.

secure a dominant position.[23] While aid was granted to the institution at various times by the Proprietors, the King, the city, and the legislature, none of these authorities assumed responsibility for the control or the support of the college. The University of Pennsylvania, like Princeton and Rutgers, may not be regarded, therefore, in any sense as a state institution. It is apparent that none of these three colleges even approximates the type of state institution represented by some of the other colonial colleges.

In summarizing the relations of the colonial governments in eight colonies to the nine colonial colleges, it may be said that in no case did the colonial governments maintain a relationship with the colleges that was truly analogous to that maintained by the state governments with state universities established at a later date. In every case the colonial governments refused to assume primary responsibility for the control and support of the institutions established in their midst. The control of these institutions was turned over to self-perpetuating boards of trustees with or without state representation, and their support was left largely to private philanthropy. In cases where some measure of responsibility for control and support was retained by the colonial government, the institutions may with some propriety perhaps be termed state colleges or universities; but even in these cases it cannot be said that precedents were established for state control and support that were significant in the shaping of the ideals of state universities which came to prevail during the Revolutionary era. These ideals were largely derived from sources other than colonial practice and precedent.

With the rise of secular and republican sentiments at the time of the Revolution, and the consequent disestablishment of the traditional churches and the overturn of the colonial governments, it was inevitable that new theories for the control and support of higher education should appear. These new theories were fundamentally opposed to the colonial theories of control and support of higher education or any modified forms of these theories. It seems clear, therefore, that colonial precedents for state control and support of higher education, in so far as they existed, proved a negligible factor in the rise of the movement for state universities

[23] See Smith, E. F., *William Smith, D.D.*, p. 6, 1927 (pamphlet). See also Cheyney, E. P., *University of Pennsylvania*, pp. 81, 88, 1901.

during the Revolutionary period.[24] The early trend of Revolutionary thought demanded a radical reconstruction of the existing colonial colleges so that they would be directly and fully responsible to the new state governments. When efforts in this direction proved largely unavailing, the leaders of this "revolutionary" movement in higher education bent their efforts to create new and separate universities that would more completely embody the ideals of a new social and political order. It is to the early movement for the reconstruction of the colonial colleges that we now turn our attention.

REVOLUTIONARY EFFORTS TO RECONSTRUCT THE COLONIAL COLLEGES

With the rise of the spirit of political independence and the development of secular interests during the eighteenth century, a new conception of the rôle of the state in the control and support of higher education came into prominence. Whereas in colonial times, as has been pointed out, it was assumed that the primary responsibility for higher education rested with the church, it was now held by many that higher education was primarily a function of the state. A growing distrust of existing church institutions manifested itself in various quarters and a desire for a new type of state institution of higher education made itself felt in many parts of the country. Under the influence of these sentiments, reinforced as they were by French ideals that were current in that day, determined efforts were made to transform some of the colonial colleges into institutions that would be more completely responsive to the needs of a new era. Of the nine colonial colleges, six were subject to attempts on the part of the new legislatures to bring them more closely under the control of the state, while three—Brown, Princeton, and Rutgers—were allowed to remain relatively free from interference on the part of the state.

While *Harvard University,* the oldest of the colonial colleges, was able in large measure to retain its traditional position as a private institution throughout the Revolutionary and post-Revolutionary eras without drastic interference on the part of the state, in part because of its consistent policy of providing for a large

---

[24] This conclusion departs from the generally accepted one which states that the colonial practices in the matter of control and support were significant precedents in the development of state universities in this country.

measure of state representation on its Board of Overseers, and in part because of the fact that it was located in a state where the Puritan Church was established until 1833, it was nevertheless subject to various attempts on the part of the legislature to exercise more fully its visitorial powers upon the institution. In the constitution of 1780, the legislature reaffirmed and strengthened its former representation on the Board of Overseers.[25] Legislative action taken in 1810, 1812, and 1814 revealed a measure of conflict between the interests of the college and the state over the matters of state representation.[26] The question of the right of the legislature to exercise visitorial powers over the college was agitated at subsequent dates, though with decreasing effectiveness up to 1833, by which time the Revolutionary interests in the state had largely subsided and the college had become too strongly entrenched to be seriously affected by occasional agitation.[27] Thus it will be seen that Harvard, by maintaining a more or less close association with the interests of the state, was able to nullify in large part the efforts that were made to bring it more directly in line with the "revolutionary" ideals of the day, and at the same time to prevent any possible movement for the establishment of a rival state institution in Massachusetts.

The *College of William and Mary,* the next college to be founded in the colonial period, was not so fortunate as Harvard in its efforts to maintain its privileged position in higher education in the state during the Revolutionary era. This was due in part to factors entirely outside its control, and in part to its own unwillingness to ally itself later with the new state government after disestablishment had become an accomplished fact. On account of its attachments to the Anglican Church the college suffered a serious loss of prestige and influence at the time of the Revolution. Although the college had maintained, as we have seen, a traditional policy of associating itself with the state throughout the colonial period, and had allowed in practice for a large measure of state representation, this policy proved no longer feasible with the changes that took place in Virginia, unless the college was willing to give up in large measure its association with the church. This it was unwilling to do. Follow-

[25] Bartlett, L. W., *State Control of Private Incorporated Institutions of Higher Education,* p. 83, 1926. State representation was increased from 74% to 86%.
[26] *Ibid.,* p. 83.
[27] See Gray, F. C., *Letter to Governor Lincoln in Relation to Harvard University,* April 16, 1831. Boston, Second Edition 1831, pamphlet (by a friend of Harvard).

ing the Revolution, efforts were made by friends of the college, chief among whom at first was Thomas Jefferson, to transform the college into a state institution in the fuller sense of the term. A bill was introduced into the legislature in 1779 providing for this change, but, for a number of reasons, no action was taken.[28] The College of William and Mary finally chose to ally itself with the newly formed Episcopal Church, and the efforts on behalf of the establishment of a state university were turned in another direction. The establishment of the University of Virginia—a state institution of an "advanced" type—was the ultimate outcome of these efforts. Thus in Virginia a situation resulted which was in sharp contrast to the situation which came to prevail in the other states in the Union where colonial colleges had been established, namely, the establishment of a state university as a rival institution of a former colonial college.

The position of *Yale University* at the time of the Revolution was quite different from that of either Harvard or William and Mary. The traditional policy of this institution had indeed been to associate itself with the interests of the state as far as possible, yet no legal provision or informal agreement was made at the outset or at any subsequent time, as we have seen, for even a measure of state representation. In fact, proposals for such representation had at various times been strenuously opposed.[29] New demands were made on the institution, however, with the advent of the Revolutionary era. A petition was finally presented to the legislature of Connecticut in 1784, demanding that either the charter of Yale be altered to provide for state representation or a rival institution be established by the state under state control. While this petition was not acted upon at the time, a reorganization of the Corporation was effected in 1792 by the legislature in response to these demands, and provision was made for a large measure of state representation by the addition of the Governor, Lieutenant Governor, and six state officials to the Corporation as ex-officio members.[30] By acceding to this radical change in policy at a time when

---

[28] See Adams, *op. cit.*, pp. 37-38, for account of the bill of 1779. See also Bell, S., *The Church, the State, and Education in Virginia*, p. 176, 1930, quoting Jefferson's statement of the main reason for the defeat of the bill.

[29] See Woolsey, T. D., *An Historical Discourse*, August 14, 1850, pp. 11, 12, 30, *New Haven, Conn.*, 1850, for the memorials of 1761 and 1763, and the defense of the college by President Clap based on principles later used in the Dartmouth College Case decision.

[30] *Ibid.*, pp. 35-38. See also the controversial pamphlets referred to in Purcell, R. J., *Connecticut in Transition*, p. 23, 1918.

the Puritan establishment in the state was still strong, Yale was able to maintain its privileges in the field of higher education in the state as a private institution, and at the same time to prevent the possible establishment of another institution more directly under state control. This adjustment of the relations of the college and state served to propitiate the revolutionary party, and, moreover, to give considerable satisfaction to the Yale interests, as indicated in the following statement by President Stiles: "A noble condescension, beyond all expectation! Especially that the civilians acquiesce in being a minority in the corporation." [31] The worst fears of Yale were allayed, and the attempts to establish a state university in Connecticut were effectively postponed and, as it proved, permanently nullified.

The situation in which *Princeton University* found itself at the time of the Revolution was again different from that of the other colonial colleges thus far considered. It had been founded in a colony where a more or less liberal policy characterized the relations of church and state, and where a large measure of religious freedom existed. While the Governor of the colony was, as we have seen, an ex-officio member of the Board of Trustees, this representation of the state was largely formal. For the most part, the institution maintained a status independent of the state, and closely allied with the Presbyterian Church.[32] At the time of the Revolution, the Presbyterians took an active part in the movement for independence. The new state government, moreover, soon came to be dominated by Presbyterian interests. This situation accounts in large part for the fact that no efforts were made during or after the Revolution to transform Princeton into a state university, and also explains why no attempts were made to found another institution under more direct state control.[33]

During the later colonial period, *Columbia University* was able to maintain its privileged position in New York, as we have seen, because of its attachments to the Anglican Church and to British interests as well as because of its provision for a large measure of state representation on its board. At the time of the Revolution,

[31] Stiles, Ezra, *Ecclesiastical Constitution of Yale College*, p. 423.
[32] Murray, D., *History of Education in New Jersey*. U. S. Bur. Ed. Cir. Inf., 1899, no. 1, pp. 212-220.
[33] No evidence has been found of such efforts in New Jersey. A letter to the writer from V. L. Collins, Secretary of Princeton University, under date of December 28, 1931, tends to confirm the statement that no efforts were made either to transform Princeton into a state university or to establish a separate state university in the state.

however, these attachments proved a liability rather than an asset, and the provision for state representation gave it no immunity from Revolutionary attack. The sad plight of Columbia during the Revolution was due in fact in large measure to these very attachments to the Anglican Church and to the Tory Party.[34] When the new state government came into power, the early movement for the founding of a state university was revived.[35] This popular and republican movement was, however, captured for a time by the aristocratic and federalist interests in the state, associated with the new Episcopal Church, that now came to the support of Columbia.[36] The Act of 1784, with its amendment of the same year, was a victory for the latter interests. Columbia was able to secure a preponderant influence as the central unit in the new University of the State of New York created by this Act.[37] This Act soon proved unsatisfactory, however, to all parties in the struggle for the control of higher education in the state, and another compromise was arranged by the Act of 1787. This new Act through a skillful resolution of conflicting interests gave each party a large measure of control in its own sphere.[38] Columbia became a private institution largely associated with the new Episcopal Church, while secondary and higher education in the state were placed under the supervision of the University of the State of New York, a comprehensive organization which was a state university only in name. This resolution of competing interests in higher education was definitive in nature and distinctive in character. A new precedent in the organization of higher education was thereby established in this country. While this precedent exerted a wide influence on higher education, particularly in the western states, it was not, however, fully accepted by any one state.

The *University of Pennsylvania* was a private institution established in a colony where a diversity of religious interests prevailed and a large measure of religious freedom existed. No state representation had been provided for in the original organization. The institution, although initiated under nonsectarian influences, had come, as we have seen, to be attached rather closely to the

---

[34] Moore, *op. cit.*, pp. 57-64.

[35] See *ibid.*, pp. 9-15, for an account of the movement initiated by Wm. Livingston.

[36] See Fox, D. R., *The Decline of Aristocracy in the Politics of New York*, 1918.

[37] Sherwood, S., *The University of the State of New York*, U. S. Bur. of Ed. Cir. Inf., 1900, no. 3, pp. 48-57.

[38] *Ibid.*, pp. 57-81.

Anglican Church and to Tory interests. Thus at the time of the Revolution it was fated to suffer serious opposition on the part of Revolutionary interests in the state. Efforts were made to refound the institution as a state university. In 1779 the charter of the college was revoked and a new institution, known as the University of the State of Pennsylvania, was established. In this new university, the state was given a controlling representation.[39] For a period of ten years the University of the State of Pennsylvania and the old college of Philadelphia existed side by side as two rival institutions, the latter protesting against the revocation of its charter. In 1789, due to a realignment of interests in the state, the original charter of the college was reinstated. The university was retained, however, for a period of two years. In 1791, when it became clear that the movement for a state university of a "revolutionary" type in Pennsylvania had largely lost its vitality, the two institutions were merged under a single board, on which the state was represented by only the Governor acting in an ex-officio capacity.[40]

Brown University was able to maintain an independent and exclusive position in the state of Rhode Island throughout the Revolutionary and post-Revolutionary periods without interference on the part of the state, largely because its interests were more or less identical with the interests of the state where the Baptist Church was the dominant church. No legal provision had been made in the original charter for state representation for reasons that have been noted in a previous connection. The institution had from the beginning maintained an unusually broad policy in regard to the representation on its board of other sectarian interests in the state, thus effectively uniting the varied interests of the state in its support.[41] In the light of these circumstances, it was natural that the rise of any movement during the Revolutionary period directed either toward the transformation of Brown University into a state-controlled institution or toward the establishment of a rival state university would be largely precluded.[42]

Rutgers University was founded in New Jersey in 1766 as a private institution under the auspices of the Dutch Reformed

[39] Bartlett, *op. cit.*, p. 87.
[40] Thorpe, *op. cit.*, p. 239.
[41] Bronson, *op. cit.*, Chap. 1.
[42] No evidence has been found by the writer revealing efforts in either of these directions. Bronson, *op. cit.*, p. 50, refers to an unsuccessful attempt in 1770 to secure a charter for a rival college at Newport, but this college was not designed as a state university of a "revolutionary" type.

Church. It occupied a subordinate position to Princeton even in colonial days, largely because of the limited constituency which it served. State representation had been provided for, as we have seen, in the original charter, but this provision was only of a formal nature. As there was no established religion in the colony, Rutgers, like its neighbor, Princeton, was able to preserve an independent status with relation to the colony up to the time of the Revolution. During the Revolution the college, being in the path of the Revolutionary armies, suffered a considerable setback, but it was able before long to reorganize on its former basis. Following the rise of Presbyterian influence in the state, a proposal was made in 1793 to merge Rutgers and Princeton in one institution.[43] This proposal was never carried out, and the two institutions remained as separate colleges, joined, however, as elder and younger sisters in the bond of a common Calvinistic faith.[44] The virtual establishment of the Calvinistic interests in the state precluded, as is indicated in a later connection, the establishment of a state university in New Jersey and probably prevented any serious efforts from being made in the legislature to transform either Rutgers or Princeton into state universities.

Dartmouth College, the last of the colonial colleges to be founded, was established in 1769 as a private institution under Congregational influences. Provision was made, as we have seen, for state representation only to the extent of allowing for the membership of the Governor acting ex-officio on the Board of Trustees. Congregational interests became increasingly dominant in the colony as well as in the college, ensuring an essential identity of interest, and thus no serious efforts were made during the Revolutionary period to change the character of the college. With the accession of John Wheelock to the presidency of the college in 1799, the situation became quite different. Difficulties arose between the President and the Board of Trustees, since John Wheelock tended to depart from the religious and political principles that had become traditional in the management of the college under his father's administration. Moreover, the rising republican interests in the state supported a movement for the reorganization of Dart-

---

[43] Demarest, *op. cit.,* pp. 173-180. Proposals had been made in colonial days for merging Rutgers at one time with Columbia, and at another with Princeton.

[44] Rutgers was closed from 1795-1807 on account of difficulties in gaining support for the college. See Murray, D., *History of Education in New Jersey.* U. S. Bur. of Ed. Cir. Inf., 1899, no. 1, p. 293.

mouth College on the plan of a state university of a "revolutionary" type. President Wheelock took a prominent part in forwarding this movement, and thus aroused the Board of Trustees to a series of drastic actions.

On August 26, 1815, John Wheelock was removed from office and the Rev. Francis Brown appointed President. Thereupon the republican interests in the state, which came into power in the legislature in 1816, took it upon themselves by legislative act to reorganize the college on June 27, 1816. The Act of 1816 transformed the college into a state university, under the name of the Dartmouth University, with a dual system of control dominated by the state.[45] The original Board of Trustees vigorously protested against the Act, and finally brought suit against the state in the Superior Court. Thus a contest was precipitated between the Federalist and Congregational interests in the state which supported the college and the Republican interests in the state which were intent on establishing a state university. The decision of the Court was in favor of the latter interests. An able opinion handed down by Chief Justice Richardson, which might well be read in this connection, was clearly based on the principles of Jeffersonian democracy as applied to the field of higher education. The decision of this Court, however, was carried by appeal of the college, on writ of error, to the Supreme Court of the United States, and Daniel Webster was engaged as one of the counsel for the college interests.[46]

Thus the stage was set for a contest on a grand scale. The Dartmouth College Case soon attracted the attention of the leaders in higher education throughout the country.[47] The vested rights of all private corporations were now at stake. A question that had been the subject for debate for over half a century in the field of higher education was now to be submitted to legal adjudication by the highest court in the land. The case was brought up for trial in March, 1818, but an adjournment of the Court delayed the final decision, and it was during this interim that the differences of the

[45] Under this Act, the state representation was to be 77% of the total membership. See Bartlett, *op. cit.*, p. 90.
[46] For a defense of Webster's activities in the Dartmouth College Case, see Fuess, C. M., *Daniel Webster*, 1930. It is to be recalled, however, that Webster was a staunch Federalist and Congregationalist.
[47] See *North American Review*, vol. 10, 1820, p. 831. Also see Lord, J. K., *A History of Dartmouth College*, vol. 1, pp. 147, 151, 1913. These references and others definitely refute the assertions of Beveridge and Warren, that the Dartmouth College Case did not attract wide attention in this country.

rival interests represented in the Court itself were finally adjusted through means that have sometimes been called in question.[48] In February, 1819, a decision was finally rendered by Chief Justice Marshall for the Court, which reversed the action of the New Hampshire Court and declared the act of the New Hampshire legislature unconstitutional and void. The unconstitutionality of the act of the New Hampshire legislature was declared to reside in the impairing of the obligations of the charter of Dartmouth College, which was to be regarded as a contract within the meaning of Article 1, Section 10, Clause 1, of the Constitution of the United States. The decision was a complete victory for the Federalist and Congregationalist interests represented at Dartmouth College. The net effect of the decision, taken together with the other factors in the situation in the state, was to check effectively and postpone indefinitely the movement for a state university in New Hampshire, and to allow Dartmouth College to retain in large part its special privileges as a private institution in the field of higher education in New Hampshire. In a contest between conservatives and liberals, Federalists and Republicans, John Marshall and Thomas Jefferson, the former in each instance had won.

The significance of this decision for higher education in this country can hardly be overestimated. Webster clearly saw that "our college cause will be known to our children's children." [49] The influence of the decision was far-reaching in determining the general direction of the movement for higher education in this country and in shaping the character of the institutions of higher education that were to be established during the middle period of our history. A competitive era in higher education, as well as in business, was ushered in, for better or for worse, when it became possible for institutions of higher education, as well as for business corporations, to remain in general free from legislative supervision or control.[50] Chancellor Kent's statement in regard to the significance of the Dartmouth College Case decision is pertinent in this connection:

[48] See Beard, C. A., and Beard, M. R., *The Rise of American Civilization*, vol. 1, pp. 818-821, 1927; Lodge, H. C., *Daniel Webster*, 1883; Shirley, J. M., *The Dartmouth College Causes*, p. 253, 1879; Lord, J. K., *op. cit.*, vol. 1, pp. 152-153, 160 footnote, 1913.

[49] Webster, D., Letter to Hopkinson, March 22, 1819. See also Emerson, C. F., "A History of Dartmouth College," in *General Catalogue of Dartmouth College (1769-1910)*, p. 31, 1910-11, and other sources referred to in another connection.

[50] The relation of the Dartmouth College Case decision to business corporations is treated in the following near-contemporary document: Henshaw, David, *Remarks upon the Rights and Powers of Corporations*, 1837 (pamphlet).

[It] did more than any other single act proceeding from the authority of the United States to throw an impregnable barrier around all rights and franchises derived from the grant of government, and to give solidity and inviolability to the literary, charitable, religious, and commercial institutions of our country.[51]

The decision implying, as it did, a victory for the religious interests in the country at large, gave these interests an unprecedented degree of freedom to develop educational institutions without fear, in general, of molestation on the part of the state. A new era of opportunity was opened up for the numerous religious groups in the country that were eager to possess the field of higher education. At the same time, it became clear that the secular or nonsectarian interests of the day were to suffer a severe setback as a result in part of the practical working out of this decision. While it is true that the way was still open for these interests to establish educational institutions, and state universities in particular, the possibility of achieving this end was rendered more remote by the fact that the forces that made for sectarian warfare and irresponsible competition were now more securely entrenched in the field of higher education. The evidence is convincing that the Dartmouth College Case decision contributed in no small measure to checking, for better or for worse, the development of state universities for at least a half century.

One of the fundamental questions involved in the Dartmouth College decision was that of the ultimate source of authority in higher education. The resolution of this question, effected in 1819, has been generally assumed to be entirely correct, especially as it was arrived at by the highest tribunal in the land; but there is evidence to show that it may not have been the wisest resolution of a fundamental question. The results of this decision in the realm of business have not always been happy, and the results in the field of higher education, as suggested above, may not all have been for the best.[52] There is abundant evidence, moreover, that Thomas

---

[51] Kent, J., *Commentaries on American Law*, vol. 1, pp. 415-416, 826-830. See also Webster's comment fifty years after the case, given in Fuess, *op. cit.*, vol. 1, p. 245.

[52] Beard and Beard, *op. cit.*, vol. 1, p. 818; Wells, W. P., *The Dartmouth College Case and Private Corporations*. Reprinted from the Report of the Transactions of the American Bar Association, 1886 (pamphlet); Sanborn, F. B., *Dartmouth College: Its Founders and Hinderers*, pp. 11-16, 1908 (pamphlet); Brown, S. G., "Historical Address," *Centennial Celebration of Dartmouth College*, p. 32, 1870 (pamphlet). For arguments advanced by prominent legal writers against the Dartmouth College Case decision, see *American Law Review*, 1874, vol. 8, pp. 189-239; 1893, vol. 27, pp. 525-539; and 1917, vol. 51, pp. 711-751.

Jefferson and other leaders in the American life of that day were fundamentally opposed to the principles upon which the Dartmouth College decision was based, and advocated an adjustment of the issue that would provide not only for private but also for public rights, premised on the view that colleges were public as well as private institutions.[53] In 1816 Jefferson wrote to Governor Plumer that

The idea that institutions established for the use of the nation cannot be touched or modified, even to make them answer their end, because of rights gratuitously supposed in those employed to manage them in trust for the public, may, perhaps, be a salutary provision against the abuse of a monarch, but it is most absurd against the nation itself. Yet our lawyers and priests generally inculcate this doctrine, and suppose that preceding generations held the earth more freely than we do; had a right to impose laws on us, unalterable by ourselves; and that we, in like manner, can make laws and impose burdens on future generations, which they will have no right to alter; in fine, that the earth belongs to the dead, and not to the living.[54]

It is indeed difficult, however, if not impossible, to appraise impartially or completely the merits or demerits of this decision, especially as such an appraisal involves prior considerations as to the nature of democratic institutions. It is not within the purpose of this study, however, to do more than suggest some of the more significant implications of this epoch-making decision of the Supreme Court for the development of higher education in this country, and in particular for the development of state universities before the Civil War.[55]

In reviewing the efforts to transform the existing colonial colleges into state universities, it is clear that these efforts were in large measure unsuccessful in achieving their purposes. In the three Puritan colonies of Massachusetts, Connecticut, and New Hampshire, the revolutionary movements for the state control of higher education were largely nullified by the continuance of a Puritan establishment. Moreover, the Federalist interests in the New England states were joined with the church in resisting the

[53] For Jefferson's opinion on the right of legislatures to control chartered institutions, see Bell, *op. cit.*, pp. 179, 297. For an opinion of Governor Tyler of Virginia on this question, see *ibid.*, pp. 186-187.

[54] Quoted in Smith, B. P., *op. cit.*, p. 101.

[55] For recent appraisals of the effects of the Dartmouth College Case decision on higher education, see Reisner, E. H., *Nationalism and Education since 1789*, p. 363, 1922; Brown, E. E., *The Origin of American State Universities*, p. 34, 1903 (pamphlet). Bartlett, *op. cit.*, pp. 25-28; and Sanborn, *op. cit.*, p. 16.

efforts of the Republican interests, which demanded state institutions of higher education of a "revolutionary" type. Harvard was able to maintain its position with the least organic change, Yale was obliged to adopt a plan for state representation, while Dartmouth, after a serious conflict with Republican interests, was able to retain intact its original privileges as a private institution. In the latter instance, the influence of the Supreme Court was brought in to finally check the efforts of the "revolutionary" party. Thus a death blow was dealt to the movement for the reconstitution of the colonial colleges. The net effect of these circumstances was to postpone indefinitely the movement for the establishment of separate state universities in the New England states. In the Anglican colonies of New York and Virginia, the "revolutionary" movement achieved greater success than elsewhere. In New York, a compromise was arranged between the interests favoring a state university and the interests of Columbia, which had come to be identified with the Episcopal Church and the Federalist Party. In Virginia, while the efforts for the reëstablishment of the College of William and Mary as a state university were unsuccessful, the movement for the founding of a state university in the state was so powerful that ultimate success was achieved in the establishment of the University of Virginia, the only state university established in a state where colonial colleges had been in existence. In the colonies of Rhode Island, New Jersey, and Pennsylvania, the "revolutionary" movement was active only in Pennsylvania. In Rhode Island the strength of the Baptist interests represented in the state and in the college precluded the possibility of any attempt being made either for the transformation of the college or for the establishment of a state university. In New Jersey, Princeton, largely because of the rise of Presbyterian influences in the state, was able to retain its identity as a private institution and to preclude the possibility of establishing a state university. Rutgers was given the right to continue its independent course as a small private institution under the control of the Dutch Reformed Church. In Pennsylvania, the "revolutionary" movement for the establishment of a state university gathered strength from the interests in the state that were sympathetic with the radical movements in the neighboring states of New York and Virginia, and found its opportunity in the conflicting situation resulting from the change from a colonial to a state government in Pennsylvania. This movement was, however, as we have seen, eventually nullified by the growth in power of the Presbyterian interests in the state following the Revolution, which finally reinstated the former college as a private institution, largely under Presbyterian influence, and effectually prevented the establishment of a separate state university. Thus it will be seen that the movement for the establishment of state universities during our early history met with serious setbacks in all the states except Virginia, where colonial colleges had established prior claims in the field of higher education. It was in the other states of the original thirteen, viz., North Carolina, South Carolina, Georgia, Maryland, and Delaware, where no colonial colleges had been established, that the movement for state universities achieved greater success. Before taking up this phase of the revolutionary movement for state universities, the relation of the problem of the separation of church and state to higher education in general, and to state universities in particular, will be discussed.

THE EFFECTS OF THE SEPARATION OF CHURCH AND STATE ON THE STATE UNIVERSITY MOVEMENT

The achievement of a separation of church and state in this country at the time of the Revolution is recognized as one of the most significant events in our national history. It was indeed an achievement both revolutionary and distinctive in character. The development of our social institutions in this country has been radically affected by this legal adjustment of the relations of church and state. Many of the more or less unique characteristics of our political, religious, and educational life may be clearly traced to this source. James Bryce has stated that "of all the differences between the Old World and the New World this is perhaps the most salient." [56] It was inevitable, therefore, that, with the acceptance of this revolutionary principle, the development of higher education in this country should depart radically from European precedents and acquire characteristics of its own that made it truly an indigenous development.

The eventual acceptance of the principle of the separation of the church and state by the thirteen original states of the Union

---

[56] Bryce, J., *American Commonwealth*, vol. 2, p. 554. Revised Edition, 1910, 2 vols. (Original Edition, 1888.)

following the Revolution, and the ultimate incorporation of this principle in the constitutions of the twenty-one new states of the Union admitted before the Civil War, opened the way for a readjustment of the interests of the church and state in the field of higher education.[57] The nature of this readjustment, although varying in certain particulars from state to state, may be expressed in general terms as follows: state institutions of higher education when established were to be free from church control, and church institutions of higher education were to be free from state control.[58] The ultimate implications of this solution of the problem of the relations of the church and state to higher education in this country are not yet entirely clear, but already evidences are not wanting to indicate that this solution was in the nature of a compromise solution from which both good and bad consequences have resulted. Even in the period before the Civil War, this supposedly fundamental and final resolution of an age-long problem proved to be less satisfactory and desirable than it at first appeared to be in the early days of our national existence. It is our task in this place to trace in brief outline the nature of the readjustments that took place in higher education following the acceptance in principle of this "revolutionary" doctrine of the complete separation of church and state. Attention will first be directed to the developments in the thirteen original states.

It will be recalled that the Anglican Church was established in six of the thirteen original states.[59] During the Revolutionary period, one of the most important issues faced by these states was that of disestablishment. The conflict that arose over disestablishment in *Virginia* was severe and prolonged, and the ultimate resolution of this conflict was definitive in nature and far-reaching in effect. The final achievement of "religious liberty" in Virginia was brought about through the working of a number of factors. The growing sentiment against the Anglican Church, due in part to its privileged position in the state and in part to its foreign attach-

[57] The Northwest Ordinance of 1787 and the Constitution of the United States (Article 6 and Amendment 1 of 1788 and 1790, respectively) affirmed the principle of the separation of church and state for the country as a whole.

[58] The significance of the Dartmouth College Case decision in the final adjustment of the relations of the church and state to higher education in this country has already been emphasized.

[59] There was considerable debate in New York as to whether the Anglican Church was legally established in the state. See Nevins, A., *The American States During and After the Revolution,* p. 426, 1927.

ments, was cumulative in its action and decisive in its result. The Anglican Church was deprived of its monopolistic position in higher education in the state and reduced to a minor church, struggling for its very existence in the new era of competition ushered in by the act of disestablishment.[60] The dissenting churches in Virginia played an important part in the disestablishment of the Anglican Church. The Presbyterian Church, in particular, took an active part in the movement and gained new power and influence in the state in the new era of religious freedom that resulted.[61] The influence of such leaders as Madison and Jefferson in the movement for the complete separation of church and state in Virginia was both impressive and definitive. The two historic documents in the struggle for religious freedom in Virginia were penned by these leaders. These documents were the "Declaration of Rights" of 1776, and the "Act for Establishing Religious Freedom" of 1786, which, because of their general significance in the struggle for religious freedom in this country, and their particular relevance to the cause of religious freedom in the field of higher education in Virginia and in the country at large, are quoted in part below:

That religion, or the duty which we owe to our CREATOR, and the manner of discharging it, can be directed only by reason and conviction, not by force or violence, and therefore all men are equally entitled to the free exercise of religion, according to the dictates of conscience; and that it is the duty of all to practice Christian forbearance, love and charity towards each other.[62]

That no man shall be compelled to frequent or support any religious worship, place or ministry whatsoever; nor shall be enforced, restrained, molested or burthened in his body or goods, nor shall otherwise suffer on account of his religious opinions or belief; but that all men shall be free to profess and by argument to maintain their opinions in matters of religion, and that the same shall in no wise diminish, enlarge or affect their civil capacities.[63]

The acceptance of these new principles demanded radical adjustments in the field of higher education in Virginia. The College of William and Mary was obliged, under the circumstances, to alter its

---

[60] The Anglican Church underwent a process of nationalization after the Revolution, and rose, as it were, from the ruins as the Protestant Episcopal Church. See Sweet, W. W., *The Story of Religions in America*, chap. 13, 1930.

[61] This church was prevented from setting up a virtual establishment in the state mainly because of the strength of the secular and republican interests in the state.

[62] Hening, W. W., *Statutes-at-Large*, vol. 9, pp. 111-112, 1823.

[63] Hening, *op. cit.*, vol. 12, p. 86.

historic policies. The college was shorn of its former prestige and reduced to a state of ineffectiveness from which it had great difficulty in extricating itself. Although efforts were made to transform the college into an institution more in harmony with the new ideals of higher education held by certain "revolutionary" leaders, these efforts failed, as we have previously noted, largely because of the opposition of the Presbyterian interests in the state which feared a new establishment, and because of the unwillingness of the new Episcopal interest in the state to lose control over its one institution of higher education.[64] Already the principle of the separation of church and state was working both to the advantage and to the disadvantage of the various religious interests in this state, as it did later in other states. The religious interests in the state combined to forestall the establishment of a state university, while at the same time certain religious interests maneuvered to secure a dominant position in the open field of higher education. Unlike the situation in many other states, however, the movement for the establishment of a state university in Virginia was too strong to be diverted from its purpose, and the final establishment of the state university meant, in this case, that no one church could achieve a dominance in higher education. The religious and secular interests in Virginia thus finally parted company for better or for worse. The University of Virginia was established in 1819 as a state university of a "revolutionary" type. Although, contrary to the principle of the separation of the church and state, the religious interests in the state succeeded in securing a measure of control over this institution for a time during the middle period,[65] it was able to maintain its identity as a state university more completely, perhaps, than any other state university in the country. It will be seen that in Virginia, therefore, the acceptance of the principle of the separation of church and state not only resulted in a parting of the ways of the church and state in higher education, but also brought in a variety of complications which had been foreseen by only a few of the leaders of the Revolutionary period.

Following the Revolution, the Anglican or Episcopal interests in *New York* were able, as we have seen, to regain much of their influence because of their continued alliance with the old aristocracy. The opposing group of interests in the state had for long,

[64] See p. 144, footnote 28.
[65] See Bell, *op. cit.*, pp. 381-391.

however, advocated the founding of a state university, and the rising Presbyterian interests in the state joined in the demand for equal rights in the field of higher education.[66] Thus, when the new era of religious liberty was ushered in by the acceptance of the principle of the separation of the church and state, a severe struggle ensued for the control of higher education in the state between these three groups of interests. By the final Act of 1787, the general organization of the state university was retained, with certain modifications agreeable to the Presbyterian interests, while Columbia was given a more or less independent status under its original charter of 1754. This compromise solution reconciled in large part the conflicting interests in the state.

It will be seen that, unlike the situation in Virginia, no state university of the type of the University of Virginia was finally established in New York; neither were the church colleges in the state, with the exception of Columbia, granted the measure of freedom enjoyed by the church colleges of Virginia. Moreover, the situation was unlike that in Massachusetts and Connecticut in that the leading college in the state was not allowed finally to occupy the privileged position in the state of a semi-state institution, such as that occupied by Harvard and Yale. In the final adjustment of conflicting interests in New York, the interests favoring a "revolutionary" type of state university were able to achieve a partial victory in the establishment of the University of the State of New York, which was in reality a general supervisory body over secondary and higher education in the state; the Presbyterian interests were able to win a partial victory by securing the right to establish church colleges that would be free from undue interference on the part of the state or other competing church interests; while the Anglican, or Episcopal interests won a partial victory by securing a more or less independent status for Columbia at the price of giving up their former special privileges in the field of higher education.[67] It is difficult to appraise the merits and demerits of this final compromise of 1787 adopted in an attempt to adjust the

[66] Sherwood, *op. cit.*, chap. 2, gives an excellent treatment of the conflicting interests in higher education in New York state, but points taken from this chapter are used in this study only when indicated by footnote reference.

[67] Upper New York state was at first largely given over to the Presbyterian interests, which established Union and Hamilton colleges in that region, while lower New York was given over to Episcopal interests. The Presbyterian interests, however, invaded the territory occupied by Columbia in 1831, when New York University was established in New York City on a liberal foundation largely under Presbyterian influence. Hobart College was established in upper New York in 1825 under Episcopal auspices.

interests of church and state in the new era of religious liberty in New York, but it is at least clear that the separation of church and state in New York ushered in a situation which was strikingly different from that which came to exist in other states in the country.

In the four other states where the Anglican Church was established, viz., North Carolina, South Carolina, Georgia, and Maryland, a separation of the church and state was achieved at the time of the Revolution. Since no institutions of higher education had been founded in these states during the colonial period, the field was largely open for the founding of a state university, of church colleges, or of both in each of these colonies. In *North Carolina, South Carolina,* and *Georgia,* state universities were first in the field and maintained a monopoly over higher education for a considerable period.[68] These state universities held the field under more or less liberal influences until certain church interests came to dominate in their councils, thus negating some of the original purposes of disestablishment, and likewise nullifying in a sense the principle of the separation of church and state. It was not until other church interests grew powerful enough to break up this second establishment that the church and state in these three states decided definitely to part company and follow, for better or for worse, separate paths in the field of higher education.[69] In *Maryland,* a somewhat peculiar situation developed that demands special attention in this connection.[70] Directly following the Revolution, Washington College and St. John's College were founded under Anglican or Episcopal auspices. There was an attempt in 1785 to unite these two institutions under a general organization known as the University of Maryland. This arrangement, however, proved unsuccessful, largely because of the fear of the former dissenting groups of a new establishment in the state on the part of the Episcopalians. Thus the two institutions remained as independent church colleges. Some thirty years later, in 1812, another University of Maryland, of a more advanced type, was established in the city of Baltimore. Maryland thus finally came to adopt the general pattern of many other states by requiring that church and state each keep within its own sphere. The complexities introduced into higher education by

[68] See pp. 175-179.
[69] See pp. 175-179.
[70] See pp. 179-180.

the acceptance of the principle of the complete separation of church and state are again revealed in the histories of the four states just considered.

In the Puritan states of Connecticut, Massachusetts, and New Hampshire, where the Federal Party was in power, the separation of church and state was fully achieved in theory at a much later date than in the southern states.[71] In *Connecticut,* full legal disestablishment was not brought about until 1818. Yale had successfully resisted attempts during the Revolutionary period to establish a state university in Connecticut, as we have seen, by acceding to the demand for state representation on its Corporation. Thus it was able, especially as disestablishment was delayed, to maintain its privileged position in the state over a long period. Even after disestablishment, Yale continued to serve in place of a state university of a "revolutionary" type.[72] Two other colleges were eventually founded in the state, but they were placed in a position of more or less unequal competition with Yale. It will be seen that Connecticut furnished a type of adjustment of the interests of church and state in the field of higher education which was quite different from that which came to exist in most of the other states, in that a church institution was allowed to serve in lieu of a state university representing the state as a whole. Thus the necessity of creating two spheres of influence in higher education, one largely secular in character and the other definitely religious in character, was obviated.

In *Massachusetts,* disestablishment was not fully effected until 1833. Harvard, having maintained a consistent policy of association with the state, with provision for state representation on its Board of Overseers, as we have seen, had weathered the Revolutionary crisis rather effectively. It was obliged, however, to pass through a long period of criticism and opposition, because of being at the same time a semi-state institution and an institution associated with the Unitarian Church.[73] It was able in the end, how-

[71] Cobb, *op. cit.,* pp. 513, 515, 517, gives dates of full disestablishment in Connecticut, Massachusetts, and New Hampshire, respectively. In the Southern colonies, the disestablishment of the Anglican Church was effected at an earlier date and in a more drastic manner largely because of its foreign attachments.

[72] President Timothy Dwight deprecated the separation of church and state, even up to the time of his death. Cobb, *op. cit.,* p. 513.

[73] For evidence of continued criticism of Harvard, on account of the Unitarian associations, see: *Report on Filling up Vacancies in the Clerical Part of the Permanent Board of Overseers of Harvard College* (pamphlet), 1845; and *A Memorial Concerning the Recent*

ever, to maintain its privileged position in the state by yielding at various times to the pressure to widen its basis of sectarian representation. Other colleges were reluctantly allowed a place in the field of higher education in Massachusetts.[74] Thus we find a situation in Massachusetts largely analogous to that in Connecticut after disestablishment, with Harvard serving in place of a state university and effectually preventing a parting of the ways between church and state that took place in other states.

In *New Hampshire,* full legal disestablishment was not achieved until 1819. In this year the decision of the Dartmouth College Case brought to an end the attempt to create a state university of the "revolutionary" type. Moreover, by this decision, the rights of church colleges were given the highest judicial sanction and legislative immunity. In this situation it was natural that Dartmouth College, a Puritan institution, should continue to occupy a privileged position in the state for some time. It is significant that no state university was created in the state and no other church colleges were established in the state before the Civil War. Thus Dartmouth, with only a formal provision for state representation, served in place of a state university up to the time of the Civil War. In this case, the separation of church and state meant that higher education was largely turned over to the dominant church party in the state, as it was in other states where Calvinistic influences were powerful.

In the four states of Pennsylvania, New Jersey, Delaware, and Rhode Island, a virtual separation of church and state had been effected from the earliest days of settlement. In *Pennsylvania* alone serious difficulties arose during the revolutionary period over the adjustment of the relations of church and state in the field of higher education. The Anglicans at first had attempted to gain a privileged position in the state and in the University of Pennsylvania.[75] With the Revolutionary crisis and the reaffirmation of disestablishment in the state, the Anglican interests were . finally defeated. Efforts were made during this same period by various interests representing both the dissenters and the new secular and republican groups in the

History and the Constitutional Rights and Privileges of Harvard College Presented by the President and Fellows to the Legislature on January 17th, 1851, 1851 (pamphlet).

[74] Tufts College, an institution associated with the Universalist Church, was not granted a charter until 1852. Holy Cross College, a Catholic institution, was refused a charter until 1865. For references on Holy Cross College see Bibliography, Section B.

[75] See p. 141, footnote 23.

state, to establish a state university of a "revolutionary" type. With the eventual failure of this attempt, the University of Pennsylvania was reinstated as a private institution associated with the Presbyterian interests which had come to hold a position of dominance in the state.[76] It will be seen that the separation of church and state in Pennsylvania, with the consequent rise in power of the Presbyterian Church, meant the nullification of the movement for a state university. Thus Pennsylvania, like Massachusetts, Connecticut, and New Hampshire, remained without a state university, and the field of higher education was given over to the church interests, with the Calvinistic interests in a privileged position.

In *New Jersey* a somewhat similar situation developed, but the difficulties experienced in Pennsylvania were not encountered. At the time of the reaffirmation of religious liberty in the state during the Revolutionary era, Princeton and Rutgers were the only colleges in the field. The fortunes of Rutgers were rudely shaken by the Revolution.[77] Proposals were made for uniting the institution with Princeton, as we have seen, but eventually the institution retained its identity and took its place as one of the church colleges in the state. Princeton, on the other hand, came through the Revolutionary crisis with added prestige and striking success.[78] No attempts were made in the state to establish a state university of the "revolutionary" type, and Princeton, being the stronger institution, came to serve the state in place of a state university. The Calvinistic interests thus achieved a dominance in New Jersey, as in the other states previously considered, and a similar adjustment of the relations of church and state to higher education came in time to exist in this state.

In *Delaware,* the principle of the separation of church and state was reasserted at the time of the Revolution. No institutions of higher education had been established in colonial times, so the field was open for advance in a number of directions. Efforts were made in 1821 to establish a state university by the name of Delaware College.[79] A charter was secured, which provided for a Board of

[76] Wood, G. B., *Early History of the University of Pennsylvania,* p. 94, Third Edition, 1896 (First Edition 1833). In 1792 the Rev. John Ewing, a Presbyterian divine, was made Provost of the institution. See Cheyney, *op. cit.,* pp. 82, 101.

[77] For information on the part taken by Rutgers leaders and alumni in the Revolution, see Humphrey, *Nationalism and Religion in America,* p. 109, 1924.

[78] On the prominent part taken by Princeton leaders and alumni in the Revolution, see Humphrey, *ibid.,* p. 82.

[79] Powell, L. P., *The History of Education in Delaware,* U. S. Bur. of Ed. Cir. Inf., 1893, no. 3, p. 90.

Trustees appointed by the Legislature, but the institution was never organized, largely on account of the opposition of the Presbyterian interests which had become dominant in the state. These interests established an institution by the name of Newark College in 1833, which was to be controlled by a more or less representative Board of Trustees, self-perpetuating in character, but with no legal provision for state representation.[80] This institution, which was named Delaware College in 1843, served in place of a state university up to the time of the Civil War, when it was reorganized as a state university under the name of the University of Delaware.[81] It will be seen that in Delaware, following the separation of the church and state, a situation developed which was analogous to that existing in the other states considered above where Calvinistic interests were largely dominant, and where a private institution largely under Calvinistic influence was allowed to serve the state in lieu of a state university.[82]

In *Rhode Island,* a large measure of religious liberty had prevailed from the earliest days of settlement. Brown University was able, as we have seen, to pass through the Revolutionary crisis without serious opposition. Although the state was not legally represented on the Governing Boards of Brown, there existed an essential identity between the dominant Baptist interests of the state and the interests of the college which had always been associated with the Baptist Church.[83] In this situation it was possible for Brown University to serve the state in place of a state university. Once again, the separation of church and state meant that the dominant church in a state might, by the adoption of a more or less liberal policy of sectarian representation, retain its privileged position in the field of higher education and at the same time prevent the serious parting of the ways of church and state which characterized the development of higher education in other parts of the country.

In the twenty-one new states admitted to the Union before the Civil War, the principle of the separation of church and state was written into the constitutions adopted at the time of their ad-

---

[80] *Ibid.,* pp. 90-91.

[81] *Ibid.,* p. 121. For criticisms of Delaware College as a sectarian college and a plea for a state university of a "revolutionary" type, see articles by "A Friend of Education" in the *Delaware Gazette* for 1847.

[82] It needs to be kept in mind that the Calvinists historically favored a union of church and state.

[83] Powell, *op. cit.,* pp. 9-10, 500-507, gives charter in full.

mittance.[84] Thus, at the very start, the way was open for those new states to work out a satisfactory adjustment of the relations of church and state in the field of higher education. Few vested interests were represented in these new states, and there existed no tradition of an established church to complicate the situation.[85] However, despite these favoring circumstances the lines between church control and state control over higher education became confused as the situation developed, and a struggle ensued in every state over the respective rights of church and state in the field of higher education. While the new states were able to draw on the experience of the older states in the east, this experience was indeterminate in nature and inconclusive in character. Furthermore, although the new states had in most cases the benefit of Congressional land grants which gave the movement for the establishment of state universities in these states an initial impetus, these grants were generally so badly managed and hence so largely unproductive that the state universities that were established were often placed in a more disadvantageous position financially than the church colleges.[86] Moreover, forces inimical to the cause of state universities became active during the middle period of our national development. The revived interest in religion throughout the country following the Revolution tended to complicate the issue, and made it extremely difficult to work out a satisfactory adjustment of the interests of the church and state in higher education. In some cases, the religious interests were able to delay or prevent the establishment of state universities, reserving the field of higher education largely for themselves. In other cases, the state universities that were established in the west were subjected to sectarian influences for a greater part of the period before the Civil War. In either case, it is clear that the conflicts between the church and the state in the field of higher education in the new states in the west, as in the older states in the east, were not resolved by the mere affirmation of the principle of the separation of the church and state.

A long period of trial and experimentation proved necessary, as the succeeding sections of this study will more fully reveal, to

[84] Vermont did not allow for full religious liberty until 1807. See Cobb, *op. cit.*, p. 517.
[85] In Vermont and Maine, the Puritan Church was able, even after disestablishment, to maintain for some time its traditional position of dominance.
[86] See Knight, G. W., *History and Management of Land Grants in the Northwest Territory*, 1885.

work out a more or less satisfactory resolution of this perplexing problem. The people of this country, particularly in the middle period of our history, when religious interests were dominant, tended to reject the full implication of the principle of the separation of the church and state, which, in the days of republican enthusiasm, they had adopted and written into their laws. The full implication of this principle which they so consistently refused to accept, and perhaps rightly so, was that the church and state should part company in such a way that state institutions of higher education would be in effect "godless" institutions without responsibility for the religious nurture of students, while religious institutions of higher education would be responsible for the religious nurture as well as for the general education of students—a situation which gave the state institutions superior advantages in the new competitive era of higher education.[87] Even as late as the time of the Civil War, leaders in religion and education insisted that the only acceptable interpretation of the principle of the separation of church and state was that higher education should be left entirely to the various religious sects. It was then too late to win universal acceptance of this interpretation. After making repeated efforts to control the new state universities in the interests of religion, and in the end losing out, the religious forces of the country bowed to the logic of events and accepted the full implication of the "revolutionary" doctrine of the complete separation of church and state. As evidence of the reluctance of the religious leaders of that day to accept the full implications of this historic principle, the following statement made by President Tyler of Amherst is quoted in concluding this discussion of one phase of the movement for the founding of state universities in this country.

To pass over other advantages and peculiarities of the voluntary system that prevails in this country, it is the only one that harmonizes with our religious institutions. In a country where there are so many different denominations of Christians and no established religion, there is no other way of providing for that decided religious influence which is indispensable to the safety and well-being of the young men in our colleges. . . . Few parents are willing to risk the character and happiness of their sons in a college which is hostile to religion, or even indifferent to it. Other things being equal, the great majority of parents, whether professed Christians or not, will choose

[87] Excellent statements of the relation of state universities to religion may be found in the contemporary sources dealing with the University of Michigan and the University of South Carolina, referred to in a later connection.

to send their sons to that college which, without too palpable a sectarian influence, sustains the highest character as a truly Christian college. And that can not be a state institution. With intuitive sagacity, not however, without some additional light derived from experience, the people of the United States, especially the enlightened Christian public, have seen the incompatibility of state colleges with the genius of our institutions, and have taken the work into their own hands.[88]

THE STATE UNIVERSITIES FOUNDED BEFORE THE CIVIL WAR

At this point in the discussion of the development of state universities in this country, a list of the twenty-one state universities that were founded before the Civil War will be presented. This list was constructed specifically for the purposes of the present study on the basis of an extensive research in legal and official sources. It has been made definitive in character in order to bring some order into the prevailing confusion in regard to certain factual aspects of the development of state universities. The general principles governing the making of this list are similar to those set forth in connection with the "List of Permanent Colleges and Universities Founded before the Civil War" given at the end of the first chapter of this study. The present list of state universities is not intended to be final in any sense of the term, nor is it intended to be used as a basis for establishing claims for priorities in founding, for such finalities and such claims must necessarily turn on the matter of definition. The priorities that are indicated in the following list (Table XXII) rest solely on the definitions set up for the purposes of this particular study.

A state university is defined in this study as a degree-conferring institution of higher education placed by legal stipulation under the predominant control of the state. State universities that were originally organized as private or semi-private institutions are included in the list only in cases where a legal succession from pre-Civil War times has been established. The date taken as the definitive date for the founding of each state university in the list is that of the charter of the original institution, provided that the institution was authorized to confer academic degrees, and provided that the institution was actually organized for the purposes

[88] Tyler, W. S., *Colleges: Their Place among American Institutions*, pp. 10-11, 1857 (pamphlet). Evidences from other contemporary sources are submitted in later sections of this study.

TABLE XXII

LIST OF STATE UNIVERSITIES FOUNDED BEFORE THE CIVIL WAR

S.N.	I.N.	CHANGES IN NAME AND LOCATION	CHARTER-DEGREE DATE

1   A14   UNIVERSITY OF GEORGIA................... *January 27, 1785*
     Athens, Ga.   (Ga. Laws, Vol. 1, p. 560)

2   A17   UNIVERSITY OF NORTH CAROLINA......... *December 11, 1789*
     Chapel Hill, N. C.   (Nash Digest, N. C. Vol. 2, p. 427)

3   A18   UNIVERSITY OF VERMONT................ *November 3, 1791*
     Burlington, Vt.   (Vt. Laws, 1791-92, p. 302)

4   A22   UNIVERSITY OF TENNESSEE (1879)
     Knoxville, Tenn.
     East Tennessee University (1840)
       Knoxville, Tenn.
     East Tennessee College (1807)
       Knoxville, Tenn.
     Blount College...................... *September 10, 1794*
       Knoxville, Tenn.   (Tenn. Laws, 1794, chap. 18)

5   A28   OHIO UNIVERSITY (1804)
     Athens, O.
     American Western University............ *January 9, 1802*
       Athens, O.   (1 Sess. 2 G.A.T., p. 161)

6   A26   UNIVERSITY OF SOUTH CAROLINA (1906)
     Columbia, S. C.
     South Carolina College (1890)
       Columbia, S. C.
     University of South Carolina (1887)
       Columbia, S. C.
     South Carolina College (1882)
       Columbia, S. C.
     South Carolina Col. of Agric. and Mech. (1880)
       Columbia, S. C.
     College of South Carolina (1878)
       Columbia, S. C.
     University of South Carolina (1866)
       Columbia, S. C.
     South Carolina College................ *December 14, 1805*
       Columbia, S. C.   (S. C. Laws, 1805, p. 83)

7   A30   MIAMI UNIVERSITY..................... *February 17, 1809*
     Oxford, Ohio   (Ohio Laws, Vol. 7, p. 184)

8   A48   UNIVERSITY OF MARYLAND................ *December 29, 1812*
     Baltimore, Md.   (Md. Laws, 1812, p. 177)

9   A37   UNIVERSITY OF VIRGINIA (1819)
     Charlottesville, Va.
     Central College...................... *February 14, 1816*
       Charlottesville, Va.   (Va. Laws, 1816, p. —)

TABLE XXII—*Continued*

S.N.	I.N.	CHANGES IN NAME AND LOCATION	CHARTER-DEGREE DATE
10	A50	UNIVERSITY OF ALABAMA . . . .*December 18, 1821* Tuscaloosa, Ala.	(Ala. Laws, 1821, p. 8)
11	A46	INDIANA UNIVERSITY Bloomington, Ind. Indiana College . . . . *January 24, 1828* Bloomington, Ind.	(Ind. Laws, 1828, p. 115)
12	A84	UNIVERSITY OF DELAWARE (1921) Newark, Del. Delaware College (1843) Newark, Del. Newark College . . . . *February 5, 1833* Newark, Del.	(Del. Laws, 1830, p. 283)
13	A187	UNIVERSITY OF KENTUCKY (1917) Lexington, Ky. State University of Kentucky (1907) Lexington, Ky. Kentucky University (1858) Harrodsburg, Ky. Lexington, Ky. 1865 Bacon College . . . . *February 23, 1837* Georgetown, Ky. Harrodsburg, Ky. 1839	(Ky. Laws, 1837, p. 274)
14	A51	UNIVERSITY OF MICHIGAN . . . .*March 18, 1837* Ann Arbor, Mich.	(Mich. Laws, 1837, p. 142)
15	A70	UNIVERSITY OF MISSOURI (1909) Columbia, Mo. University of the State of Missouri . . . . . . *February 11, 1839* Columbia, Mo.	(Mo. Laws, 1838-39, p. 181)
16	A114	UNIVERSITY OF MISSISSIPPI . . . .*February 24, 1844* Oxford, Miss.	(Miss. Laws, 1843-44, p. 227)
17	A120	STATE UNIVERSITY OF IOWA . . . .*February 25, 1847* Iowa City, Ia.	(Ia. Laws, 1846-47, p. 188)
18	A124	UNIVERSITY OF WISCONSIN . . . .*July 26, 1848* Madison, Wisc.	(Wisc. Laws, 1848, p. 38)
19	A154	UNIVERSITY OF MINNESOTA . . . .*February 13, 1851* Minneapolis, Minn.	(Minn. Laws, 1850-51, p. 142)
20	A194	LOUISIANA STATE UNIVERSITY (1870) Baton Rouge, La. Louisiana State Seminary of Learning . . . . . *March 31, 1853* Alexandria, La.	(La. Laws, 1852-53, p. 49)
21	A195	UNIVERSITY OF CALIFORNIA (1868) Berkeley, Cal. College of California . . . . *April 13, 1855* Oakland, Cal.	(Cal. Board of Ed.)

of college instruction under the terms of the charter. Changes in the name and location of each institution are given, together with legal dates of such changes. The documentary sources used in constructing this list are to be found in the Bibliography given at the end of the study.

From the map which serves as the frontispiece, it will be seen that in twenty of the thirty-four states of the Union before the Civil War twenty-one state universities were founded in the period before the Civil War.[89] These twenty states may be divided into two general groups, viz., the six original states in the east, where six state universities were established without the aid of Congressional land grants, and the fourteen new states situated in most cases in the west, where fifteen state universities were established, generally with the aid of Congressional land grants. The founding of state universities in these two general groups of states will be discussed separately in the concluding sections of this chapter. The fourteen states in which no state universities were established before the Civil War may also be divided into two general groups, viz., the seven original states in the east, and the seven new states situated in most cases in the west. As the situation relative to the founding of state universities in the first group of seven original states in the east has been discussed in previous sections of this chapter, it remains to consider in the next section the situation that existed in the second group of seven new states. The table on the following page (Table XXIII) gives a recapitulation of the facts set forth in the preceding paragraph.

In the seven new states of Illinois, Maine, Arkansas, Florida, Texas, Oregon, and Kansas, no state universities were established before the Civil War. All these states except Maine and Texas received Congressional land grants for the establishment of a state university, but these grants were not applied to this purpose before the Civil War. The situation that led to the nullification of the state university movement in each of these states will be briefly considered.[90] In *Illinois*, the denominational interests were strong from the very beginning,[91] and these interests were able effectually to check the movement for a state university up to the time of the

[89] In Ohio two state universities were founded before the Civil War, viz., Ohio University and Miami University.
[90] The seven states are considered in the order of their admittance as states to the union.
[91] See Rammelkamp, C. H., *Centennial History of Illinois College*, 1928.

TABLE XXIII

SUMMARY TABLE OF STATE UNIVERSITIES FOUNDED IN THIRTY-FOUR STATES
OF THE UNION BEFORE THE CIVIL WAR

*A. Fourteen States Where No State Universities Were Founded
Before the Civil War*

SEVEN ORIGINAL STATES *		SEVEN NEW STATES †	
1.	NEW HAMPSHIRE	1. ILLINOIS	1818
2.	MASSACHUSETTS	2. MAINE	1820
3.	RHODE ISLAND	3. ARKANSAS	1836
4.	CONNECTICUT	4. FLORIDA	1845
5.	NEW YORK	5. TEXAS	1845
6.	NEW JERSEY	6. OREGON	1859
7.	PENNSYLVANIA	7. KANSAS	1861

*B. Twenty States Where State Universities Were Founded
Before the Civil War*

SIX ORIGINAL STATES *	FOURTEEN NEW STATES †				
1. GEORGIA	1. VERMONT	1791	8. ALABAMA	1819
2. NORTH CAROLINA	2. KENTUCKY	1792	9. MISSOURI	1821
3. SOUTH CAROLINA	3. TENNESSEE	1796	10. MICHIGAN	1837
4. MARYLAND	4. OHIO	1803	11. IOWA	1846
5. VIRGINIA	5. LOUISIANA	1812	12. WISCONSIN	1848
6. DELAWARE	6. INDIANA	1816	13. CALIFORNIA	1850
	7. MISSISSIPPI	1817	14. MINNESOTA	1858

* The original states are listed in the order of their treatment in the text.
† The new states are listed in the order of their admittance to the Union. The date of admittance is given in each instance.

Civil War. Although the usual Congressional land grant had been received by the state at the time of its admittance to the Union in 1818, this grant proved largely unproductive because of gross mismanagement of funds.[92] The denominational interests in the state were opposed to the assignment of the land grants to a single state university, and attempted at various times to divert the funds to other uses, including the support of the church colleges in the state. In 1835 four church colleges were chartered, three of which became permanent institutions, viz., Illinois, McKendree, and Shurtleff. Before the Civil War, nine other permanent church colleges were founded in the state. Thus the field of higher education was given over entirely to the church interests, and the possibilities of

[92] Knight, G. W., *op. cit.*, pp. 131-136.

establishing a state university were rendered remote. While the various church colleges were united in opposing a state university, it was said, on reliable authority, that largely "through the influence of the founders and early friends of Illinois College, the idea of a state university was abandoned."[93] It was not until after the Civil War that the movement for the founding of a state university in Illinois achieved sufficient strength, with the aid of the Morrill land grant, to bring about in 1867 the establishment of the Illinois Industrial University. This institution became the University of Illinois in 1885.

Maine was separated from Massachusetts in 1820 and admitted to the Union in the same year. At that time Bowdoin College was the only college in the state. This institution had been established in 1794 as a private college associated with the Congregational and Federalist interests dominant in the district of Maine. It was organized under a dual system of control similar in general to that prevailing at Harvard and Brown. Unlike Harvard, however, no legal provision for state representation on its Board of Overseers had been made. Nevertheless there existed an essential identity of interest between the state and the college before 1820. Thus Bowdoin was able to maintain its privileged position in Maine during the early part of its history.[94] When the district of Maine became a separate state in 1820, the democratic and dissenting interests in the state came into power, and the privileged position of Bowdoin was seriously challenged. In that year, Colby College, a Baptist venture, was granted a college charter,[95] and legislative measures were taken to bring Bowdoin under state control.[96] Successive measures gradually transformed Bowdoin into more or less of a state institution. The Dartmouth College Case decision could not be appealed to in this situation by the original Bowdoin interests on account of a number of complicating factors.[97] In the test case of Allen vs. McKeen, of 1833, however, the issue between the college and the state was brought up for adjudication.[98] This case was decided in the spirit of the Dartmouth decision in favor of the original interests represented in the college. Thus

[93] *Twentieth Report of the S.P.C.T.E.W., 1863*, p. 42.
[94] Disestablishment was not brought about in Maine until 1820.
[95] See the original petition on behalf of Colby College in Hall, E. W., *History of Higher Education in Maine*. U. S. Bur. of Ed. Cir. Inf., 1903, no. 3, pp. 96-97.
[96] Hatch, L. C., *The History of Bowdoin College*, pp. 41-46, 1927.
[97] *Ibid.*, pp. 72-84. Also Hall, *op. cit.*, pp. 57, 68, 69.
[98] Shirley, *op. cit.*, pp. 351-355.

Bowdoin was permanently granted a status largely independent of the state. By virtue of this judicial decision the movement for a state university in Maine was effectually checked.[99] It was not until 1865 that the Maine State College of Agriculture and Mechanic Arts was established with the aid of the Morrill land grant.[100] This institution became the University of Maine in 1897.

Arkansas was admitted to the Union as a state in 1836. It remained for a considerable period a state with a sparse population and inadequate resources. While a Congressional land grant had been given to the state at the time of its admittance to the Union, this grant was not applied to the purposes for which it was intended until after the Civil War. Three more or less temporary church colleges were established before the Civil War.[101] The church interests represented by these colleges were opposed from the very beginning to the establishment of a state university, and thus little was done in the direction of state-controlled higher education before the Civil War. It was not until 1871 that the Arkansas Industrial University was established with the aid of the Morrill land grant. This institution became the University of Arkansas in 1898.

Florida was admitted to the Union as a state in 1845. It remained for a long time a state with a sparse population and inadequate resources. The Congressional land grant received by it was not applied for the purposes of higher education under the control of the state before the Civil War, but was used for the promotion of secondary education. An act of 1851 designated two seminaries of secondary level in the state as the recipients of the grant.[102] The movement for the establishment of a state university in Florida lacked popular support and the necessary leadership. It was not until 1905 that a number of state-supported institutions of higher education in the state were united as the University of Florida.

Texas was admitted to the Union as a state in 1845, but it was not made the recipient of the usual Congressional land grant for higher education on account of the fact that its public lands were not turned over to the United States. Thus Congress was not in a

---

[99] Richardson, C. F. and Clark, H. A., *The College Book*, pp. 202-203, 1878.

[100] It needs to be kept in mind that Maine was not entitled to a share in the Congressional land grants which had been received by most of the newer states following the precedent of 1787.

[101] Shinn, J. H., *History of Education in Arkansas*, U. S. Bur. of Ed. Cir. Inf., 1900, no. 1, pp. 9, 33-35, 64. The colleges were St. John's, Cane Hill, and Arkansas.

[102] Bush, G. G., *History of Education in Florida*, U. S. Bur. of Ed. Cir. Inf., 1888, no. 7, pp. 31, 32.

position to grant aid to the state for higher education. Provision had been made, however, by the Republic of Texas in 1839, for the reservation of 211,400 acres of land for the establishment of two state seminaries. On account of the opposition of a number of interests in the state to the idea of state-controlled education, these resources were not applied to their intended purpose.[103] An act passed in 1858 for the establishment of a state university was never carried out for the same reason.[104] Among the interests opposed to a state university the church interests were the strongest. These interests had become strongly intrenched in the field of higher education, and two permanent colleges, viz., Baylor and Austin, as well as a number of other colleges of a more or less temporary character, had been established in the state. The movement for the founding of a state university of a "revolutionary" type thus met with serious opposition from the religious interests represented in these colleges. The University of Texas was not chartered until 1881.

Oregon was admitted as a state in 1859 and received a Congressional land grant for the establishment of a state university in that year. Two church colleges, viz., Willamette and Pacific, had been founded during territorial days. The continuing influence of these institutions was in part responsible for the delay in applying the Congressional land grant to the establishment of a state university.[105] Other factors in the situation, such as the sparseness of population and the inadequacy of resources, contributed to the failure in Oregon to establish a state university before the Civil War. The University of Oregon was not chartered until 1872, when the Morrill land grant gave an additional impetus to the movement for a state university.

Kansas was the last of the new states to be admitted to the Union before the Civil War. It was admitted to the Union as a free state on January 21, 1861, only a short time before the War. On January 29, 1861, the new state was made the recipient of a Congressional land grant for the establishment of a state university. Although the movement for the founding of a state university in Kansas had been strong, even in the territorial days, the opposition

[103] Eby, F., *The Development of Education in Texas*, pp. 284-286, 1925.
[104] Lane, J. J., *History of Education in Texas*, U. S. Bur. of Ed. Cir. Inf., 1903, no. 2, p. 128.
[105] Blackmar, F. W., *Federal and State Aid to Higher Education*, U. S. Bur. of Ed. Cir. Inf., 1890, no. 1. The Constitution of 1857 provided that no part of the land grant funds should be expended until 1867, indicating that powerful interests were opposed to a state university.

of the church interests, which were already represented in the field by one permanent college, viz., Baker University, under Methodist auspices, and a number of other colleges, which proved to be more or less temporary in character, rendered the immediate organization of a state university impossible.[106] Moreover, the coming of the War put an end to any advance whatsoever in the field of higher education. The University of Kansas was, however, chartered on March 1, 1864, near the conclusion of the War, and a new era in higher education was inaugurated in the state.

This survey of the difficulties experienced by seven new states in establishing state universities before the Civil War gives further evidence of the fact that the period before the Civil War was essentially a religious one. It was clearly an era in which higher education was primarily regarded as a function of the church rather than of the state. In the discussion that follows of the eventual founding of state universities in twenty states in the Union, added confirmation will be given to the fact that the middle period of our history was religious rather than secular in character, at least in the sphere of higher education, for the universities that were established in these states were in most cases dominated by religious interests. It is to the situation existing in these states that we now turn our attention.

THE FOUNDING OF STATE UNIVERSITIES IN SIX ORIGINAL STATES

The new ideals of a state university which came in with the Revolutionary era were first put into practice in six original states in the east. It will be recalled that four of the thirteen original states in the East, viz., Massachusetts, Connecticut, Rhode Island, and New Jersey, resolutely refused to follow these new ideals of higher education, while three, viz., New York, Pennsylvania, and New Hampshire, after a brief period of experimentation, finally decided not to follow the new and "revolutionary" conceptions of a state university, advocated in that day. In six of the original states, viz., Georgia, North Carolina, South Carolina, Maryland,

---

[106] Blackmar, F. W., *Higher Education in Kansas.* U. S. Bur. of Ed. Cir. Inf., 1900, no. 2, pp. 23-39. Two semi-state institutions, viz., "The University of Lawrence" of 1859 under Presbyterian auspices and "The Lawrence University of Kansas" of 1861 under Episcopalian auspices, preceded the establishment of "The University of Kansas," but neither bore any legal relationship to the final state university of 1864, and neither survived the exigencies of time and circumstance.

Virginia, and Delaware, however, state universities of a more or less "revolutionary" type were established on a permanent basis before the Civil War. In these six original states, the movement for the founding of state universities in this country achieved a measure of success. The state universities that were established were able to carry on even in a religious era, in spite of inadequate support from state or national sources,[107] and in the face of opposition on the part of religious and political interests. The measure of success that was achieved was truly significant. Although most of the state universities begun in this era were at one time or another under the domination of religious interests, and were for a part or the whole of the time under self-perpetuating Boards of Trustees, nevertheless, considerable progress was made eventually toward a more advanced system of state-controlled higher education in these states. In the following discussion, the vicissitudes of the six state universities that were founded in these eastern states will be briefly considered.

Georgia was the first of the states in the Union to establish a state university. The University of Georgia was chartered as a degree-conferring institution in 1785, and was placed largely under state control. This was not long after the Treaty of Paris, which ended the Revolutionary War.[108] With the acceptance by Georgia in 1777 of the principle of the separation of church and state, the way had been opened for the establishment of church colleges or a state university or both. Since the group of leaders in control of the new state government were sympathetic toward the eighteenth century philosophy of higher education so ably advocated by Thomas Jefferson and others at that time, a radical departure from the traditional patterns of higher education was made in Georgia by the establishment of the University of Georgia in the early years of statehood.[109] This institution maintained a monopoly over higher education in the state for fifty years.

---

[107] The thirteen original states were not included in the plan for the Congressional land grants to higher education in spite of the fact that they had given up their claims to the western lands from which such grants were made in 1787. Maryland, in 1821, led in protesting against this seeming injustice. See Ten Brook, A., *American State Universities*, pp. 385-400, 1875.

[108] The charter of 1785 gave the University of Georgia a priority in founding among state universities in this country under the definition accepted for the purposes of this study.

[109] Coulter, E. M., *College Life in the Old South*, pp. 7, 11, 12, 23, 1928. It is to be noted that the university was located in Athens in the up-country, away from the more settled regions of Georgia.

The control of this new institution was vested by the terms of the charter of 1785 in a bicameral body termed the Senatus Academicus, consisting of a Board of Visitors made up of the Governor, the State Councillors, the Speaker of the House, and the Chief Justice, and of a Board of Trustees comprising a self-perpetuating body of citizens.[110] This arrangement provided for a large measure of state control over the institution, while a grant of 40,000 acres of land in 1784 gave the institution an initial source of state support. With this rather auspicious beginning, the University of Georgia was launched on its career.[111] But forces which had not been present in the early years of statehood soon began to exercise a retarding influence on the development of the institution. The rise of powerful sectarian groups and new political parties in the state brought in an era of rivalry and competition in the field of higher education, and led to a struggle for the control of the state university. It was charged by the interests opposed to the state university that it was "the illegitimate child of the state," and was born of a *mésalliance* with Jeffersonian democracy.[112] In time, sectarian influences came to dominate in the control of the university, and the promise of the early years was largely unrealized. The first president, Meigs, a Jeffersonian Democrat, was forced to resign in 1816 and give way to leaders more conservative in religion and politics. Popular support was before long transferred to the church colleges that were established in various parts of the state.[113] Thus the "advanced" ideals of state education embodied in the establishment of the University of Georgia were allowed to remain largely in eclipse in Georgia before the Civil War.

In *North Carolina* a university was established in 1789. This institution was a child of the Constitution of 1776, which provided that "all useful learning shall be duly encouraged and promoted in one or more universities." [114] The movement for the founding of a state university in North Carolina was initiated by a group of dissenters from the former established order, among which the Presbyterians were the leaders. These dissenting interests had been

---

[110] Jones, C. E., *Education in Georgia*, U. S. Bur. of Ed. Cir. Inf., 1888, no. 4, p. 43.
[111] See Letter of President Meigs to Governor Milledge under date of May 11, 1808.
[112] Quoted in Coulter, *op. cit.*, p. 225.
[113] See Appendix for list of colleges founded in Georgia beginning with the decade of the thirties.
[114] *Colonial Records of North Carolina*, vol. 10, p. 1012. This clause was taken from the Pennsylvania Constitution of 1776, drawn up and approved several months before the North Carolina Constitution.

twice rebuffed by the colonial government in their attempts to found a college before the war.[115] Prominent among the founders of the University of North Carolina was the Reverend Davie, who, unlike many of his Presbyterian compatriots, although a Federalist in politics, had become infected with the "revolutionary" doctrines of Jefferson in higher education. While the early enthusiasm for these doctrines on the part of Davie and others gave an initial impetus to the movement for a state university, the institution that was actually established by the terms of the charter of 1789 provided for a self-perpetuating Board of Trustees, a feature that was characteristic of Calvinistic and Federalist areas in the country. As a result of this situation, the more orthodox Presbyterian and Federalist interests that were dominant in the state were able to secure a large measure of control over the institution during its early years.

With the coming of the era of Jeffersonian democracy in 1800, a struggle for the control of the institution ensued.[116] While the new democratic interests that became powerful in the state at that time were able in 1804, 1805, and 1821 to amend the charter so that in the end all vacancies on the Board of Trustees were to be filled by the General Assembly, the Presbyterian interests were so securely lodged in the control of the state and the institution that these measures failed in the end to alter appreciably the religious character of the university.[117] The University of North Carolina remained throughout the greater part of the period before the Civil War largely under the dominance of church control. Thus again we observe the serious difficulties with which the new state universities established in this country during the middle period of our history were faced in their endeavor to realize the advanced ideals of higher education advocated during the Revolutionary era.

It was in *South Carolina* that the first "revolutionary" type of state university in the east was established on a permanent basis.[118]

[115] Drake, W. E., *Higher Education in North Carolina before 1860.* Unpublished dissertation of the University of North Carolina in 1930, pp. 25-28, for a discussion of the vetoed Act of 1771 for Queen's College, and pp. 52-54 for a discussion of the influence of Davie.

[116] Battle, K. P., *History of the University of North Carolina,* vol. 2, p. 2, 1907. The Board of Trustees from the beginning were Presbyterians in religion and Federalists in politics. Princeton and Yale were closely related to the development of the university.

[117] Smith, C. L., *The History of Education in North Carolina,* U. S. Bur. of Ed. Cir. Inf., 1888, no. 2, pp. 68-69. The Rev. Joseph Caldwell, a prominent Presbyterian divine, was made president of the institution in 1804, and under his leadership the University of North Carolina took shape as a state institution under Presbyterian and Federalist influence. Gilpatrick, D. H., *Jeffersonian Democracy in North Carolina (1789-1816),* pp. 129-130, pp. 142-145.

[118] The universities of Georgia and North Carolina were not originally placed under full legislative control. The University of Vermont was not placed under full state control

South Carolina College was granted its original charter in 1801 and given the right to confer degrees in 1805. The latter date has been taken as the definitive date for this study. By terms of the original charter, the institution was placed wholly under the control of the state, provision being made for the election of all members of the Board of Trustees by the legislature. The success of this radical departure from traditional practice was assured by the political situation existing at that time in South Carolina. The state government was under the control of the democratic party which drew its inspiration from the doctrines of Thomas Jefferson. Under these circumstances it was natural that the state university in South Carolina should be patterned after Jeffersonian ideals of higher education and should receive a large measure of popular support in the state. The institution was located at Columbia, in the up-country region of the state, where the democratic party was strongest, rather than in the low-country section, where the older established interests in religion and politics were dominant.[119] Under the able leadership of Jonathan Maxey as president, the institution flourished for a considerable period without undue influence from denominational interests.

The administration of the second president, Thomas Cooper, however, proved too radical for the denominational groups that were increasing in power and influence in the state.[120] It was felt that

the College had lost the confidence of the people; it lived upon their breath, and it must die if that breath was withheld. The cry of "revolution" "reorganization" was again to be heard echoing and re-echoing from the mountains to the seaboard.[121]

Thomas Cooper was forced to resign in 1834, and for the remainder of the period before the Civil War the institution was presided over

at first. Ohio University, however, was placed under such control in 1804, thus giving it priority as a "revolutionary" type of state university in the country at large. If the date of the original charter of the University of South Carolina is taken as definitive, it may be regarded as the first "revolutionary" type of state university to be established in this country.

[119] Attempts had been made by the state in 1785, 1795, and 1797 to establish five small semi-state colleges in various parts of the state, but only one of these, viz., the College of Charleston, was permanently successful. This last became a municipal institution in 1838. See La Borde, M., *History of South Carolina College*, p. 19, 1859.

[120] A "pamphlet war" ensued over the state university. For a statement of the position of the Trustees in 1835, see *An Appeal in Behalf of the South Carolina College*, 1835 (pamphlet).

[121] La Borde, M., *op. cit.*, p. 160. This history of South Carolina College was written in 1859 by an authority that approved of the changes that transformed the institution into a religious college.

by men with more orthodox religious views. It was decreed at that time that

> . . . a religion "pure and undefiled" was to be preached to the youth of the State; and from the College, as from a fountain, were to go forth the waters of salvation. An experiment was to be made; Christian doctrine was to be taught from the pulpit, and from the Professor's chair; Christian influences were to pervade the Campus; and a noble Literary Institution was now to have emblazoned upon its portals the significant inscription "the Christian's God alone is to be worshipped in these walls." [122]

Thus it was proved once again that the American people were not willing, at least in this era, to have a "godless state university." [123]

The movement for the founding of a state university in *Maryland* was unique in many of its features. In the early years of the colony, there existed a considerable degree of religious liberty. Later, however, the Anglican Church became the established church of the colony. With the coming of the Revolution and the enactment of disestablishment, other religious interests in the state became powerful. In this situation an attempt was made at first to unite two private colleges, viz., Washington and St. John's, which had been established in association with the new Episcopal Church, under a comprehensive organization known as the University of Maryland, which was to provide for a liberal representation of the various religious interests in the state. This unique type of institution proved abortive, and the two colleges remained private colleges associated largely with Episcopalian interests.[124] A second attempt, entirely separate from the first, to establish a state university was more successful. In 1812 the College of Medicine in Baltimore was made the basis of the new University of Maryland.[125] This institution was also distinctive in that it provided for control on the part of a Board of Regents made up of the members of the four faculties

---

[122] *Ibid.*, p. 227. See also Thornwell, J. H., *Letter to Governor Manning on Public Instruction in South Carolina*, 1853 (pamphlet). This has been called the "Bible" of South Carolina College.

[123] It is to be noted that the change in policy of the institution did not preclude the eventual establishment of a number of rival denominational colleges in the state. The state university held a monopoly in the field of higher education in the state for almost fifty years. See Meriwether, C., *History of Higher Education in South Carolina*, U. S. Bur. of Ed. Cir. Inf., 1888, no. 3, p. 169. Erskine College, for example, was unable to secure a charter from the legislature for a long period of years because of the opposition of friends of the University of South Carolina. *Ibid.*, p. 89.

[124] Steiner, B. C., *History of Education in Maryland*, U. S. Bur. of Ed. Cir. Inf., 1894, no. 2, pp. 69-71.

[125] The University of Louisville and Tulane University were also established on the basis of medical schools.

of the new institution. Thus a more or less autonomous institution was created to serve the varied interests of the state in the field of higher education.

It was not long, however, before active opposition to this new institution developed on the part of various interests in the state, and the legislature was induced in 1826 to abolish the Board of Regents and substitute a Board of Trustees. The Governor was made an ex-officio member of the board and invested with sole authority to supply all vacancies.[126] For thirteen years this reorganized institution functioned with some measure of success as a state university, in the full sense of the term.[127] The old Board of Regents were able, however, in 1838 to reinstate themselves in the position of control over the institution, by securing a decision from the Supreme Court of the state declaring the Act of 1826 unconstitutional and void.[128] Thus the principles of the Dartmouth College decision were reaffirmed and the rights of a private corporation were reëstablished in this instance. The University of Maryland remained a private institution serving the interest of the state in lieu of a state university until 1920, when it was united with the Maryland State College and brought entirely under state control.[129] It is evident that Maryland was able, during the period before the Civil War, to realize only partially the ideals of a state university advocated during the Revolutionary era.[130]

It was in *Virginia* that the most advanced and complete type of state university in the country was established before the Civil War. While the movement for the founding of a state university encountered more serious and determined opposition in Virginia than in any other state, perhaps, the success that was achieved was undoubtedly greater than that achieved in any other state in the Union. The greater success attained in this state was due in large part to the powerful leadership of Thomas Jefferson, who, in season and out of season, for a period of almost half a century, advocated the establishment of a state university. The ideals of eighteenth century liberalism, which were derived in part from France, pro-

[126] Steiner, *op. cit.*, p. 129.

[127] During this period the Baltimore College was annexed to form a part of the University. See *Memorial of the Trustees of the University of Maryland and the Trustees of Baltimore College to the Legislature of Maryland* (pamphlet), 1830.

[128] Steiner, *op. cit.*, p. 124.

[129] *Catalogue of the University of Maryland for 1927-28.* "Historical Statement."

[130] For a scholarly and impartial history of the University of Maryland, see Cordell, E. F., *University of Maryland,* vol. 1, 1907.

vided the stimulus and sanction for this movement in Virginia for a new and revolutionary philosophy of higher education.[131] The type of state institution so ably advocated by Jefferson was to be, according to his view, more consonant with the principles of political and religious freedom than the traditional institution of higher education of the colonial era. It was, however, on these very grounds of political and religious principle that the opponents to a state university in Virginia took their stand. The interests of both Federalists and religionists were opposed to the establishment of an institution that would most certainly be, in their view, republican and secular in character.[132] Thus the stage was set for a historic struggle in the field of higher education.

With the achievement of disestablishment and the acceptance of the principle of the separation of church and state, the way was open in Virginia for advance in the field of higher education. The early efforts of the leaders in the movement for the establishment of a state university were directed toward the end of transforming the College of William and Mary into a state institution. The abandonment of these efforts has been referred to in another connection.[133] The next step that was taken by the leaders of the movement was to lay the foundations of an institution that might ultimately become a state university of a "revolutionary" type. An academy that existed only by charter enactment was reconstituted as a college in 1816, and given the name of Central College. This institution, situated as it was in the central part of the state, and placed as it was under full state control, became the foundation of the University of Virginia.[134] In 1819 the legislature was persuaded to recharter Central College on a liberal and comprehensive plan under the new name of the University of Virginia. Provision was made for the control of the institution by a Board of Visitors appointed by the Governor. It was also provided that the institution "should in all things and at all times be subject to the control of the legislature."[135] A large measure of financial support was se-

[131] The acceptance of French ideas on the part of Jefferson was rigidly selective, and only those ideas that were thought to be "good for us" were adopted. See Letter of Thomas Jefferson to Peter Carr in *Niles Register for March 16th, 1816.*

[132] A fuller discussion of this point and other related points growing out of this discussion of the founding of the University of Virginia is precluded by the limits of this study. Excellent references on the whole subject may be found in Adams, H. B., *Thomas Jefferson and the University of Virginia,* U. S. Bur. of Ed. Cir. Inf., 1888, no. 1.

[133] See p. 144, footnote 28.

[134] Adams, *op. cit.,* p. 68.

[135] *Revised Code of Virginia,* chap. 34, sec. 9.

cured from the legislature in order to ensure the success of the institution. Thus launched upon its career, the University of Virginia was enabled to enter upon a long period of service to the state and to the country at large.

In an era when religious interests became increasingly dominant in the field of higher education, the University of Virginia was able in part to retain its distinctive character. During the period before the Civil War, its initial organization was not significantly altered. Following the death of Jefferson, however, the rising denominational forces in the state concentrated their attacks on the institution and succeeded in introducing a strong religious influence on the campus. Thus, for the remainder of the period before the Civil War, the University of Virginia, while retaining its legal associations with the state, took on in large part the character of a religious institution. Reference to this change is made in the following observation of an English visitor of strong religious sympathies in 1840:

> The University of Virginia, founded and endowed through the influence and exertions of President Jefferson, languished and became almost extinct, till a Christian influence was infused into its management; then it "practised and prospered." [136]

Delaware was the last of the eastern states before the Civil War to initiate a movement for the founding of a state university. While this movement was even less successful than similar movements in some of the other states that have been considered, at least it may be said that a beginning was made. In 1821 an abortive attempt was made to establish a state university under the name of Delaware College. This institution was granted a charter providing for a full measure of state control through the election of the members of the Board of Trustees by the legislature. On account of a growing opposition on the part of religious interests to this feature of the charter, the organization of the institution was indefinitely postponed.[137] In 1833 the Presbyterian interests in the state, which had been active in education and politics from the very beginning, took the initiative in securing another charter for an institution to be known as Newark College. The charter for this institution provided for a self-perpetuating Board of Trustees, and for the

[136] Lang, J. D., *Religion and Education in America*, p. 284, 1840.
[137] Powell, L. P., *The History of Education in Delaware*, U. S. Bur. of Ed. Cir. Inf., 1893, no. 3. p. 90.

repeal of the charter of 1821. While a group of representative citizens were chosen as members of the first Board of Trustees of Newark College, and the institution was granted a measure of state support, it became increasingly clear that this new institution was to be a private one largely under the control of the Presbyterian church.[138] Although the name of the institution was changed to Delaware College in 1843, and a real effort was made on the part of the institution to serve the interests of the state as well as the church, active opposition was encountered from interests in the state which demanded a state university of a more advanced type. An able writer in 1847 states that "Delaware College as it now stands can be compared to the last flickering of an expiring candle showing momentary evidences of life," and proposes that a new state university be established in Wilmington, as Newark was suitable only for "a monastery, a friary, or a nunnery, but not for a college." [139] These efforts to bring about a fundamental change in the policy of the institution were unavailing, however, and it was not until after the Civil War that the state was given a share in the control of the institution. In 1913 the state took over complete control of the institution. In 1921 Delaware College became the University of Delaware.[140] From this account of the movement for the founding of a state university in Delaware, it is clear that the situation existing in the state before the Civil War was far from favorable to the realization of the "advanced" ideals of a state university that were advocated during the Revolutionary epoch. Again it was shown that the forces that were in control of higher education in the era before the Civil War were largely religious in character.

THE FOUNDING OF STATE UNIVERSITIES IN FOURTEEN NEW STATES

The movement for the founding of state universities in the new states in the west received an initial impetus and a financial backing from the national government that were lacking in the case of the original states in the east. It was literally true that most of

[138] *Ibid.*, p. 106. In 1840 it was agreed that vacancies on the Board of Trustees should be filled by Presbyterians.
[139] Quoted in Powell, *op. cit.*, p. 112. The new charter of 1851, however, introduced no fundamental changes in the control of Delaware College.
[140] *Catalogue of the University of Delaware for 1927-28*, "Historical Statement."

the state universities that were established in the new states of the Union owed their very existence to the national government. The statement found in the charter of the University of Alabama which reads, "the University of Alabama was called into existence by the generosity of the Congress," gives evidence of the dependence of the state university movement in the west on the land grant policy of the national government.[141] If it had not been for the fact that most of the new states in the West were granted two townships of public land for the purposes of a seminary of learning, it is a real question whether these states would have established state universities at all before the Civil War. The prevailing sentiments of a religious era were definitely in favor of the establishment of small denominational colleges throughout the country, as has been brought out in other parts of this study, and the movement for the establishment of state universities would undoubtedly have been set back even more seriously than it was in the period before the Civil War had it not been for the propelling force of the land grants received by the individual states and the moral and legal obligations arising therefrom to establish some type of state institution of higher education within their borders.

The national government, in initiating a policy of federal aid to higher education in the early days of our history, through the provision of land grants to individual states, was not so much concerned with the furtherance of the cause of higher education as it was with settlement of the vexed problem of the reduction of the public debt. The evidence is convincing that the primary reason for the adoption of the policy of setting aside public land for the purposes of higher education in the western territory was that of providing an additional inducement to settlers to buy land in the west.[142] As time went on, the precedent established by Congress in its early history became the settled policy of the national government. The lack of specific design on the part of Congress in its early grants of public land led to a long period of uncertainty on the part of the individual states as to the type of higher institutions which should be established. In most states, as we shall see in the following discussion, a long period of experimentation in the field of higher education was necessary before it became apparent that

[141] Act of December 18, 1821, reprinted in Toulmin, *Digest of Alabama Laws*, p. 552. Also note statements regarding the other universities, e.g., the University of Missouri in Lowry, T. J., *A Sketch of the University of the State of Missouri*, p. 4, 1890 (pamphlet).
[142] Reisner, E. H., *op. cit.*, pp. 338-45. Also Knight, G. W., *op. cit.*, pp. 11-15.

the church and state should part company in the field of higher education, and that the land grants should be applied solely to institutions of higher education of a more or less secular nature. It is not within the purpose of this study to discuss the ultimate implications of this more or less distinctive western development,[143] but rather to discuss the general features of the movement for the founding of state universities in the west before the Civil War. It will be necessary at first to relate in some detail the steps in the adoption by Congress of the policy of land grants for higher education in the new states in the west.

It was at the instance of the Ohio Company of Associates, a group of New Englanders desirous of promoting the settlement of the western territory, that the Continental Congress inserted in the Northwest Ordinances of 1785 and 1787, and subsequent Acts, provisions for the encouragement of education in the Northwest Territory. In the Ordinance of May 20, 1785, it was provided that "there shall be reserved the lot No. 16, of every township, for the maintenance of public schools." [144] In the Ordinance of July 13, 1787, the well-known clause relating to the encouragement of education was inserted, viz., "Religion, morality, and knowledge being necessary to good government and the happiness of mankind, schools and the means of education shall be forever encouraged." [145] In the Bill of Sale to the Ohio Company of July 23, 1787, Congress was led to insert the provision that "not more than two complete townships to be given perpetually for the purposes of an University . . . to be applied to the intended object by the legislature of the state." [146] This latter provision established a precedent of far-reaching significance for the development of higher education in the new nation. All the twenty-one new states admitted to the Union before the Civil War, with the exception of Vermont, Kentucky, Maine, and Texas, were made the recipients of land grants by Congress, following the precedent established in 1787 in the grant of land to the Ohio Company.

When Ohio was admitted to the Union in 1803, as the first state to be carved out of the Northwest Territory, the original grant of two townships of land to the Ohio Company, and the grant of one

---

[143] In some of the eastern states, the church and the state eventually parted company in the field of higher education.
[144] Peters, W. E., *Legal History of Ohio University*, 1910.
[145] *Ibid.*, p. 36.
[146] *Ibid.*, p. 40.

township of land made subsequently to John Cleves Symmes, were entrusted to the state legislature. When the four states of Indiana, Illinois, Michigan, and Wisconsin were later formed out of the Northwest Territory and admitted to the Union, Congress granted to each one two townships of public land in the same manner as in the case of Ohio. By a special adjustment of its land claims in 1806, Tennessee was granted four townships for the endowment of higher education. In 1790, Congress extended its land grant policy to the territory south of Tennessee, and thus when the states of Mississippi, Alabama, and Florida were admitted to the Union, they were made the recipients of similar land grants for higher education. Following the Louisiana Purchase, the states that were formed out of this new domain were in like manner made the beneficiaries of the national government. In this vast territory, the states of Louisiana, Missouri, Arkansas, Iowa, Minnesota, and Kansas were admitted to the Union before the Civil War, and each one, at the time of its admittance to the Union, was made the recipient of public land for the purposes of higher education. The states of California and Oregon on the western coast were likewise granted public land for higher education at the time of their admittance to the Union.

Thirteen state universities were established before the Civil War in twelve of the seventeen new states referred to above which were made the recipients of Congressional land grants. These twelve states were Tennessee, Ohio, Louisiana, Indiana, Mississippi, Alabama, Missouri, Michigan, Iowa, Wisconsin, California, and Minnesota. No state universities were established before the Civil War in the remaining five new states receiving Congressional land grants, viz., Illinois, Arkansas, Florida, Oregon, and Kansas. Two other state universities were established before the Civil War in two of the four new states which failed to receive Congressional land grants, viz., Vermont and Kentucky. No state universities were established before the Civil War in the remaining two states not receiving Congressional land grants, viz., Maine and Texas. In the succeeding sections of this chapter the founding of these fifteen state universities in fourteen of the twenty-one new states admitted before the Civil War will be considered in detail in order to supplement the discussion, given in a preceding section, of the six state universities that were founded in six of the original states. Before entering upon a consideration of the founding of these fifteen state universities, a summary of the Congressional land grants made to the seventeen new states is given in Table XXIV.

TABLE XXIV

SUMMARY TABLE OF CONGRESSIONAL LAND GRANTS FOR HIGHER EDUCATION MADE TO SEVENTEEN STATES OF THE UNION BEFORE THE CIVIL WAR *

NO.	STATE	DATE OF ADMITTANCE	LAND GRANTS	CONGRESSIONAL ACTS
1	TENNESSEE ***	1796	100,000 acres	1806
2	OHIO	1803	69,120 acres	1792, 1803
3	LOUISIANA	1812	46,080 acres	1806, 1811, 1827
4	INDIANA	1816	46,080 acres	1804, 1816
5	MISSISSIPPI	1817	46,080 acres	1803, 1819
6	ILLINOIS **	1818	46,080 acres	1804, 1818
7	ALABAMA	1819	46,080 acres	1818, 1819
8	MISSOURI	1821	46,080 acres	1818, 1820
9	ARKANSAS **	1836	46,080 acres	1836
10	MICHIGAN	1837	46,080 acres	1804, 1826, 1836
11	FLORIDA **	1845	92,160 acres	1823, 1845
12	IOWA	1846	46,080 acres	1840, 1845
13	WISCONSIN	1848	92,160 acres	1838, 1846, 1854
14	CALIFORNIA	1850	46,080 acres	1853
15	MINNESOTA	1858	82,640 acres	1857, 1861, 1870
16	OREGON **	1859	46,080 acres	1859, 1861
17	KANSAS **	1861	46,080 acres	1861

* This table is constructed on the basis of information found in the following sources, with corrections and adaptations in subject matter and presentation: Blackmar, *op. cit.*, p. 338; Hinsdale, B. A., "Documents Illustrative of American Educational History," vol. 2, pp. 1225-1414. *Report of the United States Commissioner of Education for 1892-93;* and Addis, W., "Federal and State Aid to Establish Higher Education," vol. 2, pp. 1137-1164.
** States in which no state universities were established before the Civil War.
*** Tennessee was made a recipient of a Congressional land grant by a special act of 1806.

Vermont was the first of the new states to be admitted to the Union. The Constitution of 1777 had declared that "one university in the state ought to be established by direction of the General Assembly." [147] Although this declaration was omitted from the succeeding Constitution of 1786, largely on account of difficulties arising out of negotiations with Dartmouth College, the idea of a state university was revived in 1791, at the time that Vermont was admitted to the Union. In that year the University of Vermont was established.[148] The control of this institution was vested by the

[147] *Vermont Historical Society Collections,* vol. 1, p. 63 (2 vols), 1870-71. Compare the clause in the Constitution of Pennsylvania and North Carolina.
[148] Vermont was one of the four new states that did not receive a Congressional land grant before the Civil War.

terms of the charter in a self-perpetuating, not a state-appointed, Board of Trustees. Provision was made only for the ex-officio representation of the Governor and the Speaker of the House on the Board of Trustees. While certain features of the charter indicate that the founders of the University of Vermont favored a state institution of higher education of a more or less advanced type, other features, such as those just referred to, indicate that the controlling Puritan and Federalist interests in the legislature favored a more conservative type of state institution. The anomalous position of the university was revealed when a movement was initiated by the more conservative religious and political interests in the state to found another institution at Middlebury, only thirty-three miles from Burlington. These interests desired an institution more definitely designed to serve the interests of the church and more directly under the control of the church. Middlebury College was chartered in 1801, and a powerful group in the state withdrew its support from the University of Vermont.[149] As a result, the state university was left in a weakened condition, not knowing which way to turn for support.

In 1810, with the increase in influence of republican and dissenting interests in the state, the charter of the university was amended by the legislature in such a way as to give the state the right to elect all the members of the Board of Trustees.[150] This radical action was taken, it will be noted, before the Dartmouth College Case. For a period of eighteen years the University of Vermont maintained itself as a state university of a "revolutionary" type, but with only a small measure of success. Following the Dartmouth College Case decision of 1819, increasing objection was made by conservative interests to the confiscatory act of the legislature. In 1828, three years after the Rev. James Marsh, an able Congregational divine, was elected president of the university, the more conservative interests in the state were able to induce the legislature to revoke its former action and reaffirm the original charter of the university.[151] Religious influences now came to dominate the policies

[149] Wheeler, J., *Historical Discourse*, p. 17, 1854, pamphlet. For evidence of Federalist and Puritan activity, see Wilbur, J. B., *Ira Allen, Founder of Vermont*, vol. 2, p. 302 (2 vols.), 1928.

[150] Benedict, R. D., *Charter History of the University of Vermont*, p. 42, 1892 (pamphlet). Also Wilbur, *op. cit.*, vol. 2, p. 423. In 1807, disestablishment was brought about in Vermont.

[151] Bush, G. G., *History of Education in Vermont*, U. S. Bur. of Ed. Cir. Inf., 1900, no. 4, p. 146.

of the institution. In view of this fact a larger measure of success was vouchsafed the institution for the remainder of the period before the Civil War. It was not until after the Civil War that the legal status of the university was changed so as to make it more fully a state university. A reorganization was effected in 1865 which united the University of Vermont and the new State Agricultural College.[152] In this reorganization equal representation was given on the Board of Trustees to state and private interests. Thus the University of Vermont came to assume a closer legal relation to the state and to approximate more closely the "revolutionary" ideals of a state university.

Kentucky was admitted to the Union in 1792. During the early territorial days, Transylvania University had been established in the central part of the state, and came to be regarded as a state institution. When Kentucky was admitted to the Union as a state, Transylvania continued to receive the patronage of the legislature and the people.[153] It was, however, an institution placed under the control of a self-perpetuating Board of Trustees made up largely of representatives of the Presbyterian Church, and thus may not be regarded as a state university in the full sense of the term. Although the principle of the separation of church and state had been accepted in theory by the people of Kentucky, there existed for a considerable period in the state a virtual union of the church and state, at least in the field of higher education. After a long career of service as a semi-state institution in the days of Presbyterian ascendency, Transylvania lapsed into a condition of ineffectiveness, and suffered under the hands of various denominations that successively took over its management.[154] The period of Presbyterian hegemony in the state ended with the decade of the twenties, and the field of higher education was given over to a large number of competing religious sects.

During this period of denominational activity, Bacon College was founded by the Disciples Church. This institution, chartered in 1837, proved to be the forerunner of the University of Kentucky.

---

[152] *General Catalogue of the University of Vermont, 1927-28,* "Historical Statement."

[153] Kentucky was one of the four new states that did not receive a Congressional land grant for a state university.

[154] Lewis, A. F., *History of Higher Education in Kentucky,* U. S. Bur. of Ed. Cir. Inf.. 1899. no. 3, pp. 16, 57. Transylvania was placed under the more direct control of the state at various times, but in every instance the denominational interests were able to regain a dominant position on the Board of Trustees. After the Presbyterians relinquished their control, the Baptists, Episcopalians, Presbyterians, Methodists, and Disciples successively took over control.

It was at first a private college under the control of a self-perpetuating Board of Trustees made up largely of representatives of the Disciples Church.[155] While it achieved for a while some success as a college, it was forced to discontinue in 1850. With the rise in power of the Disciples in the state, a new and broader institution by the name of Kentucky University was established in 1858 on the foundation of Bacon College. This institution was intended to serve as a state institution in the same manner as Transylvania had served in the previous era of Presbyterian ascendency in the state, and the legislature readily agreed to a provision that two-thirds of the self-perpetuating Board of Trustees should be members of the Disciples Church.[156] Following the Civil War, a still more ambitious reorganization of the institution was effected. A new charter was granted in 1865 to Kentucky University, consolidating the old Kentucky University, Transylvania University, and the new Agricultural and Mechanical College. This larger institution remained largely under the control of the Disciples. In 1878 the Agricultural and Mechanical College separated itself from Kentucky University largely because the denominational character of the university proved uncongenial. In 1907 a state university of a "revolutionary" type, by the name of the State University of Kentucky, was established on the foundation of the Agricultural and Mechanical College.[157] In 1917 the name of the state university was changed to the University of Kentucky. From this brief survey of the movement for the establishment of a state university in Kentucky, it will be seen that the dominance of religious interests throughout the early history of the state tended to retard in a very serious fashion the development of a state university. It was not until very recent times that a state university of a "revolutionary" type was finally established in this state.

Tennessee was admitted to the Union as a state in 1796. Two years previous to this date, Blount College had been established as a private college under Presbyterian influence. This institution was the precursor of the University of Tennessee. In 1806 the United States Congress, in adjusting the land claims of Tennessee, granted the state 100,000 acres for the establishment of two universities,

---

[155] *Kentucky Laws*, 1837, p. 274.
[156] *Ibid.*, p. 86.
[157] The former Kentucky University of 1865 adopted the name of Transylvania University in 1908 after the organization in 1907 of the State University of Kentucky. See *General Catalogue of Transylvania College, 1927-28*, "Historical Statement."

one in the western part of the state and the other in the eastern part.[158] This Congressional grant was divided between Cumberland College, a Presbyterian college in the central part of the state, and East Tennessee College, a Presbyterian college established on the foundation of Blount College in the eastern part of the state. The former institution was reorganized in 1826 as the University of Nashville, and served as a semi-state institution with Presbyterian affiliations for a long period of years.[159] The latter institution took its place as a semi-state institution with Presbyterian affiliations serving the interests of the eastern part of the state. In 1840 this institution was renamed East Tennessee University, but its status remained largely unchanged. It was not until 1879 that the institution became in fact a state university of a "revolutionary" type, by the name of the University of Tennessee.[160] The day of Presbyterian influence in the state was now past, and, with the decline of the University of Nashville, the resources of the state were concentrated on the development of a single state university.

When *Ohio* was admitted to the Union in 1803, it was charged with the management of three townships of public land previously granted by Congress to the Ohio Company and to John Cleves Symmes for the development of higher education. Thus Ohio was the first state in the Union to benefit by the land grant policy initiated by Congress. The precedent established by Congress in this state was followed in most of the other states of the Union, and was responsible for the development of state universities in the western states. In 1802 the American Western University had been chartered by the territorial legislature, and the two townships of the Ohio Company were turned over by the legislature in trust to its Board of Trustees. In 1804 the new state legislature rechartered this institution, giving it the name of Ohio University. While the original intent of the founders of the institution was to make it a private university controlled by a self-perpetuating Board of Trustees,[161] both the charters of 1802 and 1804 decreed that the institution should be a state university with a Board of Trustees chosen

---

[158] Meriam, L. S., *Higher Education in Tennessee*, U. S. Bur. of Ed. Cir. Inf., 1893, no. 5, p. 23.

[159] *Ibid.*, pp. 60-61.

[160] Sanford, E. T., *Blount College and the University of Tennessee*, p. 74, 1894 (pamphlet).

[161] Knight, G. W., and Commons, J. R., *The History of Higher Education in Ohio*, U. S. Bur. of Ed. Cir. Inf., 1891, no. 5, p. 15. Also in Taylor, H. C., *Educational Significance of Early Federal Land Ordinances*, p. 136, 1922.

by the legislature.[162] It was decreed that the legislature might "alter, limit, or restrain any of the powers" granted to the institution, and it was later demanded that the institution make annual reports to the legislature.[163] Thus Ohio University became the first state university of a "revolutionary" type in the new states admitted to the Union. During the period before the Civil War, Ohio University served as a state institution with Calvinistic affiliations in a Calvinistic state, but with only a small measure of success, because of the increasing influence of the many other denominational colleges built up in the state, and because of the fact that the Calvinistic interests became more closely identified with such institutions as Western Reserve, Oberlin, and Marietta, which were institutions more directly under their control.[164] Evidence of the sad plight of Ohio University is given in the following summary statement:

> Almost a century has passed away, and nothing worthy of the name of a university has been realized on the spot first chosen for this enterprise.[165]

In 1809 another institution by the name of Miami University was established in the western part of the state, and granted the remaining township secured to the state by the default of John Cleves Symmes. This institution, unlike Ohio University, was not at first placed directly under the control of the state, but was given a self-perpetuating Board of Trustees. Nevertheless, the state regarded the institution as a state institution, reserving at the outset the right to "alter, limit, or restrain any of the powers" granted to the institution, and requiring later that the Trustees make a report to the legislature.[166] The anomalous position occupied by Miami University was the occasion for much controversy between the state and the institution and led in part to its decline. In 1842 it was placed more directly under the control of the state.[167] During the greater part of the period before the Civil War, Miami University was dominated by the Presbyterian interests that were active in

---

[162] Miller, E. A., *The History of Educational Legislation in Ohio from 1803 to 1850*, pp. 146-147, Chicago, 1920.

[163] Peters, W. E., *op. cit.*, pp. 89, 99, 240-243.

[164] It is to be recalled that Marietta College was founded in close proximity to Ohio University on account of the indefinite policy of that university in matters pertaining to religion.

[165] Ten Brook, *op. cit.*, p. 33.

[166] Miller, *op. cit.*, p. 149.

[167] *Laws Pertaining to Miami University*, p. 81, 1909 (pamphlet published by the university).

that part of the state. Evidence of this religious affiliation is given in the following statement by President Warfield:

> From the beginning of its history Miami University has been under distinctly religious influences; but, being a State institution, it has been entirely undenominational though with prevailing Presbyterian tendencies. From the opening till the closing, in 1873, its presidents were without exception ministers of the Presbyterian Church. The example which they set of nonsectarian, earnest Christianity is still faithfully emulated.[168]

Louisiana was admitted to the Union as a state in 1812. In its early territorial days, a comprehensive scheme for a state university was approved by the legislature. A charter was granted in 1805 to an institution which was to be known as the University of Orleans. French influences were strong in the territory from the very beginning and these influences were responsible in large part for this plan for a state university of a "revolutionary" type.[169] Although the University of Orleans was never organized, the College of Orleans, a constituent unit of the university, was established at that time under French influences in the City of New Orleans. This institution received a large measure of state support until the rise of rival interests in the state led to its abandonment. Once having adopted the policy of state aid to higher institutions of a semi-public character, the state was led to render aid to a number of colleges successively established in the state. At least six colleges were granted aid by the state in the period between 1805 and 1845, viz., the College of Orleans, referred to above, the College of Rapides, the College of Baton Rouge, the College of Louisiana, the College of Jefferson, and Franklin College.[170] These colleges were affiliated with the various political, racial, and religious interests that were struggling for a position of dominance in the state. All these institutions ended in failure, and thus the policy of state aid to higher education in Louisiana was seriously called into question.

The Constitution of 1845 marked a turning point in the educational history of the state. Thenceforth efforts were largely concentrated on the development of a single state university. Louisiana had in its early years been granted two townships of public land by

[168] Knight and Commons, *op. cit.*, p. 34. "Miami University—Sketch by President E. D. Warfield."

[169] Fay, E. W., *The History of Education in Louisiana*, U. S. Bur. of Ed. Cir. Inf., 1898, no. 1, pp. 45-46.

[170] *Ibid.*, pp. 63-67. The College of Rapides was not strictly a college, as it was not granted the legal right to confer degrees.

Congress for the purposes of "a state seminary of learning." This grant of land had been held inviolate up to 1845. The Constitution of that year declared that the funds arising from the sale of these lands should still be reserved for the establishment of a state seminary.[171] It was not until 1853 that the legislature established the Louisiana State Seminary of Learning as a "revolutionary" type of state university. It was provided in the charter that the Trustees should be appointed by the Governor, that the Board of Trustees should make an annual report to the legislature, that the institution should not be subjected to control of any religious denomination, and that the institution should in all things and at all times be subject to the control of the legislature.[172] The Congressional land grant was turned over to the seminary for its use. The institution was located near Alexandria, and was opened for students in 1860. In 1870 it was renamed the Louisiana State University and moved to Baton Rouge, while in 1877 it was merged with the Louisiana Agricultural and Mechanical College, an institution which had been established in 1874 with the aid of the Morrill land grant.[173] Thus after a long period of experimentation with the policy of state aid to semi-public institutions situated in different parts of the state, Louisiana finally decided to center its efforts more definitely on the development of a single state university.

Indiana was admitted to the Union as a state in 1816. While it was still a territory, the legislature granted a charter to a semi-public institution by the name of Vincennes University, which was to be located in the southern part of the state. This institution of 1806 was placed under a self-perpetuating Board of Trustees and entrusted with the one township of public land granted by Congress to the territory in 1804. It was, however, much delayed in organization, and in 1816 the state transferred the grant to another institution. Vincennes University was formally declared to be extinct by the legislature in 1824.[174] It was, however, revived as a private institution in 1838, and claims were made on the state for the original land grant. Although the legislature stated in 1852 that another institution was now definitely recognized as the university of the state, the Superior Court, on appeal, acknowledged the prior claim

[171] Fay, *op. cit.*
[172] *Louisiana Laws*, 1852-53, pp. 48-49.
[173] *General Catalogue of Louisiana State University, 1927-28,* "Historical Statement."
[174] Woodburn, J. A., *Higher Education in Indiana*, U. S. Bur. of Ed. Cir. Inf., 1891, no. 1, p. 33.

of Vincennes University to the original land grant.[175] During the long period of controversy between the state and Vincennes, the state was patronizing the Indiana State Seminary established in pursuance of a clause in the Constitution of 1816, which stated that

. . . it shall be the duty of the General Assembly, as soon as circumstances will permit, to provide by law for a general system of education ascending in a regular gradation from township schools to a State University, wherein tuition shall be gratis and equally open to all. [176]

The Indiana State Seminary was chartered in 1820 and located in Bloomington in the central part of the state. This institution was given the use of the township granted by Congress in 1806, as we have seen, as well as the additional township granted in 1816. It was not at first placed directly under state control nor was it granted the power to confer degrees. In 1828, however, the institution was raised to a collegiate level, given the name of Indiana College, and brought more closely under state supervision. A dual form of control, consisting of a self-perpetuating Board of Trustees and a Board of Visitors chosen by the state, was provided by the new charter.[177] By such a form of control, a check was placed upon an institution which had from the beginning been dominated largely by Presbyterian interests.[178] When it finally became apparent in Indiana, during the decade of the thirties, that the state and the church must part company in the field of higher education, a number of colleges were established in different parts of the state by the church interests,[179] while Indiana College was gradually brought into closer relation with the legislature and the state. In 1838 the legislature rechartered Indiana College, and gave it the name Indiana University. By this charter and subsequent acts of the legislature following the Civil War, the institution was in time transformed into a state university of a "revolutionary" type.[180]

[175] Wylie, T. A., *Indiana University—Its History (1820-1890)*, p. 30, 1890; Woodburn, *op. cit.*, p. 34.

[176] Harding, S. B., Editor, *Indiana University (1820-1904)*, p. 2, 1904.

[177] Woodburn, *op. cit.*, pp. 79-80. A Board of Visitors was first appointed in 1827 for the State Seminary in response to a movement for freeing the institution from sectarian control.

[178] *Ibid.*, p. 78. The situation was further complicated in Indiana because of the conflicts between Old School and New School Presbyterians in the state. For additional evidence of Presbyterian influence, see Banta, A. A., *Indiana University (1820-1920) Centennial Memorial Volume*, pp. 68, 102, 1921.

[179] The state university, while under Presbyterian influence, was able to maintain a virtual monopoly over higher education in the state. The first denominational college was chartered in 1833.

[180] Wylie, *op. cit.*, p. 31.

Mississippi was admitted to the Union in 1817, but it was not until a much later date that a state university of a "revolutionary" type was established in the state. The territorial legislature had chartered in 1802 an institution by the name of Jefferson College, and had entrusted to it the one township of public land granted by Congress in 1803.[181] While this institution was regarded at the time as a state institution, it was placed under a self-perpetuating Board of Trustees and subjected to the influence of church interests. At various times in its early history it was placed more directly under state control, but in 1844 it was finally turned over to church interests.[182] In 1830 another state institution by the name of Mississippi College was established and placed under a self-perpetuating Board of Trustees. This institution was placed under more direct state control in 1833, but was turned over to Presbyterian interests in 1842, and finally to Baptist interests in 1850.[183] Meanwhile the legislature had been led to adopt a policy of granting charters to denominational colleges situated in different parts of the state. Thus the movement for the founding of a state university in Mississippi was checked in large part by the efforts of the various religious interests in the state for a policy of decentralization in higher education. Other factors were, however, also responsible for the delay in establishing a central university under the control of the state. The decided preference of many settlers of the wealthier class for northern and eastern colleges led to a lack of interest in the plan for a state university. Moreover, the resources of the state were still largely undeveloped and the population was sparse and widely scattered. These factors combined to postpone the founding of a state university in Mississippi.[184]

It was not until the decade of the forties that the movement for a state university was revived. Conditions had radically changed. The population had increased and prosperity had resulted from the successful trade in cotton. A new loyalty to southern ideals created a desire for a worthy institution of higher education at home.[185] The people of wealth came to demand an institution of a "revolutionary"

---

[181] Waddel, J. N., *Historical Discourse, June 25, 1873*, 1873 (pamphlet).

[182] Weathersby, W. H., *A History of Educational Legislation in Mississippi from 1798 to 1860*, pp. 82-85, 1921.

[183] *Ibid.*, pp. 86-88.

[184] Mayes, E., *History of Education in Mississippi*, U. S. Bur. of Ed. Cir. Inf., 1899, no. 2, pp. 125-128.

[185] It may be said that the University of Mississippi developed in large part out of the new enthusiasm for state rights, which arose in the decade of the forties in the south.

type in the state and challenged the rights of the church in the field of higher education. The University of Mississippi was established in 1844 and located at Oxford. This new institution was entrusted with the additional township granted by Congress to the state in 1819.[186] While the Board of Trustees was at first self-perpetuating in character, its personnel was representative of the more liberal elements in the state. In 1848 the institution was opened to students. Charges of creating an "infidel institution" were soon leveled at the sponsors of the university, and the institution was characterized as a "rich man's college." [187] By the adoption of a wise policy of conciliation at this time and by the selection of an able faculty, however, the university was able to proceed and to achieve a large measure of success before the Civil War. In 1857 the Governor was made an ex-officio member of the Board of Trustees, and in 1861 the legislature provided that all vacancies on the board were to be filled by the state.[188] Thus after a long and more or less fateful period of experimentation in the field of higher education, the state of Mississippi was able to bring about the establishment of a successful state university.[189]

Alabama was admitted to the Union as a state in 1819, two years after Alabama Territory was separated from the original territory of Mississippi. In 1820 the legislature made provision for the establishment of a state university under the direct control of the legislature.[190] The University of Alabama was granted the right to confer degrees in 1821, and was opened in 1831. The Congressional land grants of 1818 and 1819 were entrusted to the Board of Trustees, and the institution was launched on its unusually successful career. It was located at Tuscaloosa, and enjoyed a patronage from all parts of the state. By the policy of conciliation with the dominant religious interests in the state,[191] the university was able to proceed on its course with less difficulty than was the case

[186] *General Catalogue of the University of Mississippi, 1927-28.* "Historical Statement." In addition to the grant of one township of 1819, the university received from Congress in 1894 a second township in lieu of the one granted to Jefferson College in 1803. See, in this connection, *Memorial to the Congress of the United States from the Board of Trustees of the University of Mississippi,* 1894 (pamphlet).

[187] Waddel, *op. cit.*

[188] Mayes, *op. cit.*, pp. 152, 157.

[189] It is of interest to note that F. A. P. Barnard, later president of Columbia University, was called to the University of Mississippi in 1854 after serving seventeen years at the University of Alabama.

[190] Clark, W. G., *History of Education in Alabama,* U. S. Bur. of Ed. Cir. Inf., 1889, no. 3, p. 32.

[191] The first two presidents, Woods and Manly, were Baptist clergymen, and the Baptists were influential in the direction of the policy of the university.

with state universities in a number of other states. The presence of an able faculty, including such men as F. A. P. Barnard, lent distinction to the institution. The support of powerful interests drawn from the wealthier classes of a prosperous state gave an added measure of stability to the University of Alabama.[192] It is of interest to compare the relative progress of Mississippi and Alabama with respect to the movement for the founding of a state university. Although Mississippi was admitted to the Union two years before Alabama, the University of Mississippi was not founded until 1844, and it was not until 1861 that this institution was placed under the direct control of the state. Alabama, on the other hand, was able to establish a state university under direct state control in 1821, forty years earlier. A large number of reasons might be given for the contrast in the situation between the two states, but it is not possible to present these reasons in this place.[193] It must be added, however, that when Mississippi finally established its state university, the success of the institution soon came to parallel that enjoyed by the University of Alabama.

Missouri was admitted to the Union as a state in 1821. As a border state it was subject to intense partisan strife between the interests of the North and the South with respect to the slavery question throughout the pre-Civil War period. This situation, combined with the sparsity of population and the inadequacy of resources during the early years of its statehood, led to a considerable delay in the organization of a state university. The religious interests in the state, moreover, were consistently opposed to the idea of a state university, and these interests were active in promoting the cause of denominational colleges. The growth of denominational colleges in the state proved inimical to the development of the state university, which was characterized as a "godless institution." In spite of these untoward circumstances, the movement for the establishment of a state university achieved a measure of success before the Civil War.

In 1831 Congress authorized the state to sell the two townships of public land originally reserved in 1818 and 1820, and to apply the interest on the proceeds to the establishment of a state seminary of learning. While the proceeds derived from the sale of these lands

---

[192] Clark, *op. cit.*, p. 33. The invention of the cotton gin in 1795 soon made the cotton trade a lucrative one. In 1827 the population was double that of 1820.

[193] Standard histories of Mississippi and Alabama reveal the differences as well as the similarities in the general development of these two states.

proved to be woefully inadequate, the people in many sections of the state rallied for a time to the support of the proposed institution. In 1839 the Geyer Act was passed. This provided for a comprehensive state university, similar in many respects to the original conceptions of a state university advocated in Virginia by Thomas Jefferson and carried out to some degree in Michigan.[194] The University of the State of Missouri was incorporated by this same Act of 1839, and placed under the direct control of the state. The university was located at Columbia, and was opened in 1841.[195] The relation of the university to the elementary and secondary school system of the state, contemplated in the Act of 1839, was never put into effect, and in 1843 the legal relation between the two was dissolved. During this period, the University of the State of Missouri made some progress in realizing the high ideals of a state university embodied in the Geyer Act; but largely on account of the opposition of religious interests and the increasing partisan feeling in the state over the slavery question, the university was greatly hindered in its development.[196] It was not until after the Civil War that the institution was able to enter into a period of effective service to the state and to the west in general.

One of the most successful state universities in the west before the Civil War was established in *Michigan,* the thirteenth of the new states to be admitted to the Union. A number of favoring circumstances were responsible for the more successful outcome of the movement for a state university in this state. In the earlier years of territorial settlement, the French elements in the population predominated, and some of the features of the Napoleonic "University of France" were adopted by the leaders in the territory in a plan for a comprehensive and centralized system of education.[197] Thus an institution to be known as the University of Michigania, or Catholepistemiad, was chartered in 1817. While this more or less grandiose plan for higher education was not put into actual effect, the general outlines of the scheme were followed to some extent in the later attempts to found a state university. In 1821 a charter was granted

[194] Hough, F. B., *Historical Sketches of the Universities and Colleges of the United States,* p. 13, 1883. The moving of the original tombstone of Thomas Jefferson to the campus of the University of Missouri gives evidence of the lasting respect of the people of Missouri for his influence on the development of their state university.

[195] Lowry, *op. cit.,* p. 14, states that the university was opened for students in 1844, but that date refers to the opening under a reorganized plan.

[196] *Ibid.,* pp. 63, 64.

[197] The charter of the "University of Michigania" is given in full in Ten Brook, *op. cit.,* pp. 91-93, 98.

for the establishment of another institution to be known as the University of Michigan, which was in effect an adaptation of the former institution to the changing character of the territory, in which "Yankee" elements had now come to predominate. This attempt was likewise abortive, largely on account of the lack of an adequate population in the state.

It was not until the migration of eastern settlers assumed large proportions in the decade of the thirties, and the territory became strong enough to take on the rights and obligations of statehood, that a successful institution of higher education was established in Michigan. In 1837, the same year that Michigan became a state, the definitive charter of the University of Michigan was granted by the new state legislature, and launched under a new enthusiasm for higher education on the part of certain interests in the state, who were in this case more or less sympathetic with the German schemes for state education.[198] This institution, like the two former institutions, was to be under direct state control.[199] The Board of Regents was to be appointed by the Governor who, together with the Lieutenant Governor and the Justices of the Supreme Court, were to be ex-officio members of the Board. When these appointments were made by the Governor, they consisted of leaders in the political life of the state to the exclusion of clergymen. Thus the university took on a definite political character at the outset. Congressional land grants of 1826 proved to be unusually successful, as compared with the management of these grants in other states, so the institution was provided from the start with a large measure of financial support. With this auspicious beginning, the University of Michigan entered upon a career of increasing effectiveness.

Serious obstacles, however, were placed in the path of the university from time to time. The denominational interests in the state made an effort to block the university at the outset, and all but succeeded in diverting the purpose of the land grants to their own ends. A change in policy on the part of the University of Michigan, involving the appointment of clergymen on the Board of Trustees,

---

[198] McLaughlin, A. C., *History of Higher Education in Michigan*, U. S. Bur. of Ed. Cir. Inf., 1891, no. 4, pp. 34-35. The influence of Crary and Pierce was determinative.

[199] The University of Michigan of 1837 was declared by the Supreme Court of the state in 1852 to be the legal successor of the universities of 1817 and 1821, but neither of the two earlier dates may be regarded as the definitive date for the founding of the University of Michigan as neither of these institutions was actually organized for purposes of college instruction.

and the appointment of professors representing the religious interests of the state, especially in the branch colleges of the university,
served to rally the support of the denominational groups around
the university for a while and to break down some of the opposition
to the undertaking.[200] Up to the year 1855, the university, by reason of this new coöperative policy, was able to establish a virtual
monopoly over higher education in the state, and denominational
colleges were excluded from the state in a more rigid manner than
in any other state in the Union.[201] By the Constitution of 1850, the
granting of charters to denominational colleges was strictly pro-
hibited. In 1852 Henry P. Tappan was elected to the presidency
of the University of Michigan. Under his influence the institution
was even more closely patterned on the German ideals of higher
education, which were largely secular in character.

In 1855, when the Republican party secured a dominant position
in the state, it brought about the enactment of an act permitting
the establishment of denominational colleges.[202] Thereafter the denominations largely withdrew their support from the university
and set about to establish colleges of their own.[203] Meanwhile the
state university had entered into a new period of power and influence as a state university of a "revolutionary" type under the able
leadership of President Tappan. Thus we find in Michigan a
situation with respect to the development of a state university that
differs markedly from the situation that existed in other states, and
one that more nearly approximated the situation in Virginia in the
east in certain of its aspects than that existing in any other state
in the Union. The University of Michigan, because of its unusual
success as a state university was able to exert a profound influence
upon the development of the state university in the west in the
period before the Civil War.

Iowa was admitted to the Union as a state in 1846. In its territorial days, an institution by the name of Iowa University was in-

[200] An important statement of the religious policy adopted by the University of Michigan
was made in 1838. For text of the same, see Ten Brook, *op. cit.*, pp. 158-59.
[201] The only denominational colleges chartered before 1855 were Marshall College,
chartered in 1839, and Michigan Central College, chartered in 1845 but not given the
right to confer degrees until 1850. See McLaughlin, *op. cit.*, pp. 126, 127; Ten Brook,
op. cit., p. 188; and Michigan Laws, 1839, p. 111.
[202] McLaughlin, *op. cit.*, p. 127.
[203] The opposition of the Methodists to the university in 1857 was in sharp contrast
to their support of the university in the earlier years. The Methodists were even accused,
in the early years, of having a preponderate influence over an institution which the
Presbyterians had the larger share in initiating on rather broad and liberal lines. For
Methodist criticisms of the university in 1857, see Ten Brook, *op. cit.*, pp. 223-224.

corporated and placed under the direct control of the legislature.[204] This institution of 1840 was never organized, however, largely on account of the increasing preference of the Iowa settlers for denominational institutions. In 1847, one year after Iowa became a state, the State University of Iowa was incorporated as a "revolutionary" type of state university, in accordance with the provisions of the Constitution of 1846 and under the stimulus of the land grants approved by Congress in 1840 and 1845.[205] Active opposition on the part of denominational interests to the new state university manifested itself at the outset and served seriously to hinder the development of the institution.[206] After considerable delay, the university was finally opened for students in a limited way at Iowa City in 1855.

Attempts were made during the first ten years to decentralize the university, and branches were actually established at different points in the state, but these branches were all legally severed from the university in 1857.[207] During the same period the denominational interests in the state were able to establish five permanent colleges and a number of other more or less temporary colleges in different parts of the state. These colleges achieved a dominant influence in the state in the period before the Civil War and effectually nullified the movement for the building up of a strong state university. In 1858 the State University of Iowa was placed under the control of the State Board of Education, and in this relationship devoted itself in large part to the work of teacher training. It was not until 1864 that the state university was again brought under direct legislative control. A reorganization of the work of the university was gradually effected, and the State University of Iowa entered upon a career of increasing usefulness to the state.[208]

Wisconsin was admitted to the Union in 1848 as the last of the states to be formed out of the Northwest Territory. During the twelve-year period that it was a separate territory, three abortive attempts were made to establish a state university. Wisconsin University at Belmont, Wisconsin University at Green Bay, and the University of the Territory of Wisconsin were duly incorporated

[204] *Iowa Laws*, 1839-40, p. 126.
[205] Parker, L. F., *Higher Education in Iowa*, U. S. Bur. of Ed. Cir. Inf., 1893, no. 6, pp. 76, 78.
[206] Blackmar, *op. cit.*, p. 291. The denominational interests found the following clause in the Act of 1847 quite disconcerting, viz., "the said university shall never be under the exclusive control of any religious denomination whatever."
[207] *Ibid.*, p. 292.
[208] Aurner, C. R., *History of Education in Iowa*, vol. 4, pp. 42, 46, 1914-20 (5 vols.).

The Founding of State Universities 203

during this period, but were never organized along the lines of a state university.[209] In 1848, the year in which Wisconsin was admitted to the Union, the University of Wisconsin was established as a state university of a "revolutionary" type and located at Madison. It was entrusted with the Congressional land grants of 1838.[210] From the outset the university was faced with a difficult situation, placed as it was in a state where powerful religious interests were entrenched in such denominational colleges as Beloit and Racine, associated with the Congregational and the Episcopal interests, respectively.

In the period between 1855 and 1858, after the state university had fairly started on its career, a severe struggle took place between these interests and the small group of friends of the state university. The very existence of the institution hung in the balance during these years, as successive proposals were made in legislative session for the abandonment of the state university and the division of the land grant funds among the denominational colleges.[211] By the year 1858 the University of Wisconsin clearly saw "the handwriting on the wall" and set about to reorganize its program in such a way as to conciliate the religious interests on the one hand and the popular interests on the other. Henry Barnard was called to the Chancellorship of the University in 1859,[212] and the work of the institution was directed into the channels of the practical sciences and teacher-training subjects which met the popular demands of the day, while less emphasis was put on the classical and liberal subjects which the religious interests regarded as their special preserve. Thus, as the Civil War approached, the University of Wisconsin was on the way to making a real place for itself in the state as a new type of state university. Following the War, the institution was able to carry on more fully its program along these lines with the aid of the Morrill grant, and eventually to broaden its program with the passing of the era of religious controversy.[213]

[209] Allen, W. F. and Spencer, D. E., *Higher Education in Wisconsin*, U. S. Bur. of Ed. Cir. Inf., 1889, no. 1, pp. 11-12.

[210] Thwaites, R. G., *The University of Wisconsin—Its History and Its Alumni*, p. 65, 1900. In 1854 Congress granted to the state of Wisconsin two additional townships as a substitute for a previous grant of two townships of "saline land," making a total grant of four townships for the support of the state university.

[211] Pyre, J. F. A., *Wisconsin*, pp. 108-111, 1920. Of special significance in this connection were the speeches in 1856 and 1858 of Senators Clement and Bennett, respectively, representing Racine College and Beloit College interests. See also, Thwaites, *op. cit.*, pp. 65-72.

[212] Allen and Spencer, *op. cit.*, p. 27. Henry Barnard was forced to resign in 1860 on account of ill health.

[213] Thwaites, *op. cit.*, p. 84. After the reorganization act of 1866, the University of Wisconsin entered upon an era of larger usefulness.

California was admitted to the Union as a state in 1850. The Constitution of 1849 had declared in favor of the establishment of a state university, and in the early sessions of the new state legislature a number of bills calling for the establishment of this institution were introduced. These bills were never passed upon, however, because of a growing sentiment in the state in favor of the establishment of denominational colleges.[214] In 1850 an act was passed providing for the incorporation of colleges in the state by the Supreme Court, and a number of denominational colleges were granted charters under the provisions of this act. Thus the field of higher education in California was given over for the time being to the religious interests. Meanwhile Congress had in 1853 granted the state two townships of public land for a state university. This grant was the subject of much discussion in the state, and the religious interests made several attempts during the ensuing years to divert the grant to the support of denominational colleges in the state. The funds derived from this grant were, however, held inviolate by the legislature for the purposes of a state university.[215]

In 1855 the Act of 1850 was revised in such a way as to give the Board of Education the right to incorporate colleges. Under this revised act, a number of other denominational colleges were granted charters. One of these colleges was the College of California, an institution established in 1855 in Oakland under the auspices of the Congregational and Presbyterian denominations.[216] This institution is of special significance because it proved to be the precursor of the University of California. The friends of the College of California hoped that their institution would in time establish itself so securely in the affections of the state that a state university would be deemed unnecessary. There was the hope that this institution would come to serve the state in the same capacity as Harvard and Yale served the states of Massachusetts and Connecticut.[217] These hopes were soon seen to be illusory, as the movement for the establishment of a state university of a "revolutionary" type gained in power with the passing of the years, and as the fortunes of the College of California were seriously affected by the failure of the de-

---

[214] Jones, W. C., *Illustrated History of the University of California*, pp. 10-13, 1895.
[215] Ferrier, W. W., *Origin and Development of the University of California*, pp. 28, 29, 1930.
[216] Willey, S. H., *A History of the College of California*, p. 8, 1887.
[217] See the "Appeal" of Dr. Horace Bushnell on behalf of the College of California, given in Willey, *op. cit.*, pp. 21-34. See also the proposal for following the plan of the University of the State of New York, Ferrier, *op. cit.*, p. 266.

nominational interests to come to the college's support. Following the Civil War, when the Morrill grant was received by the state, the Trustees of the College of California became convinced that the wisest policy for the institution under the circumstances was to turn over its property and its rights to the state and become incorporated as a constituent and central unit in the projected university. Formal action was taken on these lines and acquiesced in by the state.[218] Thus, in 1868, the University of California was established on the foundation of a private institution and launched upon a distinctive career in the field of higher education in the state.

Minnesota was admitted to the Union as a state in 1858. In 1851, during its early territorial days, the University of Minnesota was incorporated as a state university of an advanced type. This institution was not, however, organized for the purposes of college instruction until after the Civil War. During the intervening years, the Regents of the University were engaged chiefly in handling the finances of the prospective institution. A grant of 46,080 acres, or two townships, of public land was "reserved" for the territory in 1851 by Congress for the support of a seminary of learning.[219] This grant was not "donated" to the state until 1861, but meanwhile the Regents had embarked upon a perilous financial program based on the hope of receiving large dividends from the land grant, which brought the institution to the point of insolvency at the time of the panic of 1857. In that year Congress was induced to grant in the enabling act of the state two townships of public land for the benefit of the state university in addition, it was assumed by the state, to the two townships previously granted to the territory.[220] At a later date, the General Land Office of the United States refused to turn over these additional townships on the ground that it had not been explicitly stated in the Act of 1857 that the grant was to be an additional one. It was not until 1870 that Congress was persuaded to pass a special Act authorizing the additional townships.[221]

[218] Jones, *op. cit.*, pp. 38-39. For added points of significance relating to the movement for a state university in California, see *ibid.*, pp. 34, 37, and Willey, *op. cit.*, pp. 57, 58, and Ferrier, *op cit.*, p. 281.

[219] Greer, J. N., *History of Education in Minnesota*, U. S. Bur. of Ed. Cir. Inf., 1902, no. 2, p. 95. The territory had petitioned for a grant of one hundred thousand acres.

[220] Gilfillan, J. B., "History of the University of Minnesota," *Collections of the Minnesota Historical Society*, vol. 12, p. 61, 1908. In the Act of 1857, the usual clause specifying that the two townships were not an additional grant but a confirmation of a previous grant was omitted. Stephen A. Douglas was instrumental in phrasing this particular Act.

[221] Johnson, E. B., Editor, *Forty Years of the University of Minnesota*, p. 90, 1910.

In these circumstances it was inevitable that the development of the University of Minnesota should be for a number of years seriously retarded. An attempt was made in 1860 to reorganize the institution in order that it might be possible to initiate instruction at least along the lines of teacher training,[222] but this attempt proved largely unsuccessful. With the approach of the Civil War the interests of the people were turned aside, and the continued opposition of the religious interests in the state made it impossible to carry out the "revolutionary" ideals of the friends of the state university.[223] Following the Civil War, however, the Morrill Act gave a new impetus to the movement for the organization of the state university, and in 1868 the University of Minnesota was reorganized under a new and comprehensive charter, and launched upon a career of real usefulness to the state and the nation.

In the light of this general survey of the movement for the founding of state universities in this country, it will be seen that the "revolutionary" ideals of higher education advocated during the early years of our national life were realized in practice in only a few of the state universities before the Civil War.[224] In almost every instance, the state institutions that were established encountered serious opposition from the religious interests which were in control of higher education during the middle period of our history. The American people, it would seem, were not willing in that era to accept the apparent implications of the principle of the separation of church and state, which called for state universities of a more or less secular character. Thus the state universities of this country were obliged to pass through a long period of disfavor before they finally won for themselves a secure place in the affections of the people. With the profound changes that took place during the period immediately preceding and following the Civil War, there arose a popular demand for a type of higher education that would be more directly responsive to the needs of a new day. Increasing dissatisfaction with the reign of sectarianism in higher education manifested itself in many parts of the country.[225] The field of higher education had too long been regarded as the private preserve

---

[222] Greer, *op. cit.*, p. 97.

[223] *Ibid.*, p. 100, footnote, which indicates the type of opposition encountered by the state university throughout the pre-Civil War period.

[224] The University of Virginia in the east and the University of Michigan in the west were able to achieve greater success during the period before the Civil War than perhaps any of the other state universities in the country.

[225] Sturtevant, J. M., Jr., Editor, *Autobiography of J. M. Sturtevant*, p. 189, 1896.

of the denominations. In response to the new social, political, and economic ideals of the day, the state university movement soon took on new strength and power. Thus the state universities in this country were enabled to enter upon a larger sphere of influence in American life. The purposes of higher education, so boldly set forth in the following quotation from the report of Thomas Jefferson on the University of Virginia, were now to find a larger fulfillment in the state universities of this country:

To form the statesmen, legislators, and judges, on whom public prosperity and individual happiness are so much to depend; to expound the principles of government, the laws which regulate the intercourse of nations, those formed municipally for our own government, and a sound spirit of legislation, which, banishing all arbitrary and unnecessary restraint on individual action, shall leave us free to do whatever does not violate the equal rights of another; to harmonize and promote the interests of agriculture, manufactures, and commerce, and by well-informed views of political economy to give free scope to the public industry; to develop the reasoning faculties of our youth, enlarge their minds, cultivate their morals, and instill into them the precepts of virtue and order; to enlighten them with mathematical and physical sciences, and advance the arts and administer to the health, the subsistence, and the comforts of human life; and finally to form them into habits of reflection and correct action, rendering them examples of virtue to others and of happiness within themselves. These are the objects of that higher grade of education, the benefits and blessings of which the Legislature now propose to provide for the good and ornament of their country, and the gratification and happiness of their fellow-citizens.[226]

[226] *Proceedings and Report of the Commissioners for the University of Virginia,* presented December 8, 1818, Richmond, Va.

Appendix

APPENDIX

LIST OF PERMANENT COLLEGES AND UNIVERSITIES FOUNDED BEFORE THE CIVIL WAR ARRANGED BY STATES

This list is a rearrangement according to states of the general list given at the end of Chapter I, and provides a basis for a more intensive study of the development of higher education in each of the states. A summary table of this list is given on page 31.

1. *ALABAMA*

S.N.	I.N.	PRESENT NAME AND LOCATION	CHARTER-DEGREE DATE
1	A50	University of Alabama, Tuscaloosa (State)	*December 18, 1821*
2	A75	Spring Hill College, Spring Hill (Catholic)	*January 9, 1836*
3	A103	Howard College, Birmingham (Baptist)	*December 29, 1841*
4	A131	Birmingham-Southern College, Birmingham (Methodist)	*January 25, 1856*

2. *ARKANSAS*

(No permanent colleges chartered before the Civil War.)

3. *CALIFORNIA*

1	A171	College of the Pacific, Stockton (Methodist)	*July 10, 1851*
2	A195	University of California, Berkeley (Congregational-Presbyterian, then State)	*April 13, 1855*
3	A177	Santa Clara College, Santa Clara (Catholic)	*April 28, 1855*
4	A162	St. Ignatius College, San Francisco (Catholic)	*April 30, 1859*

4. *CONNECTICUT*

1	A3	Yale University, New Haven (Congregational)	*October 16, 1701*
2	A39	Trinity College, Hartford (Episcopal)	*May 22, 1823*
3	A65	Wesleyan University, Middletown (Methodist)	*May 26, 1831*

5. *DELAWARE*

S.N.	I.N.	PRESENT NAME AND LOCATION	CHARTER-DEGREE DATE
1	A84	University of Delaware, Newark.........*February 5, 1833*	
		(Presbyterian, then State)	

(*DISTRICT OF COLUMBIA*)

1	A33	Georgetown College, Washington.........*March 1, 1815*	
		(Catholic)	
2	A38	George Washington University, Washington.*February 9, 1821*	
		(Baptist)	

6. *FLORIDA*

(No permanent colleges chartered before the Civil War.)

7. *GEORGIA*

1	A14	University of Georgia, Athens...........*January 27, 1785*	
		(State)	
2	A76	Oglethorpe University, Atlanta...........*December 21, 1835*	
		(Presbyterian)	
3	A78	Emory University, Atlanta ....*December 10, 1836*	
		(Methodist)	
4	A89	Wesleyan College, Macon...............*December 23, 1836*	
		(Methodist)	
5	A74	Mercer University, Macon ....*December 22, 1837*	
		(Baptist)	
6	A123	Lagrange Female College, Lagrange.......*December 17, 1847*	
		(Methodist)	

8. *ILLINOIS*

1	A62	Illinois College, Jacksonville.............*February 9, 1835*	
		(Congregational-Presbyterian, then Presbyterian)	
2	A67	McKendree College, Lebanon...........*February 9, 1835*	
		(Methodist)	
3	A82	Shurtleff College, Alton................*February 9, 1835*	
		(Baptist)	
4	A83	Knox College, Galesburg................*February 15, 1837*	
		(Congregational-Presbyterian, then Congregational)	
5	A112	Rockford College, Rockford.............*February 25, 1847*	
		(Congregational-Presbyterian, then Congregational)	
6	A169	Northwestern University, Evanston.......*January 28, 1851*	
		(Methodist)	
7	A185	Lombard College, Galesburg.............*February 15, 1851*	
		(Universalist)	
8	A188	Illinois Wesleyan University, Bloomington.*February 12, 1853*	
		(Methodist)	

8. *ILLINOIS* (*Continued*)

S.N.	I.N.	PRESENT NAME AND LOCATION	CHARTER-DEGREE DATE
9	A167	Eureka College, Eureka (Disciples)	*February 6, 1855*
10	A91	Wheaton College, Wheaton (Methodist, then Congregational)	*February 15, 1855*
11	A145	Lake Forest University, Lake Forest (Presbyterian)	*February 13, 1857*
12	A149	Monmouth College, Monmouth (Presbyterian)	*February 16, 1857*

9. *INDIANA*

1	A46	Indiana University, Bloomington (State)	*January 24, 1828*
2	A57	Hanover College, Hanover (Presbyterian)	*January 1, 1833*
3	A59	Wabash College, Crawfordsville (Presbyterian)	*January 15, 1834*
4	A96	Franklin College, Franklin (Baptist)	*January 30, 1836*
5	A73	DePauw University, Greencastle (Methodist)	*January 10, 1837*
6	A105	University of Notre Dame, Notre Dame (Catholic)	*January 15, 1844*
7	A94	Taylor University, Upland (Methodist)	*January 18, 1847*
8	A139	Earlham College, Earlham (Friends)	*January 4, 1850*
9	A107	Butler University, Indianapolis (Disciples)	*January 15, 1850*

10. *IOWA*

1	A120	State University of Iowa, Iowa City (State)	*February 25, 1847*
2	A109	Grinnell College, Grinnell (Congregational-Presbyterian, then Congregational)	*June 17, 1847*
3	A165	Central University, Pella (Baptist, then Reformed)	*June 3, 1853*
4	A136	Cornell College, Mt. Vernon (Methodist)	*February —, 1854*
5	A168	Iowa Wesleyan College, Mt. Pleasant (Methodist)	*January 25, 1855*
6	A92	Upper Iowa University, Fayette (Methodist)	*April 5, 1856*

11. *KANSAS*

S.N.	I.N.	PRESENT NAME AND LOCATION	CHARTER-DEGREE DATE
1	A134	Baker University, Baldwin	*February 12, 1858*
		(Methodist)	

12. *KENTUCKY*

1	A24	Transylvania College, Lexington	*May 5, 1783*
		(Presbyterian, then Others)	
2	A35	Centre College, Danville	*January 21, 1819*
		(Presbyterian)	
3	A47	Georgetown College, Georgetown	*January 15, 1829*
		(Baptist)	
4	A61	St. Mary's College, St. Mary's	*January 21, 1837*
		(Catholic)	
5	A187	University of Kentucky, Lexington	*February 23, 1837*
		(Disciples, then State)	
6	A90	University of Louisville, Louisville	*February 7, 1846*
		(Municipal)	

13. *LOUISIANA*

1	A43	Centenary College of Louisiana, Shreveport .	*February 18, 1825*
		(Semi-State, then Methodist)	
2	A121	Tulane University, New Orleans	*February 16, 1847*
		(Semi-State)	
3	A194	Louisiana State University, Baton Rouge . .	*March 31, 1853*
		(State)	

14. *MAINE*

1	A20	Bowdoin College, Brunswick	*June 24, 1794*
		(Congregational)	
2	A49	Colby College, Waterville	*June 19, 1820*
		(Baptist)	

15. *MARYLAND*

1	A10	Washington College, Chestertown	*April —, 1782*
		(Episcopal)	
2	A13	St. John's College, Annapolis	*November —, 1784*
		(Episcopal)	
3	A48	University of Maryland, Baltimore	*December 29, 1812*
		(State)	
4	A72	Mt. St. Mary's College, Emmitsburg	*February 27, 1830*
		(Catholic)	
5	A87	Loyola College, Baltimore	*April 13, 1853*
		(Catholic)	

16. *MASSACHUSETTS*

| 1 | A1 | Harvard University, Cambridge . . . . | *October 28, 1636* |
| | | (Congregational, then Unitarian) | |

16. *MASSACHUSETTS* (*Continued*)

S.N.	I.N.	PRESENT NAME AND LOCATION	CHARTER-DEGREE DATE
2	A19	Williams College, Williamstown.........*June 22, 1793* (Congregational)	
3	A42	Amherst College, Amherst..............*February 21, 1825* (Congregational)	
4	A153	Tufts College, Tufts College............*April 21, 1852* (Universalist)	

17. *MICHIGAN*

1	A51	University of Michigan, Ann Arbor.......*March 18, 1837* (State)	
2	A54	Adrian College, Adrian.................*April 16, 1839* (Presbyterian, then Methodist)	
3	A175	Albion College, Albion.................*February 18, 1850* (Methodist)	
4	A144	Hillsdale College, Hillsdale ....*March 20, 1850* (Baptist)	
5	A193	Kalamazoo College, Kalamazoo ....*February 10, 1855* (Baptist)	
6	A53	Olivet College, Olivet.................——— —, *1859* (Congregational)	

18. *MINNESOTA*

1	A154	University of Minnesota, Minneapolis....*February 13, 1851* (State)	
2	A142	Hamline University, St. Paul.. ....*March 3, 1854* (Methodist)	

19. *MISSISSIPPI*

1	A55	Mississippi College, Clinton.............*December 16, 1830* (Semi-State, Presbyterian, then Baptist)	
2	A114	University of Mississippi, Oxford........*February 24, 1844* (State)	

20. *MISSOURI*

1	A79	St. Louis University, St. Louis...........*December 28, 1832* (Catholic)	
2	A70	University of Missouri, Columbia........*February 11, 1839* (State)	
3	A117	William Jewell College, Liberty..........*February 27, 1849* (Baptist)	
4	A158	Westminster College, Fulton.............*February 18, 1851* (Presbyterian)	
5	A137	Culver-Stockton College, Canton........*January 28, 1853* (Disciples)	
6	A157	Washington University, St. Louis........*February 22, 1853* (Unitarian)	

20. *MISSOURI* (*Continued*)

S.N.	I.N.	PRESENT NAME AND LOCATION	CHARTER-DEGREE DATE
7	A146	Lindenwood Female College, St. Charles (Presbyterian)	*February 24, 1853*
8	A164	Central College, Fayette (Methodist)	*March 1, 1855*

21. *NEW HAMPSHIRE*

| 1 | A9 | Dartmouth College, Hanover (Congregational) | *December 13, 1769* |

22. *NEW JERSEY*

1	A4	Princeton University, Princeton (Presbyterian)	*October 22, 1746*
2	A8	Rutgers University, New Brunswick (Dutch Reformed)	*November 10, 1766*
3	A52	Seton Hall College, South Orange (Catholic)	*March 8, 1861*

23. *NEW YORK*

1	A5	Columbia University, New York (Episcopal)	*October 31, 1754*
2	A23	Union University, Schenectady (Presbyterian and Others)	*February 25, 1795*
3	A31	Hamilton College, Clinton (Presbyterian)	*May 26, 1812*
4	A41	Hobart College, Geneva (Episcopal)	*February 8, 1825*
5	A64	New York University, New York (Presbyterian and Others)	*April 18, 1831*
6	A56	Colgate University, Hamilton (Baptist)	*March 26, 1846*
7	A108	Fordham University, Fordham (Catholic)	*April 10, 1846*
8	A104	University of Buffalo, Buffalo (Presbyterian)	*May 11, 1846*
9	A155	University of Rochester, Rochester (Baptist)	*February 14, 1851*
10	A140	Elmira College, Elmira (Presbyterian)	*January 29, 1852*
11	A135	College of the City of New York, New York (Municipal)	*April 15, 1854*
12	A152	St. Lawrence University, Canton (Universalist)	*April 3, 1856*
13	A133	Alfred University, Alfred (Baptist)	*March 28, 1857*

23. *NEW YORK* (*Continued*)

S.N.	I.N.	PRESENT NAME AND LOCATION	CHARTER-DEGREE DATE
14	A129	St. Stephen's College, Annandale......... (Episcopal)	*March 20, 1860*
15	A130	Vassar College, Poughkeepsie............ (Baptist)	*January 18, 1861*

24. *NORTH CAROLINA*

1	A17	University of North Carolina, Chapel Hill. (State)	*December 11, 1789*
2	A63	Wake Forest College, Wake Forest....... (Baptist)	*December 26, 1838*
3	A66	Davidson College, Davidson............. (Presbyterian)	*December 28, 1838*
4	A88	Greensboro College, Greensboro.......... (Methodist)	*December 28, 1838*
5	A138	Duke University, Durham............... (Methodist)	*November 21, 1852*
6	A183	Catawba College, Salisbury............. (German Reformed)	*December 17, 1852*

25. *OHIO*

1	A28	Ohio University, Athens................. (State)	*January 9, 1802*
2	A30	Miami University, Oxford.............. (State)	*February 17, 1809*
3	A40	Kenyon College, Gambier .... (Episcopal)	*January 24, 1826*
4	A44	Western Reserve University, Cleveland.... (Congregational-Presbyterian)	*February 7, 1826*
5	A68	Denison University, Granville............ (Baptist)	*February 2, 1832*
6	A71	Oberlin College, Oberlin................ (Congregational)	*February 28, 1834*
7	A69	Marietta College, Marietta.............. (Congregational)	*February 14, 1835*
8	A85	Muskingum College, New Concord....... (Presbyterian)	*March 18, 1837*
9	A192	St. Xavier College, Cincinnati........... (Catholic)	*March 5, 1842*
10	A118	Ohio Wesleyan University, Delaware...... (Methodist)	*March 7, 1842*
11	A116	Wittenberg College, Springfield.......... (Lutheran)	*March 11, 1845*
12	A176	Baldwin-Wallace College, Berea.......... (Methodist)	*December 20, 1845*

25. OHIO (*Continued*)

S.N.	I.N.	PRESENT NAME AND LOCATION	CHARTER-DEGREE DATE
13	A127	Otterbein College, Westerville .... (United Brethren)	*February 13, 1849*
14	A132	Capital University, Columbus............ (Lutheran)	*March 2, 1850*
15	A143	Heidelberg College, Tiffin............... (German Reformed)	*February 13, 1851*
16	A191	Antioch College, Yellow Springs.......... (Christian)	*May 14, 1852*
17	A150	Mt. Union College, Alliance............. (Methodist)	*January 9, 1858*

26. OREGON

1	A159	Willamette University, Salem............ (Methodist)	*January 12, 1853*
2	A170	Pacific University, Forest Grove.......... (Congregational-Presbyterian, then Congregational)	*January 13, 1854*

27. PENNSYLVANIA

1	A6	University of Pennsylvania, Philadelphia.. (Episcopal, then Presbyterian)	*June 16, 1755*
2	A12	Dickinson College, Carlisle.............. (Presbyterian, then Methodist)	*September 9, 1783*
3	A16	Franklin and Marshall College, Lancaster.. (German Reformed)	*March 10, 1787*
4	A27	Washington and Jefferson College, Washington .... (Presbyterian)	*January 15, 1802*
5	A34	Allegheny College, Meadville .... (Presbyterian, then Methodist)	*March 24, 1817*
6	A36	University of Pittsburgh, Pittsburgh...... (Presbyterian)	*February 18, 1819*
7	A45	Lafayette College, Easton............... (Presbyterian)	*March 9, 1826*
8	A80	Gettysburg College, Gettysburg .... (Lutheran)	*April 7, 1832*
9	A106	Bucknell University, Lewisburg .... (Baptist)	*February 5, 1846*
10	A115	Augustinian College of Villanova, Villanova. (Catholic)	*March 10, 1848*
11	A95	Geneva College, Beaver Falls............ (Presbyterian)	*March 7, 1850*
12	A178	Waynesburg College, Waynesburg .... (Presbyterian)	*March 25, 1850*
13	A151	St. Joseph's College, Philadelphia .... (Catholic)	*January 29, 1852*

27. *PENNSYLVANIA* (*Continued*)

S.N.	I.N.	PRESENT NAME AND LOCATION	CHARTER-DEGREE DATE
14	A190	Westminster College, New Wilmington.... *April 27, 1852* (Presbyterian)	
15	A166	Haverford College, Haverford .... *March 15, 1856* (Friends)	
16	A179	Irving Female College, Mechanicsburg .... *March 28, 1857* (Lutheran)	

28. *RHODE ISLAND*

| 1 | A7 | Brown University, Providence............ *October 24, 1765* (Baptist) | |

29. *SOUTH CAROLINA*

1	A15	College of Charleston, Charleston......... *March 19, 1785* (Episcopal, then Municipal)	
2	A26	University of South Carolina, Columbia... *December 14, 1805* (State)	
3	A189	Erskine College, Due West............. *December 20, 1850* (Presbyterian)	
4	A141	Furman University, Greenville........... *December 20, 1850* (Baptist)	
5	A160	Wofford College, Spartanburg............ *December 16, 1851* (Methodist)	
6	A184	Columbia College, Columbia............. *December 21, 1854* (Methodist)	
7	A174	Newberry College, Newberry .... *December 20, 1856* (Lutheran)	

30. *TENNESSEE*

1	A21	Tusculum College, Greeneville........... *September 3, 1794* (Presbyterian)	
2	A22	University of Tennessee, Knoxville....... *September 10, 1794* (Presbyterian, then State)	
3	A111	Maryville College, Maryville............. *January 14, 1842* (Presbyterian)	
4	A93	Union University, Jackson.............. *February 5, 1842* (Baptist)	
5	A122	Cumberland University, Lebanon......... *December 30, 1843* (Presbyterian)	
6	A163	Bethel College, McKenzie.............. *February 3, 1850* (Presbyterian)	
7	A182	Carson and Newman College, Jefferson City. *December 5, 1851* (Baptist)	
8	A156	University of the South, Sewanee......... *January 6, 1858* (Episcopal)	

31. *TEXAS*

S.N.	I.N.	PRESENT NAME AND LOCATION	CHARTER-DEGREE DATE
1	A100	Baylor University, Waco ....*February 1, 1845*	
		(Baptist)	
2	A98	Austin College, Sherman................*November 22, 1849*	
		(Presbyterian)	

32. *VERMONT*

1	A18	University of Vermont, Burlington.......*November 3, 1791*	
		(State)	
2	A25	Middlebury College, Middlebury.........*November 1, 1800*	
		(Congregational)	
3	A81	Norwich University, Northfield ....*November 6, 1834*	
		(Universalist)	

33. *VIRGINIA*

1	A2	College of William and Mary, Williamsburg.*February 8, 1693*	
		(Episcopal)	
2	A32	Washington and Lee University, Lexington.*October —, 1782*	
		(Presbyterian)	
3	A11	Hampden-Sidney College, Hampden-Sidney.*May —, 1783*	
		(Presbyterian)	
4	A37	University of Virginia, Charlottesville.....*February 14, 1816*	
		(State)	
5	A58	Randolph-Macon College, Ashland........*February 3, 1830*	
		(Methodist)	
6	A77	Emory and Henry College, Emory.......*March 25, 1839*	
		(Methodist)	
7	A101	Bethany College, Bethany (W. Va.).......*March 2, 1840*	
		(Disciples)	
8	A97	University of Richmond, Richmond.......*March 4, 1840*	
		(Baptist)	
9	A173	Roanoke College, Salem.................*March 14, 1853*	
		(Lutheran)	

34. *WISCONSIN*

1	A99	Carroll College, Waukesha...............*January 31, 1846*	
		(Presbyterian)	
2	A102	Beloit College, Beloit...................*February 2, 1846*	
		(Congregational-Presbyterian, then Congregational)	
3	A124	University of Wisconsin, Madison ....*July 26, 1848*	
		(State)	
4	A110	Lawrence College, Appleton ....*January 15, 1847*	
		(Methodist)	
5	A172	Ripon College, Ripon..................*January 29, 1851*	
6	A147	Milwaukee-Downer College, Milwaukee...*March 1, 1851*	
		(Congregational-Presbyterian, then Congregational)	

Bibliography

BIBLIOGRAPHY

A. HISTORICAL REFERENCES ON THE ONE HUNDRED AND EIGHTY-TWO PERMANENT COLLEGES FOUNDED BEFORE THE CIVIL WAR

(Arranged alphabetically to serve as an index)

A54   *Adrian College,* Adrian, Mich.

A50   *University of Alabama,* Tuscaloosa, Ala.

Barnard, F. A. P. and Pratt, J. W. Report on a Proposition to Modify the Plan of Instruction in the University of Alabama. New York, 1855 pamphlet.

Manly, B. Report on Collegiate Education. Tuscaloosa, Ala., 1852 pamphlet.

A175   *Albion College,* Albion, Mich.

A133   *Alfred University,* Alfred, N. Y.

Semi-Centennial Souvenir (1857-1907).

A34   *Allegheny College,* Meadville, Pa.

Smith, E. A. Allegheny, A Century of Education (1815-1915). Meadville, Pa., 1916.

A42   *Amherst College,* Amherst, Mass.

Constitution and System of By-Laws of the Charity Fund of Amherst College, with an Historical Appendix. Amherst, Mass., 1881.

Hitchcock, E. Reminiscences of Amherst College. Northampton, Mass., 1863.

Humphrey, H. Sketches of the Early History of Amherst College. Northampton, Mass., 1905 pamphlet.

Tyler, W. S. A History of Amherst College (1821-1891). New York, 1894.

A191   *Antioch College,* Yellow Springs, O.

Articles of Incorporation of Antioch College. Xenia, O., 1875 pamphlet.

A98   *Austin College,* Sherman, Tex.

A134   *Baker University,* Baldwin, Kan.

A176   *Baldwin-Wallace College,* Berea, O.

A100   *Baylor University,* Waco, Tex.

A102   *Beloit College,* Beloit, Wisc.

Eaton, E. D. Historical Sketches of Beloit College. New York, 1928.

Emerson, J. Address. Beloit, Wisc., 1857 pamphlet.

A101 *Bethany College,* Bethany, W. Va.
A163 *Bethel College,* McKenzie, Tenn.
A131 *Birmingham-Southern College,* Birmingham, Ala.
    Christenberry, D. P.   Semicentennial History of the Southern University (1856-1906).   Greensboro, Ala., 1908.
    Perry, W. D.   A History of Birmingham-Southern College.   1931.
A20 *Bowdoin College,* Brunswick, Me.
    Addresses and Poems on the Occasion of the One-Hundredth Anniversary of the Incorporation of Bowdoin College, June 27 and 28, 1894.   Brunswick, Me., 1894 pamphlet.
    Cleaveland, N. and Packard, A. S.   History of Bowdoin College.   Boston, 1882.
    Hatch, L. C.   The History of Bowdoin College.   Portland, Me., 1927.
    Packard, A. S.   Our Alma Mater.   Brunswick, Me., 1858.
    Smyth, E. C.   Three Discourses upon the Religious History of Bowdoin College.   Brunswick Me., 1858.
A7 *Brown University,* Providence, R. I.
    Bronson, W. C.   History of Brown University (1764-1914).   Providence, R. I., 1914.
    Brown, R. P., Editor.   Memories of Brown.   Providence, R. I., 1909.
    Celebration of the One-Hundredth Anniversary of the Founding of Brown University, Sept. 6, 1864.   Providence, R. I., 1865.
    Guild, R. A.   Early History of Brown University (1756-1791).   Providence, R. I., 1897.
    Guild, R. A.   History of Brown University.   Providence, R. I., 1867.
    Guild, R. A.   Manning and Brown University.   Boston, 1864.
    Keen, W. W.   The Early Years of Brown University (1764-1770).   Boston, 1914 pamphlet.
    Pitman, I.   Address to the Alumni Association of Brown University, Sept. 5, 1843.   Providence, R. I., 1843 pamphlet.
A106 *Bucknell University,* Lewisburg, Pa.
    Gretzinger, W. C.   An Historical Sketch of Bucknell University.   Lewisburg, Pa., 1890.
A104 *University of Buffalo,* Buffalo, N. Y.
    Park, Julian.   History of the University of Buffalo (1846-1917).   Buffalo, N. Y., 1917 in Publications of the Buffalo Historical Society, Volume 22.
A107 *Butler University,* Indianapolis, Ind.
A195 *University of California,* Berkeley, Cal.
    Ferrier, W. W.   Origin and Development of the University of California.   Berkeley, Cal., 1930.
    Jones, W. C.   Illustrated History of the University of California.   Berkeley, Cal., 1895 (Rev. Ed. 1901).

Sibley, R., Editor. Romance of the University of California. San Francisco, Cal., 1928.

Willey, S. A. A History of the College of California. San Francisco, Cal., 1887.

A132   *Capital University,* Columbus, O.

A99   *Carroll College,* Waukesha, Wisc.

A182   *Carson and Newman College,* Jefferson City, Tenn.

A183   *Catawba College,* Salisbury, N. C.

Leonard, J. C. History of Catawba College. 1927.

A43   *Centenary College of Louisiana,* Shreveport, La.

Nelson, W. H. A Burning Bush and a Flaming Fire—A Story of Centenary College of Louisiana. Nashville, Tenn., 1931.

A164   *Central College,* Fayette, Mo.

A165   *Central University,* Pella, Ia.

A35   *Centre College,* Danville, Ky.

Breckinridge, W. C. P. Address before the Alumni Association of Centre College. Danville, Ky., 1885 pamphlet.

Humphrey, E. P. Statement and Appeal in Behalf of Centre College. Catalogue of the College. 1873.

A15   *College of Charleston,* Charleston, S. C.

A49   *Colby College,* Waterville, Me.

Champlin, J. T. Historical Discourse Delivered at the Fiftieth Anniversary of Colby University. Waterville, Me., 1870 pamphlet.

Chipman, C. P. The Formative Period in Colby's History. Waterville, Me., 1912 pamphlet.

Whittemore, E. C. History of Colby College. 1927.

A56   *Colgate University,* Hamilton, N. Y.

Alton, A. E. et al., Editors. Colgate University Centennial Celebration. Hamilton, N. Y., 1920.

Bronson, B. F. et al., Editors. The First Half-Century of Madison University. New York, 1872.

Historical Sketch of Madison University. Hamilton, N. Y., 1852 pamphlet.

Rosenberger, J. L. Rochester and Colgate. Chicago, 1925.

A184   *Columbia College,* Columbia, S. C.

A5   *Columbia University,* New York, N. Y.

Jay, J. Columbia College. New York, 1876 pamphlet.

Keppel, F. P. Columbia. New York, 1914.

Keppel, F. P., Editor. History of Columbia University (1754-1904). New York, 1904.

Moore, G. H. The Origin and Early History of Columbia College. New York, 1890.

Moore, N. F. A Historical Sketch of Columbia College (1754-1876). New York, 1846. Revised in 1876 by Van Amringe.

Nelson, C. A., Compiler. Columbiana, A Bibliography. Columbia University, 1904.

Pine, J. B. King's College and the Early Days of Columbia College. New York, 1917 pamphlet.

Van Amringe, J. H. Columbia University, in Chamberlain, J. L., Editor, Universities and Their Sons. Boston, 1898. 5 vols.

A136 *Cornell College,* Mt. Vernon, Ia.

A137 *Culver-Stockton College,* Canton, Mo.

A122 *Cumberland University,* Lebanon, Tenn.

A9 *Dartmouth College,* Hanover, N. H.

Charter and Historical Sketch of Dartmouth College. Hanover, N. H., 1900 pamphlet.

Chase, F. A History of Dartmouth College (1735-1815). Cambridge, Mass., 1891.

Crosby, N. First Half Century of Dartmouth College. Hanover, N. H., 1876 pamphlet.

Gerould, J. T. Bibliography of Dartmouth College. Concord, N. H., 1894.

Lord, John K. A History of Dartmouth College (1815-1909). Concord, N. H., 1913. 2 vols.

Quint, W. S. The Story of Dartmouth. New York, 1914.

Smith, B. P. History of Dartmouth College. Boston, 1878.

Wheelock, E. A Plain and Faithful Narrative of the Moor's Charity-School at Lebanon in Connecticut. Boston, 1763 pamphlet.

A66 *Davidson College,* Davidson, N. C.

Shaw, C. R. History of Davidson College. New York, 1923.

Withers, W. A., Editor. Semicentennial Catalogue of Davidson College (1837-1887). Raleigh, N. C., 1891.

A84 *University of Delaware,* Newark, Del.

A68 *Denison University,* Granville, O.

Memorial Volume of Denison University (1831-1906). Granville, O., 1907.

Shepardson, F. W. Denison University (1831-1931). Granville, O., 1931.

A73 *DePauw University,* Greencastle, Ind.

Brown, I. F. Bulletin of DePauw University. Historical Number. 1914.

Semicentennial Reminiscences and Historical Addresses (1837-1887). Greencastle, Ind., 1887 pamphlet.

A12 *Dickinson College,* Carlisle, Pa.

Crooks, G. R. The History of a Hundred Years. 1883 pamphlet.

Himes, C. F. A Sketch of Dickinson College. Harrisburg, Pa., 1879.

King, H. C. History of Dickinson College. New York, 1897.

Narrative of the Proceedings of the Board of Trustees of Dickinson College from 1821 to 1830. Carlisle, Pa., 1830 pamphlet.

Super, C. W. A Pioneer College and Its Background. Salem, Mass., 1923.

A138   *Duke University*, Durham, N. C.
  Craven, B. Historical Sketch of Trinity College, in Centennial
   of Methodism in North Carolina.
  History of Government of Duke University, pamphlet.
  Spence, H. E. The Development of Duke University. Alumni
   Register of Duke University, January 1926.
A139   *Earlham College*, Earlham, Ind.
A140   *Elmira College*, Elmira, N. Y.
A78 *Emory University*, Atlanta, Ga.
A77 *Emory and Henry College*, Emory, Va.
  Davis, F. M. Semicentennial Bulletin.
A189   *Erskine College*, Due West, S. C.
A167   *Eureka College*, Eureka, Ill.
  Dickinson, E. J., Editor. A History of Eureka College. 1894.
A108   *Fordham University*, New York, N. Y.
  Taafe, T. G. History of St. John's College. Fordham, N. Y.,
   1891.
A96 *Franklin College*, Franklin, Ind.
  First Half Century of Franklin College. 1884.
A16 *Franklin and Marshall College*, Lancaster, Pa.
  Charters and Acts of Assembly Relating to Franklin and Marshall
   College. Lancaster, Pa., 1914.
  Dubbs, J. H. History of Franklin and Marshall College. Lan-
   caster, Pa., 1903.
A141   *Furman University*, Greenville, S. C.
  McGlothlin, W. J. Baptist Beginnings in Education: A History
   of Furman University. 1926.
A47 *Georgetown College*, Georgetown, Ky.
  Historical Catalogue of Georgetown College (1829-1917). George-
   town, Ky., 1917.
  Manly, B. Past and Future of Georgetown College.
  Meyer, L. W. Georgetown College. Louisville, Ky., 1929.
  Moreland, J. A History of Georgetown College.
  Yager, A., Historical Sketch of Georgetown College. Georgetown,
   Ky., 1904.
A33 *Georgetown College*, Washington, D. C.
  Easby-Smith, J. S. Georgetown University in the District of Co-
   lumbia (1789-1907). New York, 1907. 2 vols.
  Hodgkins, H. L. Historical Sketch. 1883.
  Shea, J. G. History of Georgetown College. Washington, D. C.,
   1891.
A38 *George Washington University*, Washington, D. C.
  Claims of the Columbian College. Washington, 1857 pamphlet.
  Cobb, R. George Washington University: Its Growth and Indi-
   viduality. Washington, D. C., 1916 pamphlet.
  History of the Columbian College.

Staughton, W.   Address Delivered at the Opening of the Columbian College in the District of Columbia January 9th, 1822. Washington, D. C., 1822.

Stockton, C. H.   A Historical Sketch of George Washington University.   Washington, D. C., 1915 pamphlet.

A14   *University of Georgia,* Athens, Ga.

Coulter, E. M.   College Life in the Old South.   New York, 1928.

Hammond, N. J.   University of Georgia.   Atlanta, Ga., 1873.

Hull, A. L.   Historical Sketch of the University of Georgia.   Atlanta, Ga., 1894.

A95   *Geneva College,* Beaver Falls, Pa.

Glasgow, W. M.   The Geneva Book.   1908.

A80   *Gettysburg College,* Gettysburg, Pa.

Breidenbaugh, E. S.   The Pennsylvania College Book.   Philadelphia, 1882.

A88   *Greensboro College,* Greensboro, N. C.

A109   *Grinnell College,* Grinnell, Ia.

Magoun, G. F.   Historical Sketch of Iowa College.   Chicago, 1865 pamphlet.

Official History of the Trustees of Iowa College.

A31   *Hamilton College,* Clinton, N. Y.

Allison, C. E.   A Historical Sketch of Hamilton College.   Yonkers, N. Y., 1889.

Davis, Henry.   A Narrative of the Embarrassments and Decline of Hamilton College.   Clinton, N. Y., 1833.

Documentary History of Hamilton College.   Clinton, N. Y., 1922.

Fisher, S. W.   Historical Discourse, July 16, 1862.   1862 pamphlet.

A142   *Hamline University,* St. Paul, Minn.

A11   *Hampden-Sidney College,* Hampden-Sidney, Va.

Grigsby, Hugh B.   Centennial Address, 1876.   Hampden-Sidney College Bulletin 1913.

Morrison, A. J.   Calendar of Board Minutes (1776-1876).   Richmond, Va., 1912.

A57   *Hanover College,* Hanover, Ind.

Dunn, W. McK.   Early History of Hanover College.   Madison, Ind., 1883.

Millis, W. A.   History of Hanover College.   Hanover, Ind., 1927.

A1   *Harvard University,* Cambridge, Mass.

Bush, George G.   Harvard, the First American University.   Boston, 1886.

Eliot, Samuel A.   Sketch of the History of Harvard College.   Boston, 1848.

Gardiner, J. H.   Harvard.   New York, 1914.

Gray, F. C.   Letter to Governor Lincoln in Relation to Harvard University, April 16, 1831.   Boston, Second Edition, 1831 pamphlet.

Hill, G. B.   Harvard College by an Oxonian.   New York, 1894.

Johnson, Edward. Wonder-Working Providence in Original Narratives of Early American History. Edited by J. F. Jameson. New York, 1906.

Mather, Cotton. Magnalia Christi Americana. Hartford, Conn., 1820.

Memorial Concerning Recent History . . . of Harvard College. Cambridge, Mass., 1851 pamphlet.

Moe, A. K. A History of Harvard. 1896.

Morison, S. E. The Development of Harvard University (1869-1929).

Norton, Andrews. Speech Delivered before the Overseers of Harvard College. Boston, 1825 pamphlet.

Pierce, Benjamin. A History of Harvard University. Cambridge, Mass., 1833. 2 vols.

Quincy, J. The History of Harvard University. Boston, 1840. 2 vols.

Report on Filling Up Vacancies in the Clerical Part of the Permanent Board of Overseers of Harvard College. Boston, 1845 pamphlet.

Thayer, W. R. History of Harvard University. In Chamberlain, J. L., Editor, Universities and Their Sons. Boston, 1898. 5 vols.

Vaille, F. O. and Clark, H. A. The Harvard Book. Cambridge, Mass., 1875. 2 vols.

A166 *Haverford College,* Haverford, Pa.

History of Haverford College. Philadelphia, 1892.

Sharpless, I. The Story of a Small College. Philadelphia, 1918.

A143 *Heidelberg College,* Tiffin, O.

Williard, G. W. History of Heidelberg College. Cincinnati, O., 1879.

A144 *Hillsdale College,* Hillsdale, Mich.

A41 *Hobart College,* Geneva, N. Y.

Turk, M. W. Hobart, the Story of a Hundred Years (1822-1922). Geneva, N. Y., 1921.

A103 *Howard College,* Birmingham, Ala.

Garrett, M. B. Sixty Years of Howard College (1842-1902). In Howard College Bulletin, October 1927.

A62 *Illinois College,* Jacksonville, Ill.

Baldwin, T. Historical Sketch of the Origin, Progress, and Wants of Illinois College. New York, 1832 pamphlet.

Barton, C. B. The Founders and Founding of Illinois College. Jacksonville, Ill., 1902 pamphlet.

Beecher, E. and Baldwin, T. Appeal in Behalf of the Illinois College Recently Founded at Jacksonville, Ill. New York, 1831 pamphlet.

Quarter Century Celebration at Illinois College. New York, 1855.

Rammelkamp, C. H. Centennial History of Illinois College (with full bibliography). New Haven, Conn., 1928.

A188   *Illinois Wesleyan University*, Bloomington, Ill.

A46   *Indiana University*, Bloomington, Ind.
> Banta, D. D. Indiana University (1820-1920) Centennial Memorial Volume. Bloomington, Ind., 1921.
> Harding, S. B., Editor. Indiana University (1820-1904). Bloomington, Ind., 1904.
> Wylie, T. A. Indiana University, Its History (1820-1890). Indianapolis, Ind., 1890.

A120   *State University of Iowa*, Iowa City, Ia.
> Pickard, J. L. Historical Sketch of the State University of Iowa. Iowa City, Ia., 1899 pamphlet.

A168   *Iowa Wesleyan College*, Mt. Pleasant, Ia.
> Jeffrey, H. N., Editor. Historical Sketch of Iowa Wesleyan College. Mt. Pleasant, Ia., 1917.
> Williams, C. S. Iowa Wesleyan University. 1905.

A179   *Irving Female College*, Mechanicsburg, Pa.

A193   *Kalamazoo College*, Kalamazoo, Mich.

A187   *University of Kentucky*, Lexington, Ky.

A40   *Kenyon College*, Gambier, O.
> Bodine, W. B. Historical Sketch of the Theological Seminary of the Diocese of Ohio, and Kenyon College. Gambier, O., 1875 pamphlet.
> Chase, P. Plans of Kenyon College. Philadelphia, 1826 pamphlet.
> Chase, P. Plea for the West. Philadelphia, 1826 pamphlet.
> Smythe, G. F. Kenyon College. New Haven, Conn., 1924.

A83   *Knox College*, Galesburg, Ill.
> Bailey, J. W. Knox College, by Whom Founded and Endowed. Chicago, 1860 pamphlet.
> Report on Knox College Presented to the General Association of Illinois. Quincy, Ill., 1861 pamphlet.
> Rights of Congregationalists in Knox College. Chicago, 1859 pamphlet.
> Webster, M. F. The Story of Knox College. Galesburg, Ill., 1912.

A45   *Lafayette College*, Easton, Pa.
> Owen, W. B. Historical Sketches of Lafayette College. Easton, Pa., 1876.
> White, H. A. Lafayette College.

A123   *Lagrange Female College*, Lagrange, Ga.

A145   *Lake Forest University*, Lake Forest, Ill.

A110   *Lawrence College*, Appleton, Wisc.
> Plantz, S. Lawrence College. Menasha, Wisc., 1922 pamphlet.
> Smith, R. Importance and Claims of the Lawrence University of Wisconsin. Boston, 1866 pamphlet.

A146   *Lindenwood Female College*, St. Charles, Mo.

A185   *Lombard College*, Galesburg, Ill.

A194   *Louisiana State University*, Baton Rouge, La.

A90   *University of Louisville*, Louisville, Ky.

A87   *Loyola College*, Baltimore, Md.

A67   *McKendree College*, Lebanon, Ill.

Walton, W. C. Centennial History of McKendree College. 1928.

A69   *Marietta College*, Marietta, O.

Addresses and Proceedings Connected with the Semi-Centennial Celebration of Marietta College. 1885.

Andrews, I. W. Historical Sketch of Marietta College. Cincinnati, O., 1876 pamphlet.

A48   *University of Maryland*, Baltimore, Md.

Cordell, E. F. University of Maryland (1807-1907). New York, 1907. 2 vols.

Memorial of the Trustees of the University of Maryland and the Trustees of Baltimore College to the Legislature of Maryland. Baltimore, Md., 1830 pamphlet.

A111   *Maryville College*, Maryville, Tenn.

Wilson, S. T. A Century of Maryville College. Maryville, Tenn., 1916.

A74   *Mercer University*, Macon, Ga.

A30   *Miami University*, Oxford, O.

Laws of the United States and the State of Ohio Pertaining to the Miami University. 1909.

Tobey, W. L. and Thompson, W. O. The Diamond Anniversary Volume of Miami University. Hamilton, O., 1899.

Upham, A. H. Centennial of Miami University. Ohio Archaeological and Historical Society Publication, Vol. 18, Columbus, O., 1909.

Upham, A. H. Old Miami—the Yale of the Early West. Hamilton, O., 1909.

A51   *University of Michigan*, Ann Arbor, Mich.

Adams, C. K. Historical Sketch of the University of Michigan. Ann Arbor, Mich., 1876.

Farrand, E. M. History of the University of Michigan. Ann Arbor, Mich., 1885.

Hinsdale, B. A. History of the University of Michigan. Ann Arbor, Mich., 1906.

Semi-Centennial Volume (1837-1887). Ann Arbor, Mich., 1888.

A25   *Middlebury College*, Middlebury, Vt.

Blake, C. E. History of Middlebury College. 1894.

A147   *Milwaukee-Downer College*, Milwaukee, Wisc.

Miner, H. A. History of Downer College. 1921.

Wight, W. W. Annals of Milwaukee College. 1891.

A154   *University of Minnesota*, Minneapolis, Minn.

Hall, C. W. The University of Minnesota: A Historical Sketch. Minneapolis, Minn., 1896 pamphlet.

Johnson, E. B., Editor. Forty Years of the University of Minnesota. Minneapolis, Minn., 1910.

Snyder, F. B. The University's Beginnings. 1921.

A55 *Mississippi College,* Clinton, Miss.
A114 *University of Mississippi,* Oxford, Miss.
  Memorial to the Congress of the United States from the Board of
  Trustees of the University of Mississippi. Nashville, Tenn., 1894
  pamphlet.
  Waddel, J. N. Historical Discourse Delivered on the Quarter-
  Centennial Anniversary, June 25, 1873. Oxford, Miss., 1873
  pamphlet.
A70 *University of Missouri,* Columbia, Mo.
  Babb, J. G. A Short History of the University. Columbia, Mo.,
  1915.
  Hough, F. B., Editor. Historical Sketches of the Universities and
  Colleges of the United States. U. S. Bureau of Education,
  Washington, D. C., 1883.
  Lowry, T. J. A Sketch of the University of the State of Missouri.
  Columbia, Mo., 1890 pamphlet.
A149 *Monmouth College,* Monmouth, Ill.
A72 *Mt. St. Mary's College,* Emmitsburg, Md.
  McSweeney, —. History of the Mountain.
A150 *Mt. Union College,* Alliance, O.
  Condensed History of Mt. Union College. Mt. Union, O., 1866
  pamphlet.
  McMaster, W. H. Historical Statement. Mount Union, O.
A85 *Muskingum College,* New Concord, O.
A174 *Newberry College,* Newberry, S. C.
A135 *College of the City of New York,* New York, N. Y.
  Cosenza, M. E. The Founding of the College of the City of New
  York. New York, 1926.
  Mosenthal, P. J. and Horne, C. F. City College, Memories of
  Sixty Years. New York, 1907.
A64 *New York University,* New York, N. Y.
  Chamberlain, J. L., Editor. New York University. Boston, 1901.
  2 vols.
  Consideration upon the Expediency and the Means of Establishing
  a University in the City of New York: Address to the Citizens.
  New York, 1830 pamphlet.
  History of the Controversy in the University of the City of New
  York with Original Documents and an Appendix by the Pro-
  fessors of the Faculty of Science and Letters. New York, 1838
  pamphlet.
A17 *University of North Carolina,* Chapel Hill, N. C.
  Battle, K. P. History of the University of North Carolina.
  Raleigh, N. C., 1907. 2 vols.
  Sketches of the History of the University of North Carolina (1789-
  1889). Chapel Hill, N. C., 1889.
A169 *Northwestern University,* Evanston, Ill.
  Ward, E. F. Story of Northwestern University. New York, 1924.

Wilde, A. H.   A History of Northwestern University (1855-1905). 1905.   4 vols.

A81   *Norwich University*, Northfield, Vt.

Dodge, G. M. and Ellis, W. A.   Norwich University (1819-1911). Montpelier, Vt., 1911.   3 vols.

Ellis, W. A.   History of Norwich University (1819-1895).   Concord, N. H., 1898.

A105   *University of Notre Dame*, Notre Dame, Ind.

Brief History of Notre Dame University (1842-1892).   Chicago, 1895.

A71   *Oberlin College*, Oberlin, O.

Fairchild, E. H.   Historical Sketch of Oberlin College.   Springfield, O., 1868 pamphlet.

Fairchild, J. H.   Oberlin, the Colony and the College.   Oberlin, O., 1883.

Leonard, D. L.   The Story of Oberlin.   Boston, 1898.

Smith, D.   A History of Oberlin.   Cleveland, O., 1837 pamphlet.

A76   *Oglethorpe University*, Atlanta, Ga.

Thornwell, J.   The Oglethorpe Story.   Atlanta, Ga.

Thornwell, J.   The Refounding of Oglethorpe University.   Atlanta, Ga.

A28   *Ohio University*, Athens, O.

Martzolff, C. L.   Ohio University—The Historic College of the Old Northwest.   Athens, O., 1910.

Peters, W. E.   Legal History of Ohio University.   Cincinnati, O., 1910.

A118   *Ohio Wesleyan University*, Delaware, O.

Nelson, E. T., Editor.   Fifty Years of History of the Ohio Wesleyan University (1844-1894).   Cleveland, O., 1895.

A53   *Olivet College*, Olivet, Mich.

Morrison, N. J.   A Memorial Address.   Lansing, Mich., 1866 pamphlet.

Williams, W. B.   History of Olivet College (1844-1900).   Olivet, Mich., 1901.

A127   *Otterbein College*, Westerville, O.

Garst, H.   Otterbein University (1847-1907).   Dayton, O., 1907.

A171   *College of the Pacific*, Stockton, Cal.

A170   *Pacific University*, Forest Grove, Ore.

A6   *University of Pennsylvania*, Philadelphia, Pa.

Cheyney, E. P. and Oberholtzer, E. P.   University of Pennsylvania. In Chamberlain, J. L., Editor, Universities and Their Sons.   Boston, 1901.   2 vols.

Dulles, C. W.   The Charity School of 1740—the Foundation of the University of Pennsylvania.   Philadelphia, 1904 pamphlet on the controversy over the origin of the University.

Gilbert, W. K.   History of the College and Academy of Philadelphia.   Philadelphia, 1863.

Lippincott, H. M. George Washington and the University of Pennsylvania. Philadelphia, 1916.

Lippincott, H. M. University of Pennsylvania—Franklin's College. Philadelphia, 1919.

Montgomery, T. H. History of the University of Pennsylvania (1749-1770). Philadelphia, 1900.

Pennypacker, S. W. The Origin of the University of Pennsylvania. Alumni Register, January 1901.

Pennypacker, S. W. University of Pennsylvania in Its Relation with the State of Pennsylvania. Philadelphia, 1891 pamphlet.

Thorpe, F. N. Benjamin Franklin and the University of Pennsylvania. U. S. Bur. of Ed. Cir. Inf., 1892, no. 2.

Wood, G. B. Early History of the University of Pennsylvania (1749-1827). Philadelphia, 1833 (Third Edition 1896).

A36   *University of Pittsburgh*, Pittsburgh, Pa.

Celebration of the One Hundred and Twenty-fifth Anniversary. University of Pittsburgh Bulletin. Pittsburgh, Pa., 1912.

Holland, W. J., Compiler. Acts of Assembly and Other Important Papers Relating to the Western University of Pennsylvania. Pittsburgh, 1859.

Holland, W. J. The Educational Needs of Appalachia. Morgantown, W. Va., 1901.

A4   *Princeton University*, Princeton, N. J.

Alexander, S. D. Princeton College in the Eighteenth Century.

Collins, V. L. Princeton. New York, 1914.

DeWitt, J. Princeton University. In Chamberlain, J. L., Editor, Universities and Their Sons. Boston, 1898. 5 vols.

Dod, W. A. History of the College of New Jersey. Princeton, N. J., 1844.

Edgar, R. Historical Sketch of the College of New Jersey. Philadelphia, 1859.

Maclean, J. History of the College of New Jersey (1741-1854). Philadelphia, 1877. 2 vols.

Norris, E. M. The Story of Princeton. Boston, 1917.

The Princeton Book. Boston, 1879.

Wallace, G. R. Princeton Sketches: The Story of Nassau Hall. New York, 1893.

A58   *Randolph-Macon College*, Ashland, Va.

Erby, R. History of Randolph-Macon College. Richmond, Va., 1899.

A97   *University of Richmond*, Richmond, Va.

A172   *Ripon College*, Ripon, Wisc.

A173   *Roanoke College*, Salem, Va.

A155   *University of Rochester*, Rochester, N. Y.

Rosenberger, J. L. Rochester, the Making of a University. Rochester, N. Y., 1927.

Rosenberger, J. L. Rochester and Colgate. Chicago, 1925.

A112 *Rockford College*, Rockford, Ill.

A8 *Rutgers University*, New Brunswick, N. J.
> Centennial Celebration of Rutgers College, June 21, 1870. Albany, N. Y., 1870.
>
> Demarest, W. H. S. A History of Rutgers College (1766-1924). New Brunswick, N. J., 1924.
>
> Lewis, J. V., Editor. Rutgers College: Celebration of the 150th Anniversary of Its Founding (1766-1916). 1917.

A162 *St. Ignatius College*, San Francisco, Cal.
> Riordan, J. W. The First Half Century. 1905.

A13 *St. John's College*, Annapolis, Md.
> Commemoration of the One-Hundredth Anniversary of St. John's College. Baltimore, Md., 1890.
>
> Fell, T., Compiler. Some Historical Accounts of the Founding of King William's School. Annapolis, Md., 1894.

A151 *St. Joseph's College*, Philadelphia, Pa.

A152 *St. Lawrence University*, Canton, N. Y.
> St. Lawrence University: Sixty Years of St. Lawrence. 1916.

A79 *St. Louis University*, St. Louis, Mo.
> Fanning, W. H. Diamond Jubilee. St. Louis, Mo., 1904.
>
> Fanning, W. H. Historical Sketch of the St. Louis University. St. Louis, Mo., 1908 pamphlet.

A61 *St. Mary's College*, St. Mary's, Ky.

A129 *St. Stephen's College*, Annandale, N. Y.

A192 *St. Xavier College*, Cincinnati, O.

A177 *Santa Clara College*, Santa Clara, Cal.

A52 *Seton Hall College*, South Orange, N. J.
> Marshall, W. F. A Sketch of Seton Hall College. 1895.

A82 *Shurtleff College*, Alton, Ill.
> De Blois, A. K. The Pioneer School: A History of Shurtleff College. New York, 1900.

A156 *University of the South*, Sewanee, Tenn.
> Fairbanks, G. R. History of the University of the South (1857-1905). Jacksonville, Fla., 1905.
>
> Haskins, D. G. A Brief Account of the University of the South. New York, 1877.

A26 *University of South Carolina*, Columbia, S. C.
> An Appeal in Behalf of the South Carolina College. Charleston, S. C., 1835 pamphlet.
>
> Centennial Celebration of South Carolina College. 1905.
>
> Green, E. L. A History of the University of South Carolina. Columbia, S. C., 1916.
>
> La Borde, K. History of South Carolina College (1801-1857). Columbia, S. C., 1859.

A75 *Spring Hill College*, Spring Hill, Ala.
> Spring Hill College (1830-1905). Mobile, Ala., 1906.

A94 *Taylor University*, Upland, Ind.

A22   *University of Tennessee,* Knoxville, Tenn.

> Karnes, T. C. The University of Tennessee.
>
> Report of Committee on the Relations between the University and the State. University of Tennessee Record, Vol. X, No. 2, 1907.
>
> Sanford, E. T. Blount College and the University of Tennessee, June 12, 1894. Knoxville, Tenn., 1894 pamphlet.
>
> White, Moses. Early History of the University of Tennessee. 1879 pamphlet.

A24   *Transylvania College,* Lexington, Ky.

> Peter, R. and Peter, J. Transylvania University: Its Origin, Rise, Decline and Fall. Louisville, Ky., 1896.

A39   *Trinity College,* Hartford, Conn.

> An Examination of the "Remarks" on Considerations Suggested by the Establishment of a Second College in Connecticut. Hartford, Conn., 1825 pamphlet.
>
> Considerations Suggested by the Establishment of a Second College in Connecticut. Hartford, Conn., 1824 pamphlet.
>
> Remarks on Washington College and on the "Considerations" Suggested by Its Establishment. Hartford, Conn., 1825 pamphlet.

A153   *Tufts College,* Tufts College, Mass.

> History of Tufts College. 1897.

A121   *Tulane University,* New Orleans, La.

> Johnson, W. P. Tulane University of Louisiana: Commencement Address, 1895.

A21   *Tusculum College,* Greeneville, Tenn.

A93   *Union University,* Jackson, Tenn.

A23   *Union University,* Schenectady, N. Y.

> Alexander, G., Editor. Union College Centennial Anniversary (1795-1895). New York, 1897.
>
> Hough, F. B. Historical Sketch of Union College. U. S. Bureau of Ed., Washington, D. C., 1876 pamphlet.

A92   *Upper Iowa University,* Fayette, Ia.

A130   *Vassar College,* Poughkeepsie, N. Y.

> Historical Sketch of Vassar College. New York, 1876.
>
> Taylor, J. M. and Haight, E. H. Vassar. New York, 1915.

A18   *University of Vermont,* Burlington, Vt.

> Benedict, R. D. Charter History of the University of Vermont: An Address, June 24, 1891. Burlington, Vt., 1892 pamphlet.
>
> Wheeler, J. F. A Historical Discourse. Burlington, Vt., 1854 pamphlet.

A115   *Augustinian College of Villanova,* Villanova, Pa.

> Middleton, T. C. Historical Sketch of the Augustinian Monastery, College, and Mission of the St. Thomas of Villanova (1842-1892). Villanova, Pa., 1893.

A37   *University of Virginia,* Charlottesville, Va.

> Adams, H. B. Thomas Jefferson and the University of Virginia. U. S. Bur. of Ed. Cir. Inf., 1888, no. 1.

A Sketch of the University of Virginia. Washington, D. C., 1859.

A Sketch of the University of Virginia. Richmond, Va., 1885.

Barringer, P. B. et al., Editors. University of Virginia. New York, 1904.

Bruce, P. A. History of the University of Virginia (1819-1919). New York, 1920-22. 5 vols.

Culbreth, D. M. R. The University of Virginia: Memories of Her Student Life and Professors. New York, 1908.

Patton, J. S. Jefferson, Cabell, and the University of Virginia. New York, 1906.

Patton, J. S. and Doswell, S. J., Editors. The University of Virginia. Charlottesville, Va., 1915.

University of Virginia: Its History, Influence, ... New York, 1904. 2 vols.

A59 *Wabash College,* Crawfordsville, Ind.

Hovey, E. O. History of Wabash College. Wabash Magazine, 1857.

Tuttle, J. F. The Origin and Growth of Wabash College. Logansport, Ind., 1876 pamphlet.

A63 *Wake Forest College,* Wake Forest, N. C.

Huffman, J. D. How We Got the Charter. In Wake Forest Student, Vol. XVII, No. 6.

Paschal, G. W. History of Wake Forest College. In Wake Forest College Bulletin, Vol. XIX, No. 4.

A10 *Washington College,* Chestertown, Md.

A157 *Washington University,* St. Louis, Mo.

A27 *Washington and Jefferson College,* Washington, Pa.

Moffat, J. D. Historical Sketch of Washington and Jefferson College. Washington, Pa., 1890 pamphlet.

Smith, J. History of Jefferson College. Pittsburgh, Pa., 1857.

A32 *Washington and Lee University,* Lexington, Va.

Washington and Lee University: Historical Papers. Baltimore, Md., 1890.

A178 *Waynesburg College,* Waynesburg, Pa.

A89 *Wesleyan College,* Macon, Ga.

Quillian, W. F. A New Day for Historical Wesleyan.

A65 *Wesleyan University,* Middletown, Conn.

A Historical Sketch of the Endowment of Wesleyan University. Middletown, Conn., 1904 pamphlet.

An Appeal to the Citizens of Connecticut in Behalf of the Wesleyan University, 1839.

Celebration of the Seventy-Fifth Anniversary (1831-1906). Middletown, Conn., 1907.

Semicentennial of Wesleyan University, 1881.

A44 *Western Reserve University,* Cleveland, O.

Cutter, C. History of Western Reserve College (1826-1876). Cleveland O., 1876.

Haydn, H. C. An Historical Sketch of Western Reserve University. Cleveland, O., 1895.

Kitzmiller, H. H. 100 Years of Western Reserve. Hudson, N. Y., 1926.

A158 *Westminster College,* Fulton, Mo.

Laws, S. S. An Address in Behalf of Westminster College. St. Louis, Mo., 1857 pamphlet.

Fisher, M. M. History of Westminster College. Columbia, Mo., 1903.

A190 *Westminster College,* New Wilmington, Pa.

Rice, J. J. History of Westminster College (1851-1903). 1903.

A91 *Wheaton College,* Wheaton, Ill.

A159 *Willamette University,* Salem, Ore.

A117 *William Jewell College,* Liberty, Mo.

Clark, J. G. History of William Jewell College.

A2 *College of William and Mary,* Williamsburg, Va.

Adams, H. P. The College of William and Mary. U. S. Bur. of Ed. Cir. Inf. 1887, no. 1.

The History of the College of William and Mary. Richmond, Va., 1874.

Tyler, L. G. The College of William and Mary (1693-1907). Richmond, Va., 1907 pamphlet.

Tyler, L. G. College of William and Mary to 1917. Williamsburg, Va., 1917 pamphlet.

A19 *Williams College,* Williamstown. Mass.

Durfee, C. A History of Williams College. Boston, 1860.

Perry, A. L. Williamstown and Williams College. New York, 1899.

Spring, E. H. Fifty Years at Williams, under the Administrations of Presidents Chadbourne, Carter, Hewitt, Hopkins and Garfield. Pittsfield, Mass., 1928.

Spring, L. W. A History of Williams College. Boston, 1917.

A124 *University of Wisconsin,* Madison, Wisc.

Butterfield, C. W. History of the University of Wisconsin from Its First Organization to 1879. Madison. Wisc.. 1879.

Carpenter, S. H. An Historical Sketch of the University of Wisconsin (1849-1876). Madison, Wisc.. 1879.

Pyre, J. F. A. Wisconsin. New York, 1920.

Thwaites, R. G., Editor. The University of Wisconsin, Its History and Alumni. Madison. Wisc., 1900.

A116 *Wittenberg College,* Springfield, O.

Clark, G. G. History of Wittenberg College. Springfield, O., 1887.

Prince, B. F. History of Wittenberg College (in manuscript).

A160 *Wofford College,* Spartanburg, S. C.

A3 *Yale University,* New Haven. Conn.

Baldwin, E. Annals of Yale College from Its Foundation to the Year 1831. New Haven, 1831.

Belden, E. P. Sketches of Yale College. New York, 1843.

Chittenden, R. H. History of the Sheffield Scientific School. New Haven, 1928. 2 vols.

Clap, T. Annals or History of Yale College (1700-1766). New Haven, 1766.

Clap, T. The Religious Constitution of Colleges, Especially of Yale College. New London, Conn., 1754 pamphlet.

Dexter, F. B. Sketch of the History of Yale University. New York, 1887.

Dexter, F. B. Yale Biographies and Annals. 4 vols.

Dexter, F. B., Editor. Documentary History of Yale University (1701-1745). New Haven, 1916.

Dexter, F. B. A Selection from the Miscellaneous Historical Papers of Fifty Years. New Haven, 1918.

Kingsley, W. L., Editor. Yale College: A Sketch of Its History. New York, 1878. 2 vols.

Oviatt, E. The Beginnings of Yale (1701-1726). New Haven, 1916.

Smith, C. H. Yale University. In Chamberlain, J. L., Editor, Universities and Their Sons. Boston, 1898. 5 vols.

Stiles, Ezra. Ecclesiastical Constitution of Yale College.

Stokes, A. P. Memorials of Famous Yale Men. New Haven, 1914. 2 vols.

Woolsey, T. D. An Historical Discourse, August 14, 1850. New Haven, 1850.

B. GENERAL PRIMARY AND SECONDARY REFERENCES ON THE FOUNDING OF AMERICAN COLLEGES AND UNIVERSITIES BEFORE THE CIVIL WAR

Adams, C. K. Review of Ten Brook's American State Universities. North American Review, Vol. 121, October 1875, pp. 365-408.

Adams, J. T. The Epic of America. Boston, 1931.

Addis, W. Federal and State Aid to Establish Higher Education. U. S. Commissioner of Education, Report of 1896-97, Vol. 2, pp. 1137-64.

Alexander, A. Biographical Sketch of the Founder and Principal Alumni of the Log College. Philadelphia, 1851.

Allison, W. H.; Fay, S. B.; Shearer, A. H., and Shipman, H. A., Editors. A Guide to Historical Literature. New York, 1931.

American Almanac and Repository of Useful Knowledge, 1830-62. 33 vols.

American Annals of Education and Instruction, 1831-39. Edited by Wm. C. Woodbridge. Boston. 9 vols.

American Journal of Education, 1826-30. Edited by Wm. Russell. Boston. 5 vols.

American Journal of Education and College Review, 1855-81. Edited by Henry Barnard and Absalom Peters. Hartford, Conn. 31 vols.

American Quarterly Register and Journal of the American Education Society, 1828-43. Andover, Mass. 15 vols.

Anderson, M. B. Voluntaryism in Higher Education. New York, 1877 pamphlet.

Andrews, B. F. The Land Grant of 1862 and the Land Grant Colleges. U. S. Bureau of Education Bulletin 1918, No. 13. Washington, D. C.

Aurner, C. R. History of Education in Iowa, 1914-20. Iowa City, Ia. 5 vols.

Bacon, L. W. A History of American Christianity. New York, 1897.

Baldwin, A. M. New England Clergy in the American Revolution. Durham, N. C., 1928.

Barnard, F. A. P. Letter to the Honorable Board of Trustees of the University of Mississippi. Tracts on Education, Vol. III, No. 27. Oxford, Miss., 1858.

—— On Improvements Practicable in American Colleges. In American Journal of Education and College Review, Vol. 1, 1856.

—— Two Papers on Academic Degrees. New York, 1880 pamphlet.

Bartlett, L. W. State Control of Private Incorporated Institutions of Higher Education. New York, 1926.

Bashford, J. W. The Oregon Missions. New York, 1918.

Beard, C. E. and Beard, M. R. The Rise of American Civilization. New York, 1927. 2 vols.

Beard, C. E. The Economic Origins of Jeffersonian Democracy. New York, 1915.

Beecher, L. A Plea for Colleges. Cincinnati, O., 2nd edition, 1838 pamphlet.

Beeman, N. S. S. Collegiate and Theological Education at the West. New York, 1847 pamphlet.

Bell, S. The Church, the State and Education in Virginia. Philadelphia, 1930.

Benedict, H. Y. A Source Book Relating to the History of the University of Texas.

Benton, G. P. State Universities and the Educational Challenge of Tomorrow. Proceedings of the National Association of State Universities. 1918.

Birdseye, C. F. Individual Training in Our Colleges. New York, 1907.

Blackmar, F. W. The History of Federal and State Aid to Higher Education in the United States. U. S. Bur. of Ed. Cir. Inf., 1890, no. 1. Contributions to American Educational History, No. 9.

Blake, S. J. Visit to Some American Colleges.

Blandin, J. M. E. History of Higher Education of Women in the South Prior to 1860. New York, 1909.

Boone, R. G. Education in the United States. New York, 1889.

—— History of Education in Indiana. New York, 1892.

Brown, E. E. The History and Development of American Education. Addresses and Proceedings of the National Education Association, 1915, pp. 599-602.

Brown, E. E.   The Making of Our Middle Schools.   New York, 1902.
—— The Origin of American State Universities.   University of California
    Publication, Vol. 3, No. 1, 1903.   Berkeley, Cal., pamphlet.
Brown University.   Notes on College Charters.   Providence, R. I., 1910.
Bryan, W. S. P.   The Church, Her Colleges and the Carnegie Foundation.
    Princeton, N. J., 1911 pamphlet.
Bryce, J.   The American Commonwealth.   New York, 1888.   Revised edition
    1910.   2 vols.
Buckham, J. W.   Progressive Religious Thought in America.
Butler, N. M.   Scholarship and Service.   New York, 1921.
—— Education in the United States.   New York, 1900.
Carleton, F. T.   Education and Social Progress.   New York, 1908.
—— Economic Influences upon Educational Progress in the United States,
    1820-50.   University of Wisconsin Bulletin 1908, No. 1.
Case, S. J., Editor.   A Bibliographical Guide to the History of Christianity.
    Chicago, 1931.
Catalogues of all colleges included in this study for 1927-28.   Historical
    Statements.
Cattell, J. M.   University Control.   New York, 1913.
Caullery, M.   Universities and Scientific Life in the United States.   Cam-
    bridge, Mass., 1922.
Chadbourne, P. A.   Colleges and College Education.   In Putnam's Maga-
    zine, September 1869.
Chamberlain, J. L., Editor.   Universities and Their Sons.   Harvard, Yale,
    Princeton, and Columbia.   Boston, 1898-1900.   5 vols.   New York
    University and University of Pennsylvania.   Boston, 1901.   2 vols.
Channing, E.; Hart, A. B., and Turner, F. J.   Guide to the Study and Read-
    ing of American History.   Boston, 1896.   Revised Edition 1912.
Christian Education Handbook for 1928.   Council of Church Boards of
    Education.   New York, 1928.
Cleveland, C. C.   The Great Revival in the West, 1797-1805.   Chicago, 1916.
Cobb, S. H.   Rise of Religious Liberty in America.   New York, 1902.
Cook, J. W.   Educational History of Illinois.   Chicago, 1912.
Cooper, D. M.   A Plea for the Smaller College.   Detroit, Mich., 1898 pam-
    phlet.
Coulter, E. M.   College Life in the Old South.   New York, 1928.
Crawford, W. H.   The American College.   New York, 1915.
Cubberley, E. P.   Public Education in the United States.   Boston, 1919.
—— History of Education.   Boston, 1920.
Davis, E.   The Half Century.   Boston, 1850.
Davis, S. E.   Educational Periodicals During the Nineteenth Century.   U. S.
    Bureau of Education Bulletin 1919, No. 28.   Washington, D. C.
Dexter, E. G.   History of Education in the United States.   New York,
    1904.
Dexter, F. B.   The Influence of the English Universities in the Development
    of New England.   Cambridge, Mass., 1880.
Dodd, W. E.   The Cotton Kingdom.   New Haven, Conn., 1919.

Drake, W. E.   Higher Education in North Carolina before 1860.   Unpublished dissertation at the University of North Carolina, 1930.

Dwight, T.   Travels in New England and New York.   New Haven, Conn., 1821-22.   4 vols.

Eby, F., Compiler.   Education in Texas: Source Materials.   University of Texas Bulletin, April 25, 1918.

—— The Development of Education in Texas.   New York, 1925.

Educational Directory: 1928.   U. S. Bureau of Education Bulletin 1928, No. 1.   Washington, D. C.

Edwards, M. L.   Religious Forces in the United States, 1815-30.   Miss. Val. Hist. Rev. X, pp. 436-449.

Elsbree, O. W.   Rise of Missionary Spirit in America, 1790-1815.   Williamsport, Pa., 1928.

Emerson, R. W.   Nature, Addresses and Lectures.   Boston, 1876.

Farrar, T.   Report of the Case of the Trustees of Dartmouth College Against William H. Woodward.   Portsmouth, N. H., 1819.

Faust, A. B.   German Element in the United States.   Boston, 1909.   2 vols.

Fay, B.   Revolutionary Spirit in France and America.   New York, 1927.

Fernald, M. C.   History of the Maine State College and the University of Maine.   Orono, Me., 1916.

Fish, C. R.   The Rise of the Common Man, 1830-50.   A History of American Life.   Edited by A. M. Schlesinger and D. R. Fox.   New York, 1927.

Fisher, S. G.   Church Colleges.   Philadelphia, 1895 pamphlet.

Flexner, A.   Universities, American, English, and German.   New York, 1930.

Ford, H. J.   Scotch-Irish in America.   Princeton, N. J., 1915.

Foster, W. T.   Administration of the College Curriculum.   Boston, 1911.

Fox, D. R.   Harper's Atlas of American History.   New York, 1920.

—— The Calvinistic Mind in America.   Proceedings of the New York State Historical Association, Vol. XIX, 1921, pp. 156-163.

—— The Decline of Aristocracy in the Politics of New York.   New York, 1918.

Gardiner, S. L.   Educational Corporations of New York State.   Albany, N. Y., 1924.

Germann, G. B.   National Legislation Concerning Education.   New York, 1899.

Gilman, D. C.   Education in America 1776-1876.   North American Review, Vol. 122, 1876.

—— On the Growth of American Colleges.   1871.

Gilpatrick, D. H.   Jeffersonian Democracy in North Carolina (1789-1816).   New York, 1931.

Goodsell, W.   Pioneers of Women's Education in the United States.   New York, 1931.

—— The Education of Women.   New York, 1923.

Graves, F. P.   The Evolution of Our Universities.   School and Society, Vol. 8, December 14, 1918, pp. 691-702.

Greene, E. B.   The Foundations of American Nationality.   New York, 1922.

Greene, M. L. The Development of Religious Liberty in Connecticut. Boston, 1905.

Grubbs, F. H. Early Oregon Schools. Oregon Pioneer Trans. 1913.

Hall, T. C. The Religious Background of American Culture. New York, 1930.

Halsey, L. J., Editor. The Works of Philip Lindsley. Philadelphia, 1864. 3 vols.

Hanna, C. A. The Scotch-Irish. New York, 1902. 2 vols.

Hansen, A. O. Liberalism and American Education in the Eighteenth Century. New York, 1926.

Harper, W. R. Prospects of the Small College. Chicago, 1900 pamphlet.

Haven, E. O. Universities in America. 1863 pamphlet.

Heatwole, C. J. A History of Education in Virginia. New York, 1916.

Henshaw, D. Remarks upon the Rights and Powers of Corporations. . . . Boston, 1837 pamphlet.

Hinsdale, B. A. Documents Illustrative of American Education History. U. S. Commissioner of Education Report 1892-93, Vol. 2.

—— Notes on the History of Foreign Influence upon Education in the United States. U. S. Commissioner of Education Report 1897-98, Vol. 1.

Hobson, E. G. Educational Legislation and Administration in the State of New York from 1777 to 1850. Supplementary Education Monograph No. 11. University of Chicago Press, 1918.

Holme, Ernest R. The American University—An Australian View. Sydney, Australia, 1920.

Holy Cross College. Commonwealth of Massachusetts. House Bill No. 130. House of Representatives, April 13, 1849. Giving Report of Joint Standing Committee on Education and Bill for Incorporation of Holy Cross College.

—— Remarks on the Petition for an Act Incorporating the College of the Holy Cross. Boston, 1849 pamphlet.

—— Speeches of Mr. Hopkins of Northampton on the Bill to Incorporate the College of the Holy Cross, 1849. Northampton, Mass., 1849 pamphlet.

Hough, F. B. Historical and Statistical Record 1784-1884 of New York (State) University. Albany, N. Y., 1885.

—— Compiler. Constitutional Provisions in Regard to Education in the Several States of the American Union. U. S. Bur. of Ed. Cir. Inf., 1875, no. 7.

Howe, M. A. DeW. Classic Shades. Boston, 1928.

Hoyt, J. W. Memorial in Regard to a National University. Washington, D. C., 1892.

Humphrey, S. F. Nationalism and Religion in America, 1774-1789. Boston, 1924.

Huntington, J. T. Our Schools and Colleges. Boston, 1866 pamphlet.

Hutchins, H. B. The State University Idea. Ann Arbor, Mich., 1921.

Iverson, A. American Education Society in the 19th Century. B.D. Thesis, University of Chicago, 1923.

Jaqua, E. J. Secondary and Higher Education in Iowa. Harvard Ph.D. Thesis, 1919.

James, E. J. The Origin of the Land-Grant Act of 1862. University of Illinois Studies, Vol. IV, No. 1. Urbana, Ill., 1910.

Jameson, J. F. The American Revolution Considered as a Social Movement. Princeton, N. J., 1926.

Kelly, R. L. Theological Education in America. New York, 1924.

Kendall, H. The College and Christian Missions. Utica, N. Y., 1862.

Kent, J. Commentaries on American Law. New York, 1826-30.

King's Chapel Lectures, 1917. Cambridge, Mass., 1917.

Kirk, E. N. The Church and the College. Boston, 1856 pamphlet.

Kirkland, J. H. Higher Education in United States of America. Vanderbilt University Quarterly, 1913 pamphlet.

Kirkpatrick, J. E. Academic Organization and Control. Yellow Springs, O., 1930.

—— The American College and Its Rulers. New York, 1926.

—— The British College in the American Colonies. School and Society, Vol. 17, April 28, 1923, pp. 449-454.

Klapper, P. College Teaching. New York, 1920.

Knight, E. W. Education in the United States. Boston, 1929.

—— Public Education in the South. Boston, 1922.

Knight, G. W. History and Management of Land Grants in the North West Territory. American Historical Association, Vol. 3. New York, 1885.

Ladd, G. T. Development of American Universities.

Lane, J. J. History of the University of Texas. 1891.

Lang, J. D. Religion and Education in America. London, 1848.

Lauer, P. E. Church and State in New England. Johns Hopkins University Studies. Baltimore, Md., 1892.

Livingston, W. The Independent Reflector. New York, 1752-53. 52 issues.

Magoun, G. F. The Source of American Education—Popular and Religious. New Englander, Vol. 36, July 1877, pp. 445-486.

—— The West: Its Culture and Its Colleges. Davenport, Ia., 1855 pamphlet.

Mathews, L. K. The Expansion of New England. Boston, 1909.

Meade, Bishop W. Old Churches, Ministers, and Families of Virginia. Philadelphia, 1857. 2 vols.

Meiklejohn, A. The Liberal College. Boston, 1920.

Miller, E. A. History of Educational Legislation in Ohio (1803-1850). Supplementary Educ. Monographs, No. 13. University of Chicago Press, 1920.

Mode, P. G. Sourcebook and Bibliographical Guide for American Church History. Menasha, Wisc., 1920.

—— The Frontier Spirit in American Christianity. New York, 1923.

Monroe, P. Cyclopedia of Education. New York, 1911-13.

Morgan, F. G. Integration in Higher Education—With Special Reference to College Mergers. University of South Carolina dissertation, 1928.

Morse, A. E. The Federalist Party in Massachusetts to the Year 1800. Princeton, N. J., 1909.

Mott, F. L. A History of American Magazines, 1741-1850.

Nevins, A. The American States during and after the Revolution. New York, 1927.

——— Illinois. New York, 1917.

New England First Fruits. Letter dated September 26, 1642. Published in London in 1843. Old South Leaflets, No. 51.

Nichols, R. H. The Growth of the Christian Church. Philadelphia, 1914. 2 vols.

Niebuhr, H. R. The Social Sources of Denominationalism. New York, 1929.

Niles Weekly Register, 1811-49. Baltimore, Md. 76 vols.

North American Review, 1815-77. Boston.

Norton, C. E., et al. Four American Universities. New York, 1895.

Orfield, M. N. Federal Land Grants to the States with Special Reference to Minnesota. University of Minnesota, 1915.

Parrington, V. L. Main Currents in American Thought, Vols. I-III. New York, 1927-31.

Parsons, E. C. Educational Legislation and Administration of the Colonial Governments. New York, 1899.

Patterson, J. K. Defense of the State College. Frankfort, Ky., 1882 pamphlet.

Paxson, F. L. History of the American Frontier, 1763-1893. Boston, 1924.

Peters, A. Discourse before the Society for the Promotion of Collegiate and Theological Education at the West. New York, 1851 pamphlet.

Pinckney, T. C. United States School and College Directory for 1874. New York, 1874.

Porter, Noah. The American Colleges and the American Public. New Haven, Conn., 1870.

Porter, N. The Educational Systems of the Puritans and the Jesuits Compared. New York, 1852 pamphlet.

Potter, E. N. Church Colleges and the Church University. Publisher not given, 1888 pamphlet.

Powell, B. E. Semi-Centennial History of the University of Illinois. Urbana, Ill., 1918.

Pratt, D. J. Annals of Public Education in the State of New York. Albany, N. Y., 1873.

Pritchett, H. S. The Relations of Christian Denominations to Colleges. Nashville, Tenn., 1908 pamphlet.

Purcell, R. J. Connecticut in Transition, 1775-1818. American Historical Association, Washington, D. C., 1918.

Raper, C. L. The Church and Private Schools of North Carolina. Greensboro-Stone, N. C., 1898.

Reisner, E. H. Nationalism and Education Since 1789. New York, 1922.

Reynolds, J. H. and Thomas, D. Y. History of the University of Arkansas. Fayetteville, Ark., 1910.

Richardson, C. F. and Clark, H. A. The College Book. Boston, 1878.

Richardson, L. B. A Study of the Liberal College. Hanover, N. Y., 1924.

Riegel, R. E. America Moves West. New York, 1930.

Riley, I. W. American Thought. New York, 1915. Rev. Ed. 1923.

Robertson, D. A., Editor. American Colleges and Universities. New York, 1928. Revised Edition, 1932.

Robinson, E. E. Evolution of American Political Parties. New York, 1924.

Robinson, M. L. The Curriculum of the Woman's College. U. S. Bureau of Education Bulletin 1918, No. 6. Washington, D. C.

Robinson, W. R. Jeffersonian Democracy in New England. New Haven, Conn., 1916.

Rowe, H. K. The History of Religion in the United States. New York, 1924.

Rusk, R. L. The Literature of the Middle Western Frontier. New York, 1925. 2 vols.

Sanborn, F. B. Dartmouth College: Its Founders and Hinderers. Concord, Mass., 1908 pamphlet.

Schlesinger, A. M. New Viewpoints in American History. New York, 1922.

Schmidt, G. P. The Old-Time College President. New York, 1930.

Schneider, H. W. The Puritan Mind. New York, 1930.

Scribner's Statistical Atlas of the United States for 1870. Plates 19 and 20. New York, 1885.

Sears, J. B. Philanthropy in the History of American Higher Education. U. S. Bureau of Education Bulletin 1922, No. 26.

Session Laws of the Thirty-Four States of the Union before the Civil War.

Sharpless, I. The American College. New York, 1915.

Shewmaker, W. O. Theological Education in America. In the Papers of the American Society of Church History, Second Series, Vol. 6. New York, 1917.

Shirley, J. M. The Dartmouth College Causes. St. Louis, Mo., 1879.

Slosson, E. E. The American Spirit in Education. Chronicles of America Series, edited by Allen Johnson, Vol. 33. New Haven, Conn., 1921.

—— Great American Universities. New York, 1910.

Smith, Francis F. College Reform. Philadelphia, 1851 pamphlet.

Smith, H. B. An Argument for Christian Colleges. New York, 1857 pamphlet.

Smith, M. The Growth of the American University. University of California Chronicle, Vol. 25, January 1923, pp. 93-98.

Smith, R. C. A Defense of Denominational Education. Milledgeville, Ga., 1854 pamphlet.

Snow, L. F. The College Curriculum in the United States. Contributions to Education, No. 10, Teachers College, Columbia University. New York, 1907.

Society for the Promotion of Collegiate and Theological Education at the West. 26 Annual Reports, 1844-69.

Statistics of Universities, Colleges, and Professional Schools, 1927-28. U. S. Office of Education Bulletin 1929, No. 38.

Steiner, B. C. History of University Education in Maryland. Johns Hopkins University Studies, Ninth Series III-IV. Baltimore, Md., 1891.

Sterling, W., Editor. Quarter-Centennial History of University of Kansas, 1866-1891. Topeka, Kan., 1891.

Storrs, R. L. Colleges, a Power in Civilization to Be Used for Christ. New York, 1856 pamphlet.

Sturtevant, J. M. An Address in Behalf of the S.P.C.T.E.W. New York, 1853 pamphlet.

—— Denominational Colleges. In the New Englander, February, 1860.

Sweet, W. W. The Story of Religions in America. New York, 1930.

Tappan, H. P. Public Education. Tracts on Education, Vol. III, No. 2. Detroit, Mich., 1857.

—— University Education. New York, 1850.

Taylor, Howard C. Educational Significance of the Early Federal Land Ordinances. Contributions to Education, No. 118, Teachers College, Columbia University. New York, 1922.

Taylor, J. M. Before Vassar Opened: A Contribution to the History of Higher Education of Women in America. Boston, 1914.

Ten Brook, A. American State Universities. Cincinnati, O., 1875.

Tenney, E. P. The New West as Related to the Christian College. Colorado Springs, Col., 1879 pamphlet.

Thompson, J. B. Evolution of the American College. Rutgers College Publications, No. 5. New Brunswick, N. J., 1894.

Thornwell, J. H. Letter to Governor Manning on Public Instruction in South Carolina. Columbia, S. C., 1853 pamphlet. Republished in Charleston, S. C., 1885.

Thorpe, F. N., Editor. The Federal and State Constitutions. A Revision of B. P. Poore's Charters and Constitutions of the United States. Washington, D. C., 1909. 7 vols.

Thurber, C. H. Fiscal Support of State Universities and State Colleges. U. S. Bureau of Education Bulletin 1924, No. 28.

Thwing, C. F. A History of Higher Education in America. New York, 1906.

—— American College in American Life. New York, 1897.

—— American and German Universities. New York, 1928.

Tocqueville, Alexis de. Democracy in America. Fourth Edition. New York, 1841. 2 vols.

Troeltsch, E. Social Teaching of the Christian Churches. New York, 1931. 2 vols.

Turner, F. J. The Frontier in American History. New York, 1920.

Tyler, W. S. Colleges: Their Place among American Institutions. New York, 1857 pamphlet.

U. S. Bureau of Education. Publications from 1867 to 1890 with Subject Index. Washington, D. C., 1891.

United States Census Volumes for 1860.

U. S. Commissioner of Education Annual Reports. Bureau of Education, Washington, D. C., 1870 on.

Van Tyne, C. H. Loyalists of the American Revolution. New York, 1902.

Vermont Historical Society Collections. Montpelier, Vt., 1870-71. 2 vols.

Walsh, L. G. and Walsh, M. F. History and Organization of Education in Pennsylvania. Indiana, Pa., 1928. 3 vols.

Warren, C. Supreme Court in United States. Boston, 1922. (Rev. Ed. Boston, 1926. 2 vols.)

Wayland, F. Report to the Corporation on Changes in the System of Collegiate Education. Providence, R. I., 1850.

—— Thoughts on the Present Collegiate System in the United States. Boston, 1842.

Weathersby, W. H. A History of Educational Legislature in Mississippi from 1798 to 1860. Supplementary Education Monographs, No. 16. University of Chicago Press, 1921.

Webster College. A Business Man's Plea for Webster College. St. Louis, Mo., 1857 pamphlet.

Weeks, S. B. Church and State in North Carolina. 1893.

Weigle, L. A. American Idealism. Pageant of America Series, Vol. 10. New Haven, Conn., 1928.

Wells, W. P. The Dartmouth College Case and Private Corporations. Reprinted from the Report of the Transactions of the American Bar Association. Philadelphia, 1886 pamphlet.

White, A. D. Advanced Education: The Relations of the National and State Governments to Advanced Education. In the National Education Association Proceedings for 1874.

Whiting, L. Address before the Society for the Promotion of Collegiate and Theological Education at the West. Boston, 1855 pamphlet.

Whitney, G. H. Wayland on College Education in America. North American Review, Vol. LXXII, January 1851, p. 82.

Wickersham, J. P. History of Education in Pennsylvania. Lancaster, Pa., 1886.

Williams, M. The Shadow of the Pope. New York, 1932.

Woody, T. A History of Women's Education in the United States. New York, 1929. 2 vols.

Wright, B. F. American Democracy on the Frontier. Articles in Yale Review, Winter Quarter, 1931.

Young, E. B. A Study of the Curricula of Seven Selected Women's Colleges in the Southern States. Contributions to Education, No. 511, Teachers College, Columbia University. New York, 1932.

C. DENOMINATIONAL HISTORIES BEARING ON THE FOUNDING OF AMERICAN COLLEGES AND UNIVERSITIES BEFORE THE CIVIL WAR

1. *BAPTIST*

American Baptist Register and Almanac. New York. Annually.

Benedict, S. General History of the Baptist Denomination in America. Boston, 1813. 2 vols.

Cathcart, W. The Baptists and the American Revolution. Philadelphia, 1876.

Cathcart, W., Editor. Baptist Encyclopedia. Philadelphia, 1883. 2 vols.

Christian, J. T. A History of the Baptists. Nashville, Tenn., 1926.

Newman, A. H. History of the Baptist Churches in the United States. American Church History Series. New York, 1894.

Riley, B. F. A Memorial History of the Baptists in Alabama. Philadelphia, 1923.

Sweet, W. W. Religion on the American Frontier—The Baptists, 1783-1830. New York, 1931.

2. *CATHOLIC*

Cassidy, F. P. Catholic College Foundations and Developments in the United States, 1677-1850. Washington, D. C., 1924.

Erbacher, S. A. Catholic Higher Education for Men in the United States, 1850-1866. Washington, D. C., 1931.

O'Gorman, T. A History of the Roman Catholic Church in the United States. New York, 1895.

Shea, J. D. G. History of the Catholic Church in the United States. New York, 1890.

3. *CONGREGATIONAL*

Bridgman, H. A. New England in the Life of the World. Boston, 1920.

Douglass, T. O. The Pilgrims of Iowa. Boston, 1911.

Dunning, A. E. Congregationalists in America. Boston, 1894.

Eaton, E. D. The Inevitable Relation of Congregationalists to Education. Chicago, 1928 pamphlet.

Walker, W. A History of the Congregational Churches in the United States. American Church History Series. New York, 1894.

4. *CHRISTIAN*

Morrill, N. T. The History of the Christian Denomination in America, 1794-1911. Dayton, O., 1912.

5. *DISCIPLES*

Garrison, W. E. Religion Follows the Frontier—A History of the Disciples of Christ. New York, 1931.

Gates, E. The Disciples of Christ. New York, 1905.

Montgomery, R. B. Education of Ministers of the Disciples of Christ. St. Louis, Mo., 1931.

Reeves, F. W. and Russell, J. D. College Organization and Administration. A Report of a Survey of Disciples Colleges. Indianapolis, Ind., 1929.

Tyler, B. B. A History of the Disciples of Christ. American Church History Series. New York, 1894.

6. *DUTCH REFORMED*

Corwin, E. T. A History of the Reformed Church, Dutch. American Church History Series. New York, 1894.

7. *EPISCOPAL*

Brewer, C. H. A History of the Religious Education in the Episcopal Church. New Haven, Conn., 1924.

McConnell, S. D. History of the American Episcopal Church. New York, 1890. Revised Edition 1916.

Tiffany, C. C. A History of the Protestant Episcopal Church in the United States of America. American Church History Series. New York, 1895.

8. *FRIENDS*

Thomas, A. C. and Thomas, R. H. A History of the Society of Friends. American Church History Series. New York, 1894.

9. *GERMAN REFORMED*

Dubbs, J. H. A History of the Reformed Church, German. American Church History Series. New York, 1894.

Good, J. I. History of the Reformed Church in the United States in the Nineteenth Century. New York, 1911.

10. *LUTHERAN*

Gotwald, F. G. Early American Lutheran Theological Education, 1745-1845. Lutheran Quarterly, January, 1916.

Jacobs, H. E. A History of the Evangelical Lutheran Church in the United States. American Church History Series. New York, 1893.

Leonard, R. J. et al. Survey of Higher Education for the United Lutheran Church in America. New York, 1929. 3 vols.

Wentz, A. R. The Lutheran Church in American History. Philadelphia, 1923.

11. *METHODIST*

Alexander, G. History of the Methodist Episcopal Church South. American Church History Series. New York, 1894.

Bangs, N. A History of the Methodist Episcopal Church. New York, 1838-41. 4 vols.

Buckley, J. M. A History of the Methodists in the United States. American Church History Series. New York, 1896.

Cummings, A. W. The Early Schools of Methodism. New York, 1886.

Duvall, S. M.   The Methodist Episcopal Church and Education up to 1869. Contributions to Education, No. 284, Teachers College, Columbia University.   New York, 1928.

Goss, C. C.   Statistical History of the First Century of American Methodism.   New York, 1866.

Methodist Almanac 1833-60 (later, Methodist Year Book).   New York. Annually.

Moats, F. I.   The Educational Policy of the Methodist Episcopal Church Prior to 1860.   Unpublished manuscript, Library of the State University of Iowa.

Norwood, J. N.   The Schism in the Methodist Episcopal Church, 1844. Alfred, N. Y., 1923.

Simpson, M.   A Hundred Years of Methodism.   New York, 1876.

—— Encyclopedia of Methodism.   5th Edition, New York, 1882.

Sweet, W. W.   Rise of Methodism in the West.   New York, 1920.

12. *PRESBYTERIAN*

Breed, W. P.   Presbyterians and the Revolution.   Philadelphia, 1876.

Foster, R. V.   A History of the Cumberland Presbyterian Church.   American Church History Series.   New York, 1894.

Glasgow, W. M.   Cyclopedic Manual of the United Presbyterian Church of North America.   Pittsburgh, Pa., 1903.

Johnson, T. C.   A History of the Presbyterian Church, South.   American Church History Series.   New York, 1894.

Nevin, A.   Encyclopedia of the Presbyterian Church in the United States of America.   Philadelphia, 1884.

Patton, J. H.   A Popular History of the Presbyterian Church in the United States of America.   New York, 1900.

Scouller, J. B.   A History of the United Presbyterian Church.   American Church History Series.   New York, 1894.

Thompson, R. E.   History of the Presbyterian Church in the United States. New York, 1895.

Weber, H. C.   Presbyterian Statistics through 100 Years, 1826-1926.   Philadelphia, 1927.

13. *UNITARIAN*

Allen, J. H.   A History of the Unitarians in the United States.   American Church History Series.   New York, 1894.

14. *UNITED BRETHREN*

Berger, D.   A History of the United Brethren in Christ.   American Church History Series.   New York, 1894.

Drury, A. W.   History of the Church of the United Brethren in Christ. Dayton, O., 1924.

Noffsinger, J. S.   A Program for Higher Education in the Church of the Brethren.   Contributions to Education, No. 172, Teachers College, Columbia University.   New York, 1925.

15. *UNIVERSALIST*

Eddy, R.   A History of the Universalists in the United States.   American Church History Series.   New York, 1894.

D. BIOGRAPHICAL MATERIAL BEARING UPON THE FOUND-ING OF AMERICAN COLLEGES AND UNIVERSITIES BEFORE THE CIVIL WAR

White, H. C.   Abraham *Baldwin*, Father of the University of Georgia. Athens, Ga., 1926.

Fulton, J.   Memoirs of Frederick A. P. *Barnard*.   New York, 1896.

Beecher, C., Editor.   Autobiography of Lyman *Beecher*.   New York, 1864-65.   2 vols.

McDowell, B.   Simeon *Benjamin*, Founder of Elmira College, 1792-1868. Elmira, N. Y., 1930 pamphlet.

Chase, P.   Reminiscences—Bishop Philander *Chase*.   Boston, 1848.   Second Edition, 2 vols.

Smith, L. C.   Life of Philander *Chase*.   New York, 1903.

Malone, D.   The Public Life of Thomas *Cooper* (1783-1839).   New Haven, Conn., 1926.

Ewing, L. E. L.   Dr. John *Ewing*.   Philadelphia, 1924.

Honeywell, R. J.   The Educational Work of Thomas *Jefferson*.   Harvard University Press, 1931.

Schneider, H. and C.   Samuel *Johnson*.   New York, 1929.   4 vols.

Lawrence, W. R., Editor.   Extracts from the Diary and Correspondence of the late Amos *Lawrence*.   Boston, 1855.

Halsey, L. J.   A Sketch of the Life and Educational Labors of Philip *Lindsley*.   Hartford, Conn., 1859.

Sedgwick, J. T.   A Memoir of the Life of Wm. *Livingston*.   New York, 1833.

Mann, M.   Life and Works of Horace *Mann*.   Boston, 1865.

Murdock, K. B.   Increase *Mather*.   Cambridge, Mass., 1925.

Meigs, W. M.   Life of Josiah *Meigs*.   Philadelphia, 1887.

Parker, W. B.   The Life and Public Services of Justin Smith *Morrill*.   Boston, 1924.

McClintock, J., Editor.   Life and Letters of Stephen *Olin*.   New York, 1853.

Babcock, R.   Memoir of J. M. *Peck*.   Philadelphia, 1864.

Taylor, J. B.   Memoir of Rev. Luther *Rice*.   Baltimore, 1840.

Smith, E. F.   William *Smith*, D.D.—First Provost of the University of Pennsylvania.   Reprint from General Magazine and Historical Chronicle of the University of Pennsylvania, January, 1927.

Smith, H. W.   Life and Correspondence of the Rev. William *Smith*.   Philadelphia, 1880.   2 vols.

Stille, C. J.   Memoir of William *Smith*.   Philadelphia, 1869.

Dexter, F. B., Editor. The Literary Diary of Ezra *Stiles*. New York, 1901. 3 vols.

Sturtevant, J. M., Jr., Editor. An Autobiography of J. M. *Sturtevant*. New York, 1896.

Magoun, G. F. Asa *Turner*—A Home Missionary Patriarch. Boston, 1889.

Carriel, M. T. The Life of Jonathan Baldwin *Turner*. Privately printed, 1911.

Wayland, F. and H. L., Editors. Reminiscences and Correspondence. Francis *Wayland*. New York, 1867.

—— A Memoir of the Life and Labors of Francis *Wayland*. New York, 1868. 2 vols.

Lodge, H. C. Daniel *Webster*. Boston, 1883.

Fuess, C. M. Daniel *Webster*. Boston, 1930. 2 vols.

Collins, V. L. President *Witherspoon*. Princeton, N. J., 1925. 2 vols.

E. U. S. BUREAU OF EDUCATION STATE HISTORIES OF HIGHER EDUCATION

Adams, H. B., Editor. Contributions to American Educational History. U. S. Bureau of Education, Circulars of Information. (No titles for Illinois, California, or Oregon.)

C.A.E.H.	YR. NO.	AUTHOR	TITLE
8	1889-3	Clark, W. G.	History of Education in *Alabama*.
26	1900-1	Shinn, J. H.	History of Education in *Arkansas*.
14	1893-2	Steiner, B. C.	History of Education in *Connecticut*.
15	1893-3	Powell, L. P.	History of Education in *Delaware*.
6	1888-7	Bush, G. G.	History of Education in *Florida*.
5	1888-4	Jones, C. E.	Education in *Georgia*.
10	1891-1	Woodburn, J. A.	Higher Education in *Indiana*.
17	1893-6	Parker, L. F.	History of Education in *Iowa*.
27	1900-2	Blackmar, F. W.	Higher Education in *Kansas*.
25	1899-3	Lewis, A. F.	History of Higher Education in *Kentucky*.
20	1898-1	Fay, E. W.	History of Education in *Louisiana*.
36	1903-3	Hall, E. W.	History of Higher Education in *Maine*.
19	1894-2	Steiner, B. C.	History of Education in *Maryland*.
13	1891-6	Bush, G. G.	History of Higher Education in *Massachusetts*.
11	1891-4	McLaughlin, A. C.	History of Higher Education in *Michigan*.
31	1902-2	Greer, J. M.	History of Education in *Minnesota*.
24	1899-2	Mayes, E.	History of Education in *Mississippi*.
21	1898-2	Snow, M. S.	Higher Education in *Missouri*.
3	1888-2	Smith, C. L.	History of Education in *North Carolina*.
23	1899-1	Murray, David.	History of Education in *New Jersey*.
22	1898-3	Bush, G. G.	History of Education in *New Hampshire*.

C.A.E.H.	YR. NO.	AUTHOR	TITLE
28	1900-3	Sherwood, S. *University of the State of New York.*
12	1891-5	Knight, G. W. and Commons, J. R. History of Higher Education in *Ohio.*
—	1892-2	Thorpe, F. N. Benjamin Franklin and the *University of Pennsylvania.*
33	1902-4	Haskins, C. H. and Hull, W. I. History of Education in *Pennsylvania.*
18	1894-1	Tolman, W. H. History of Higher Education in *Rhode Island.*
4	1888-3	Meriwether, C. History of Higher Education in *South Carolina.*
16	1893-5	Merriam, L. S. Higher Education in *Tennessee.*
35	1903-2	Lane, J. J. History of Education in *Texas.*
29	1900-4	Bush, G. G. History of Education in *Vermont.*
2	1888-1	Adams, H. B. Thomas Jefferson and the *University of Virginia.*
1	1887-1	Adams, H. B. *College of William and Mary.*
7	1889-1	Allen, W. F. and Spencer, D. E. Higher Education in *Wisconsin.*